CONSERVATION IS NOT ENOUGH

Conservation Is Not Enough

Rethinking Relationships with Water in the Arid Southwest

Janine Schipper

UNIVERSITY OF WYOMING PRESS
Laramie

© 2025 by University Press of Colorado

Published by University of Wyoming Press
An imprint of University Press of Colorado
1580 North Logan Street, Suite 660
PMB 39883
Denver, Colorado 80203-1942

All rights reserved

 The University Press of Colorado is a proud member of Association of University Presses.

The University Press of Colorado is a cooperative publishing enterprise supported, in part, by Adams State University, Colorado School of Mines, Colorado State University, Fort Lewis College, Metropolitan State University of Denver, University of Alaska Fairbanks, University of Colorado, University of Northern Colorado, University of Wyoming, Utah State University, and Western Colorado University.

ISBN: 978-1-64642-670-6 (hardcover)
ISBN: 978-1-64642-701-7 (paperback)
ISBN: 978-1-64642-702-4 (ebook)
https://doi.org/10.5876/9781646427024

Cataloging-in-Publication data for this title is available online at the Library of Congress

Schipper, J. (2018). An Ethic of Interdependence: Environmental Crisis and the Case of Water Scarcity in the American West. In S. Stanley, R. Purser, and N. Singh (Eds.), *Handbook of Ethical Foundations of Mindfulness*. Mindfulness in Behavioral Health. Springer, Cham. https://doi.org/10.1007/978-3-319-76538-9_12.

License Number: 5654920821084

Cover art © fuzzylogickate/Adobe Stock 119677903.

This book will be made open access within three years of publication thanks to Path to Open, a program developed in partnership between JSTOR, the American Council of Learned Societies (ACLS), University of Michigan Press, and The University of North Carolina Press to bring about equitable access and impact for the entire scholarly community, including authors, researchers, libraries, and university presses around the world. Learn more at https://about.jstor.org/path-to-open/.

This work is licensed under CC BY-NC-ND 4.0.

Contents

Introduction: Our Water Stories 3

1. A Culture of Conservation 25
2. The Limits of the Conservation Ethos 53
3. The Origins of the Conservation Ethos 79
4. Indigenous Water Relationships 105
5. Rethinking Water Relationships in the Arid Southwest 133

Epilogue: The Song of the Water 167

Acknowledgments 169
Appendix A: Research Overview 175
Appendix B: Demographic Information 179
Works Cited 183
Index 195

If there is magic on this planet, it is contained in water.
—*Loren Eiseley*

Water sustains all life. Her songs begin in the tiniest of raindrops, transform to flowing rivers, travel to majestic oceans and thundering clouds and back to earth again. When water is threatened, all living things are threatened.
—*Indigenous Declaration on Water, 2001*

What happens to water, happens to all of us.
—*Vernon Masayesva, former Chairman of the Hopi Tribal Council, Executive Director of Black Mesa Trust*

CONSERVATION IS NOT ENOUGH

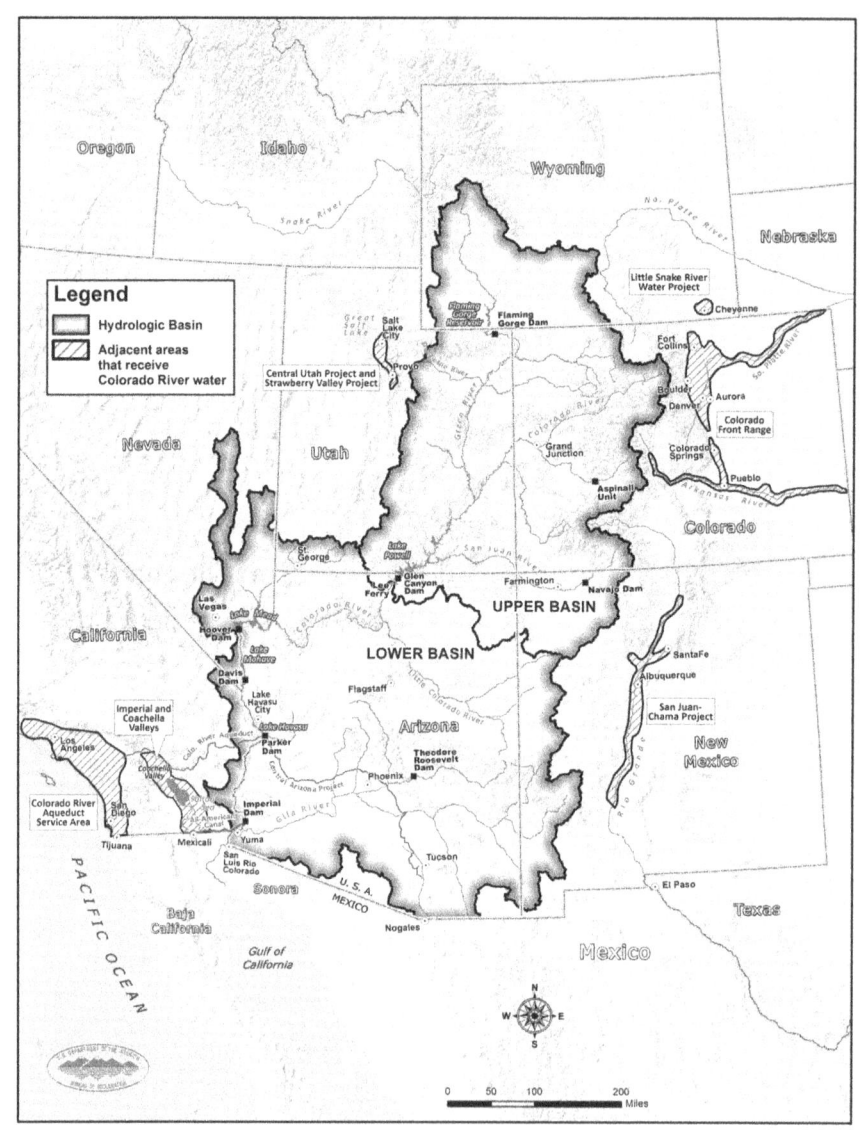

Map of the Colorado River Basin. (US Bureau of Reclamation)

INTRODUCTION

Our Water Stories

When I first arrived in Flagstaff, Arizona, in the summer of 1997, I missed the ocean. I missed looking out as far as the eye could see into the deep blue expanse. I missed the lakes, ponds, and rivers and the verdant green forests—products of a water-quenched region.

Living in my new home, in a community built on former WWII bean fields, I would gaze over the high-desert brush spread out toward the San Francisco Peaks, taking in the muted colors and dry scrub, dull and stark to my senses. This land felt bleak, and I yearned for the blue sweep of the ocean, aching for a place where my mind could expand and dance with the tossing waves.

After eighteen months of feeling homesick for the northeast coast, something began to shift in me. I found myself appreciating the subtle green buds that speckled the land as wildflowers burst open after monsoon rains. I marveled at the power of the mountain, feeling its solidity and a type of wild presence, previously unknown and unfelt by me. And one day, I gazed up at the Arizona-blue sky, and my mind took off, stretching out over the land. I realized that day that all I needed was to look up, and there was the ocean, just not where I was used to seeing it.

https://doi.org/10.5876/9781646427024.c000

In the Southwest great stretches of ocean may be seen from miles away. Whereas a thick overcast film often characterizes the New England and mid-Atlantic sky, in Arizona I could see the ocean in the form of storm clouds hurtling across the heavens. They build up momentum like great waves that suddenly come crashing down upon the land, soaking the sunbaked fields, carving out rivulets and drainages, revealing the power and majesty of the ocean, Southwest style.

Over the years, I have come to not only appreciate living in the Southwest, I have come to love living here. It's a love forged by listening, observing, connecting, and opening to something very different from anything I had ever known before. And as with everything I love, I also feel heartbreak when the land is hurt in some way.

Today, as I walk along the path behind my home, clouds gather and thicken. There's a reunion going on over the Peaks. They collect and darken, piling high, more massive than the imagination can comprehend; more massive than the greatest skyscraper; three times the size of the mountain itself. There really is no comparison.

Pregnant, heavy with the water they have collected from the ocean, they burst open, pouring over the mountain, and rushing down her massive sides. The water follows old tried paths, tumbling over rocks, twisting and turning as it rushes down, draining into rivulets that pour into streams, moving with the weight of gravity through the valley, into washes, once dried out from the hot summer sun, then into creeks. I listen to its gurgling song. There are messages in the songs of the clouds as they move down mountains, into valleys, through streams and creeks. But to hear these messages, we need to listen deeply.

Heading south, returning home, the water follows pathways to reunite with the ocean and begin the journey all over again. That is the life of a cloud. From the creeks and streams, rivulets come together, reuniting again as they once did as clouds high in the sky. I imagine them gathering together and flowing into the River, the main river of the Southwest: the Colorado. But it is unlikely that much of the rainwater actually makes it into the Colorado, as the thirsty land with its volcanic, permeable soil soaks up the rain long before it enters the river.

What rainwater does make its way off the Peaks, meeting up with creeks, streams, and tributary rivers, eventually gathers with the reduced flow of the Colorado (fed primarily by snowmelt,) and now, as one River, heads

FIGURE O.1. San Francisco Peaks during a monsoon storm. (Photograph by Sam Minkler)

south toward the Mexican border. But the Colorado is depleted. Aside from a reduced flow due to climate change, water is dammed and siphoned away to be redirected where needed: Los Angeles, Las Vegas, Phoenix, Tucson. Approximately 40 million people depend on water from the Colorado River. Nowhere else on the planet do so many people depend on a river so small.

The river continues to head south and gradually becomes a trickle, seeping slowly into the Colorado River Delta, whose thirsty parched surface, once a vibrant Garden of Eden, absorbs the remaining drops of the cloud. The cloud never makes it to the Sea of Cortez, never reunites with the Great Ocean from whence it came. The cycle has been disrupted.

The Drought in the Desert

Of course, the Southwest is a desert. It has always been dry, receiving between three and fifteen inches of precipitation annually. But a desert can have a drought too. And when a desert is in an extended drought, people begin to get nervous and wonder, will there be enough water to go around?

During the twentieth century, climate variability led to less precipitation, hotter temperatures, reduced runoff, and increased evaporation. Since 2000, the US Southwest has experienced higher than average temperatures and drought conditions, meaning less moisture through evaporation and less precipitation (EPA, 2023). The increased temperatures have resulted in less snowfall and are driving evaporation of surface water. Overuse of the two main rivers of the Southwest, the Colorado River and the Rio Grande, and their tributaries has strained water systems throughout the Southwest. As soils dry out, crops and vegetation are also stressed. As vegetation dies out, less evaporative cooling takes place, decreasing the moisture entering the atmosphere, resulting in fewer clouds, creating negative feedback loops and amplifying the drought (Southwest Climate Science Center Workshop, 2017).

Signs of extended drought, water mismanagement, and overuse abound, including declining groundwater and reservoir levels, desertification, hotter and dryer seasons, "structural deficit" (there is more Colorado River water allocated than is available), continually increasing populations (with Southwest cities being some of the nation's fastest growing), and depleted water supplies for ranching and agriculture. All of these serve as indicators of a looming water crisis, where ecosystems and human systems are driven beyond their thresholds. Across the region, there is increased discussion of water crisis and concern about a dire water future for the Southwest.

THE COLORADO RIVER: "ONE OF THE HARDEST-WORKING RIVERS IN THE WEST"

Originating as snowmelt at as high as 14,000 feet above sea level in the mountains of western Wyoming, central Colorado, and northeastern Utah, the Colorado River moves through the Canyonlands of Utah into Northern Arizona, carving out the Grand Canyon. It weaves through the drylands of the desert Southwest, forms the Arizona-California border, and finally

FIGURE 0.2. Over the past 25 years, the Salton Sea has decreased to one-third of its original water volume. In the past decade alone, the sea's area diminished by 38 square miles. Various factors have fueled this decline, including the state's drought conditions and the diminishing levels of the Colorado River. (Photograph by Janine Schipper)

> **BOX 0.1. MEGADROUGHT**
>
> Between AD 1000 and 1450, the Southwest United States experienced what scientists have come to call a "megadrought," a series of prolonged droughts, each lasting two decades or longer. During megadroughts we see less rain, depleted rivers, and dry fire-prone forests. Today, the Southwest faces what climate scientists warn may be another megadrought, the first in over 500 years, beginning in 2000 and with no end in sight. Park Williams, professor of bioclimatology at Columbia University, referencing his team's report on the latest megadrought, reports that the current drought is 62 percent more severe than it would have been without human-driven climate change (Meyer, 2018). The Intergovernmental Panel on Climate Change (IPCC) reported in 2021 that rapid warming due to human activities are leading to an intensification of the water cycle, with extreme flooding and rainfall in some regions and extreme drought in other regions (IPCC, 2021). The 2023 IPCC report indicates that approximately 950 million people residing in arid regions are expected to grapple with water stress, heat stress, and desertification. Nearly half of the world's population already faces severe water scarcity for at least one month annually (IPCC, 2023).

enters Sonora Mexico, where it once permeated and spread through an expansive, lush delta and emptied into the Gulf of California.[1]

In 1922, Aldo Leopold canoed the Colorado's verdant delta and described a "milk and honey wilderness" (Leopold, 1949/2020, p. 135) that filled him with a sense of awe as he beheld "a hundred green lagoons" (Leopold, 1949/2020, p. 131) where up to four hundred plant species and a plethora of birds, fish,

---

1 To explore additional literature on the social, cultural, political, and historical aspects of the Colorado River, please refer to the following sources: Simon Boughton, *The Wild River and the Great Dam: The Construction of Hoover Dam and the Vanishing Colorado River* (2024); Wade Davis, *River Notes: A Natural and Human History of the Colorado* (2023); Christian S. Harrison, *All the Water the Law Allows: Las Vegas and Colorado River Politics* (2021); Eric Kuhn and John Fleck, *Science Be Dammed: How Ignoring Inconvenient Science Drained the Colorado River* (2019); Cecil Kuhne, *River Master: John Wesley Powell's Legendary Exploration of the Colorado River and Grand Canyon* (2017); David Owen, *Where the Water Goes: Life and Death along the Colorado River* (2018); April R. Summit, *Contested Waters: An Environmental History of the Colorado River* (2013); Eric B. Taylor, *Rivers Run through Us: A Natural and Human History of Great Rivers of North America* (2021).

and mammals, including the great jaguar, once lived. While the delta of Leopold's wanderings spanned nearly 3,000 square miles, now it covers 250 square miles. Today, aside from the alfalfa and green onion fields, the Colorado River Delta, as described by journalist Ian James, is a "dry riverbed (that) spreads out in a dusty plain where only gray desert shrubs survive" (James, 2020).

Recognized at the turn of the twentieth century as a source for economic development and the key to westward expansion, the once wild Colorado has become one of the most managed rivers in the world. The 1,450-mile-long Colorado River currently serves about 40 million people, irrigates over 7,000 square miles of farmland (5.5 million acres), supports a $5-billion-a-year agricultural industry, and serves as the main water source for thirty federally recognized tribes, seven national wildlife refuges, four national recreational areas, and eleven national parks. The Colorado River also contributes to the Southwest's power grid, providing 4,178 megawatts of electricity to support over 782,000 households with hydropower (Thiel, 2013).

Not only is the Colorado "one of the hardest-working rivers in the West" (Nature Conservancy, n.d.), the Colorado River is also considered one of the most threatened and was named in 2013 by American Rivers as "America's Most Endangered River." The organization pronounced, "Demand on the river's water now exceeds its supply, leaving the river so over-tapped that it no longer flows to the sea" (American Rivers, 2013).

Over the past century, rising temperatures and longer periods of drought have resulted in a 20 percent decrease in the Colorado's annual flow (Milly, 2020), with scientists predicting a 40 percent decrease in the coming years. Since 2000, there has been less precipitation, including less snowmelt, which constitutes 75 percent of the Colorado's annual flow. Although agricultural lands compose a small percentage of rural land throughout the region (less than 8 percent of nonfederal rural land), they use approximately 80 percent of the region's water (USDA, 2020), and this includes over 80 percent of Colorado River water. Agricultural use combined with the needs of a growing population places additional stress on the river.

The two main reservoirs, Lake Mead and Lake Powell, have been steadily dropping due to decades of overuse, drought, evaporation from higher temperatures, and decreased snowpack in the Rocky Mountains. As the water levels drop, mineral deposits are left behind on the cliffs that surround the reservoirs, causing the infamous bathtub rings, powerful visuals symbolizing the precariousness of water in the Southwest. Lake Mead experienced a twenty-three-year downward trend. In July 2022, Lake Mead hit its lowest elevation level since the onset of the drought, plummeting to 1,040 feet (Bureau of Reclamation, 2022). Should the reservoir continue to fall and reach 950 feet, it will stop generating electricity. It will be considered a "dead pool" if it dips below 895 feet, profoundly impacting the millions of people who depend on it. As of April 2023, following an exceptionally wet winter, the US Bureau of Reclamation's five-year probabilistic forecast indicated that Lake Mead has a 50 percent chance, and Lake Powell has a 17 percent chance, of reaching critically low reservoir elevations by 2027 (Bureau of Reclamation, April 27, 2023). Despite the 2023 wet winter contributing to an increase in water levels at Lake Mead and Lake Powell, drought conditions persist. To contextualize the impact of a single favorable year, the Bureau of Reclamation has indicated that the water levels of Lake Powell and Lake Mead would experience a modest increase of 3 percent (Bureau of Reclamation, April 20, 2023).

The Colorado River is also one of the most highly contested and litigated rivers in the country. Throughout the last century, the allocation of Colorado River water has been a contentious issue involving not only the seven Colorado River states and thirty Colorado River tribes but also a diverse array of other stakeholders. This includes individuals such as irrigators, businesses, civic advocates, politicians, ranchers, government officials, engineers, and, more recently, environmental organizations and recreational users, all vying for influence in decisions regarding Colorado River water distribution (National Resource Council, 2007). Furthermore, the Colorado is overallocated. This means that there is less water in the Colorado than the states, tribes, and Mexico have rights to. To learn more about the issues around water rights and overallocation, see textbox 2.2, "Water Rights and the Law of the River," in chapter 2.

The other principal river in the Southwest, the Rio Grande, originates in the Colorado Rockies, runs 1,896 miles, and culminates in the Gulf of Mexico. As with the Colorado River, unprecedented drought combined with continued water demands have placed the Rio Grande in grave danger. In the summer of 2022, for the first time in forty years, the Rio Grande went dry in Albuquerque.

Real work needs to be done. After witnessing over twenty-four years of drought, and based on many years of researching and contemplating water sustainability in the Southwest, I feel skeptical about the main approaches driving decisions around how to create a more sustainable water future. I'm not sure that modifying laws, negotiating better ways to share the little water available, raising water prices, and launching conservation campaigns are going to be enough to solve the problems we face.

The Research for This Book

I am not trained in water management, conservation ecology, hydrology, geology, or any of the sciences typically involved in understanding and solving problems related to water. I am a sociologist. I am interested in people, our attitudes, beliefs, and underlying assumptions and behaviors, and in how we solve problems. As an environmental sociologist, my research has been devoted to exploring people's relationships with water and how the underlying assumptions about nature impact the way people relate with water and live on these lands. In my work with the public, I seek to facilitate discussions and debates that challenge taken-for-granted assumptions about water conservation. My aspiration for this book is to serve as a catalyst, inspiring individuals throughout the region to thoroughly scrutinize deeply ingrained assumptions, actively listen to diverse perspectives, contemplate fresh possibilities, and participate in meaningful dialogues about water in the Southwest.

Sociology provides a unique perspective on water issues by recognizing that they are not only technical or environmental problems but also rooted in social and cultural factors. By exploring the social and cultural factors that shape attitudes and behaviors toward water use and conservation, sociologists can help individuals and communities understand the broader structural and cultural factors that contribute to water challenges in the Southwest. This approach challenges the prevalent focus on individual behavior and lifestyle change and highlights the need for systemic change, including policy reform.

By promoting critical engagement, sociologists can help individuals gain a more nuanced understanding of the complex social dynamics involved in water issues and identify culturally appropriate solutions. Additionally, the sociological perspective can help policymakers, water managers, and conservationists question their assumptions, critically evaluate their approaches, and develop effective strategies for water sustainability that are informed by cultural considerations.

Despite the crucial role that sociology plays in understanding the social dimensions of water issues, this perspective has been largely overlooked in current discussions. Instead, the dominant discourse has prioritized technological and economic approaches, often neglecting the social dimensions of the issue. By incorporating sociological perspectives, a more comprehensive understanding of the complex social dynamics involved in water conservation can be achieved, which may lead to the identification of new possibilities and more effective solutions.

After fifteen years of drought, the sociologist in me began to wonder: How do others relate with water in this arid region of the world? What types of attitudes prevail? What wisdom is available that can guide us as we navigate this tenuous water reality? It is with these concerns, questions, and contemplations that I sought to understand how those living throughout the Southwest relate with water.

I also had a more personal reason for conducting this research. I wanted to reflect upon living in this arid region of the world. I wanted to consider what it means to love a place fiercely while knowing that, by living here, I contribute to impending water crisis. I wondered what others talk about when considering the severity of the situation. Were they concerned? Did they seek solutions? I wondered if I could get a pulse on the situation, understand the inner workings of the collective, and come out on the other side of this research with some clarity and some water wisdom to offer in pursuit of a sustainable water future.

GATHERING WATER NARRATIVES

And so, as part of exploratory research aimed at gaining a fuller understanding of the complex social dynamics involved in water issues, I began a research project with the goal of gathering "water narratives," which encompass people's stories, experiences, and relationships with water. Exploratory research is a preliminary investigation that seeks to generate insights, raise questions, and gain a broad understanding of a complex phenomenon.

Over the course of three years, 178 students became involved in the project of gathering water narratives from ninety-five individuals living throughout the Southwest. Most of the participants in the study live in Arizona, but we also collected water narratives from those living in California, southwestern Colorado, New Mexico, southern Nevada, southwestern Texas, and Utah. Participants came from a wide range of backgrounds, including a variety of cultures, ethnicities, ages, socioeconomic backgrounds, professions, political orientations, and educational levels. We interviewed water experts including hydrologists, earth scientists, municipal water treatment managers, and water conservationists.

We were not only interested in talking with those whose careers centered around water. We wanted to gather water narratives from individuals from all walks of life. We wanted to learn about the perspectives of farmers, cattle ranchers, developers, and others whose work centered around access to water. But we also interviewed an Uber driver, a hairstylist, a firefighter, a waiter, and a beekeeper. We interviewed a justice of the court, university professors, K–12 teachers, retirees, college students, an employee of an animal shelter, a camp owner, a botanical garden curator, and a ski instructor, among others. We interviewed people from a range of ethnic backgrounds, including European Americans, Indigenous Americans, Mexican Americans, African Americans, and one Pacific Islander. The ages of the interviewees ranged from eighteen to eighty-five years old. For research overview and summary of participant demographics, please see appendixes A and B.

The one universal value that defined ways of thinking about and relating with water, which spanned this cross-section of Southwestern life, was conservation. Without exception and without ever using the word *conservation* in any of the interview questions, all participants not only mentioned conservation as a core value but also expressed a belief that water conservation was critical to the future of life in the Southwest. Furthermore, each participant identified ways in which they practiced water conservation. No matter what their political orientation, age, ethnicity, profession, or educational attainment, participants were not only interested in conservation but also embraced conservation efforts to varying degrees. It appears that a conservation ethos has permeated the culture.

I became intrigued by this interest, this devotion to conservation as if it were a kind of holy grail, a strong moral precept, something that could save us. If it were, then why hasn't it? After all, water conservation has a long history, rooted in the early conservation movement of the 1850s, which ignited an interest in maintaining the scenic lands and waterways of the West.

The widespread interest in water conservation raises many questions: What do people mean when they say they value and practice water conservation? How did it get to the point where conservation appears to be universally valued? Is conservation enough to avert water crisis? What needs to be valued if conservation is not enough?

BOX 0.2. INTERVIEW QUESTIONS

1. What three words come to mind when you think of "water"?
   Can you tell us a little bit about why you chose each of those words?

2. What are your earliest memories of water?

3. Tell me about water where you currently live.
   Where does your water come from?
   How do you use water?
   Are there any restrictions on water use where you live?

4. Are there any community issues related to water or water use? What are the main issues? For each of these issues, what is your opinion or stance?
   Describe any involvement you've had at the community or grassroots level in shifting water policy.

5. Do you think there are water shortages in the Southwest?
   If yes, who or what is most responsible for creating the water shortages we see in the southwest?
   Who or what is most responsible for addressing these water shortages?

6. What do you think water looked like in this area one hundred years ago?

7. What do you think that water will look like in this area in one hundred years?

8. Have you ever changed the way you use water (whether recreationally, for landscape, or for home use)? What inspired those changes?

9. How would you define a "water ethic"? What does a "water ethic" look like to you? What's an appropriate relationship between human beings and water?

10. Do you practice a water ethic—or, how would you assess yourself in relation to your definition of a water ethic? Does your community practice a water ethic?

Central Theme: Challenging the Culture of Water Conservation in the Southwest

The research the students and I conducted over the past eight years suggests that a fundamental shift in perspective is needed to address the water challenges in the Southwest effectively. Despite the prevalent emphasis on conservation, evidenced by diverse individuals expressing their commitment to water conservation efforts, this book maintains that the utilitarian approach tied to conservation falls short of adequately addressing the region's dire water situation.

As we will see, the conservation mindset that has taken root prioritizes the utilitarian view of water as a resource to be measured, collected, moved, and utilized with economic efficiency. This approach, while not inherently negative, primarily focuses on cost-saving incentives and water efficiency, often leading to paradoxes where efficiency inadvertently results in increased water usage as conservation efforts create opportunities for further growth.

As we grapple with increasingly severe climate conditions and concerns about dwindling water levels in the Colorado River, it becomes evident that a mere utilitarian approach to conservation may not suffice. As readers engage with this book, it is my hope that they will grasp the importance of moving beyond the established conservation paradigm and consider a more transformative perspective when addressing the pressing water challenges facing the Southwest.

This shift entails moving away from an anthropocentric and utilitarian conservation ethos toward embracing a deep ecology ethos. Deep ecology advocates for a holistic view of the environment, considering the intrinsic value of all living beings and emphasizing interconnectedness and interdependence within ecosystems. Such a perspective challenges us to move beyond exploitation and prioritize a more balanced coexistence within the Earth's ecosystems.

To facilitate this transformation, the book recommends finding inspiration in Indigenous communities that have survived in arid landscapes for countless generations. These communities exemplify a relationship with water that transcends the utilitarian paradigm and the established approaches to conservation. Amplifying Indigenous leadership and integrating Indigenous wisdom could catalyze a paradigm shift toward a more holistic, interconnected, and relational approach to water issues in the Southwest. While drawing inspiration from Indigenous models and leadership is crucial, it's equally vital not to burden Indigenous communities with the sole responsibility of "saving" us from the ecological challenges we currently confront.

Ultimately, in order to navigate the complex and urgent water crisis, a profound shift in perspective is necessary. The shift suggested throughout this book involves embracing a deep ecology ethos, learning from Indigenous knowledge systems, and transitioning toward a more interconnected and relational approach to water that goes beyond conventional conservation efforts.

Understanding Conservation and Its Theoretical Dimensions

The term *conservation* is generally thought of as "the care and protection of [the Earth's] resources so that they can persist for future generations" (*National Geographic*, n.d.). Conservation involves regulating social systems so as to prevent ecological destruction, including loss in biodiversity and habitat destruction. Ultimately, water conservation is the practice of using water efficiently to protect water resources so that they are available for future generations.

In the southwestern United States, where water scarcity is a constant concern, the history of water conservation can be traced back to ancient Indigenous practices. Indigenous American tribes such as the Hopi and Navajo demonstrated an early understanding of the need for responsible water stewardship, through methods like terraced farming and the construction of intricate irrigation systems.

Upon their arrival, European settlers implemented a formalized and structured approach to water conservation efforts. The construction of dams and reservoirs in the late nineteenth and early twentieth centuries, like the Hoover Dam on the Colorado River, marked a pivotal moment in water management in the Southwest. These structures not only provided a stable water supply for growing urban populations but also facilitated the expansion of agriculture in the region. To provide water in this arid region of the world, water conservation practices became essential.

In recent decades, the challenges posed by prolonged droughts and increased demand for water resources have led to a renewed focus on water conservation in the Southwest. This has resulted in the adoption of various water-saving technologies, such as low-flow fixtures and xeriscaping, as well as the implementation of water-use regulations. The idea of conservation has evolved to encompass not only individual water-saving practices but also broader policies and community efforts aimed at ensuring a continual water supply in the face of growing environmental pressures.[2]

In our exploration of water conservation, its promise, and its shortcomings, several theoretical models are employed—social construction of conservation, deep ecology, and environmental justice theory—to provide a more complex understanding of this critical subject. These theoretical models act as lenses through which water conservation is analyzed and approached, shedding light on the underlying philosophies, ethical considerations, and practical implications that guide conservation efforts.

SOCIAL CONSTRUCTION OF CONSERVATION

This perspective recognizes that our understanding of water conservation is not a fixed, objective truth but rather a concept shaped by cultural, historical, and political factors. By examining how conservation ideas and practices are socially constructed, we gain insight into the biases, power dynamics, and cultural influences that underpin our approach to water conservation. This lens challenges us to critically assess the values and interests embedded in conservation efforts.

DEEP ECOLOGY

Deep ecology advocates for a transformation in our relationship with nature, emphasizing an eco-centric worldview. This model is central to the analysis presented in this book, as it calls for a shift from a utilitarian view of water as a resource to be exploited to a perspective that recognizes the intrinsic value of water and all living beings. By promoting a deep and interconnected relationship with the natural world, deep ecology challenges us to reorient our conservation efforts toward a more holistic and sustainable approach.

---

2   To delve further into literature regarding water conservation in the Southwest, please refer to the following sources: John Fleck, *Water Is for Fighting Over, and Other Myths about Water in the West* (2019); Robert Glennon, *Unquenchable: America's Water Crisis and What to Do about It* (2009); Heather Hansman, *Downriver: Into the Future of Water in the West* (2022); Allison Lassiter, *Sustainable Water: Challenges and Solutions from California* (2015); Sandra Postel and Brian Richter, *Rivers for Life: Managing Water for People and Nature* (2003); Brian Richter, *Chasing Water: A Guide for Moving from Scarcity to Sustainability* (2014); Melissa Sevigny, *Mythical River: Chasing the Mirage of New Water in the American Southwest* (2016); Juliet Stromberg and Barbara Tellman, *Ecology and Conservation of the San Pedro River* (2012).

ENVIRONMENTAL JUSTICE THEORY

Environmental justice theory holds a fundamental place in an exploration of water conservation in the Southwest. By addressing the disproportionate impact of environmental degradation on marginalized communities, with a particular emphasis on Indigenous communities of the region, this lens highlights the ethical dimensions of water conservation. Environmental justice compels us to consider not only the ecological aspects but also the social and economic dimensions of water conservation, with the aim of ensuring that vulnerable populations are not unfairly burdened by environmental issues.

This book draws on environmental justice theory in a way that includes but also goes beyond its traditional focus on equitable resource distribution. Environmental justice theory plays a key role in revealing how the colonial origins of conservation practices contributed to the silencing and marginalization of Indigenous voices, as well as the undervaluing of Indigenous people's ways of knowing and their holistic relationship with the environment. The theory emphasizes their unique knowledge systems and spiritual connections to water, frequently devalued in conventional conservation approaches. This exploration of Indigenous wisdom enriches the conversation about water conservation.

Additionally, an environmental justice lens directs our gaze toward the growing influence of Indigenous leadership in contemporary conservation endeavors. It spotlights the strides made by Indigenous leaders in advocating for their communities' rights and their sacred connection with water. Their leadership inspires more inclusive and equitable conservation practices.

The Flow of the Book

> This writing will be like a river, winding its way through different landscapes and concepts to show the importance of remaining connected to the world we inhabit and call home.
> —Lyle Balenquah, Hopi, *member of the Greasewood Clan from the Village of Bacavi on Third Mesa*

As the narrative unfolds through each chapter, readers are guided on a journey, beginning with the cultural foundations of conservation and culminating in the realization of the imperative need for a shift in our relationships with water in the arid Southwest. The chapters progressively build upon one another, collectively presenting a case for transforming our perception and approach to water issues. Each chapter opens with a collection of "Voices," featuring quotes from participants that highlight a range of perspectives and introduce the themes of the chapter.

Chapter 1, titled "A Culture of Conservation," embarks on a journey to unravel the complex cultural backdrop that molds dominant perspectives on water conservation. It delves into the fundamental question of "How do we think about water?" and explores the cognitive dissonance that often underlies conservation efforts, enabling us to justify our lifestyle choices while maintaining a business-as-usual approach to water despite mounting concerns. The chapter delves into individual and federal initiatives in water conservation, shedding light on the challenging decisions many of us confront when tasked with conserving water. Additionally, it scrutinizes the culture of conservation from various angles, including water management, conservation science, and a spectrum of high-tech and low-tech solutions. This exploration of the culture of conservation lays the foundation for a critical examination of the values and assumptions that underpin our approaches to water conservation.

Chapter 2, titled "The Limits of the Conservation Ethos," peels back the layers of the conservation ethos to uncover its inherent values and their associated limitations. It scrutinizes the common usage of the term *resource* for water, prompting reflection on the consequences of treating water as a mere object for utilization and wealth generation. This perspective often results in indifferent treatment of water until our own well-being is directly impacted. The chapter explores a range of other conservation values, including the perception of water as a commodity, the importance of ownership and rights to water, the value placed on efficiency, and the pursuit of unceasing growth. This exploration offers insights into the challenges posed by the conservation mindset, setting the stage for a critical examination of the ethos's origins.

In chapter 3, titled "The Origins of the Conservation Ethos," we take a historical perspective to unravel the influence of a colonial mentality on prevailing water conservation approaches. This investigation reveals how historical undercurrents propelled the belief in the need to subdue the "uncivilized wilderness" and establish water ownership through "prior appropriation" rules and laws. The chapter culminates in a poignant exploration of how the erasure of Indigenous water wisdom served as the cornerstone for the conservation ethos that permeates our present approach.

Chapter 4, titled "Indigenous Water Relationships," explores an Indigenous water ethos, highlighting its stark differences from mainstream conservation efforts. This chapter emphasizes present-day possibilities for learning from Indigenous wisdom and leadership. It underscores core Indigenous values such as respect and reverence, valuing water as a living being, and the importance of ancestral knowledge, juxtaposing them with Western values centered on utility and efficiency. The chapter places importance on the transmission of knowledge and water wisdom through generations, illuminating the interconnectedness of water within Indigenous cultures. It concludes by delving into the notion that water communicates with humans and can be engaged through ceremony, prayer, and storytelling, forging a deep connection with the water world.

In chapter 5, the pivotal chapter, titled "Rethinking Water Relationships in the Arid Southwest," we embark on a shift in perspective concerning our relationship with water in this region. The chapter begins by questioning whether our current interactions with the natural world are rooted in love, respect, and reciprocity or driven by fear and opportunism. The concept of a water ethic is introduced, drawing inspiration from Aldo Leopold's land ethic and extending it to water, emphasizing interconnected caring relations among water and all beings.

Our journey delves into the possibilities of a relational water ethos, grounded in the principles of deep ecology and enriched by Indigenous knowledge systems. Within this context, the chapter explores the intimate interconnectedness of all life-forms, emphasizing the importance of systems thinking. Furthermore, evolving perspectives on water rights and the concept of legal personhood for water bodies are investigated, showcasing communities that have embraced this idea. The chapter also examines the burgeoning recognition of water's sacredness within the dominant culture and its implications. Chapter 5 concludes by challenging the conquest mentality, advocating for a shift toward a relational mindset and highlighting the vital role of community-driven water conservation systems like acequias. Finally, it discusses the growing influence of Indigenous leadership and raises thought-provoking questions about the future of water sustainability in the arid Southwest.

Our journey comes to a reflective conclusion in the epilogue, titled "The Song of the Water," inviting contemplation of the transformational possibilities that arise when embracing a more relational approach to water.

Notes to the Reader

My intention for writing this book is to share the many voices from my research, and some of what I have learned during the process of exploring cultural perceptions of water in the Southwest. While the main message of the book is in its title, *Conservation Is Not Enough*, I do not mean to suggest that conservation should be scrapped or that it is not important. I want to acknowledge here the incredible efforts, contributions, care, and concern forged by many conservationists. Many of today's conservationists are deeply connected to the world they are trying to conserve. They have made it their life's work, as Aldo Leopold did in the 1930s and 1940s, to care for the world they love so dearly. I recently met some young environmentalists who are helping farmers switch from alfalfa farming (water intensive) to barley farming (which uses less water) in an effort to conserve water. They spoke passionately about their love of water and land and their efforts to help and "be the change they want to see in the world."

Before each of the chapters, I have included the voices of participants in response to specific interview questions. By sharing these chapter-opening quotes as well as respondent quotes sprinkled throughout the book, I hope that readers will gain a sense of the many voices and multiple perspectives that arose in the interviews. I have used pseudonyms and removed certain identifying information to maintain confidentiality. We offered participants an option to choose their own pseudonyms. I have included the pseudonyms that participants chose (some of which may appear unusual, like "Curious Coyote") in order to maintain and respect participants' approaches to identifying themselves.

In this book, I have included my personal reflections on water conservation, as well as my own approaches to addressing this issue. As a qualitative sociologist, I recognize the importance of reflexivity in conducting sociological qualitative research. This involves questioning my own assumptions and critically reflecting on how my own background and perspectives shape the way I perceive and interpret information.

Furthermore, I believe it is valuable for readers to gain insight into my personal journey and struggles regarding my approaches to water conservation. Through this research and my interactions with numerous individuals throughout the region, as well as the time I have spent with various bodies of water, I have undergone personal growth and experienced a shift in my perspectives. Sharing these experiences allows readers to understand the transformative impact that engaging with the subject matter has had on me.

Whenever possible, I have specified tribal affiliations of participants and scholars cited throughout this book. I use the term *Indigenous Americans* to indicate the original inhabitants of US land prior to European occupation and settlement. Indigenous respondents sometimes refer to themselves as "Indigenous," "Natives," "Native Americans," and "Indians." I use the name Diné throughout this book, as this is how the Diné refer to themselves. Navajo, the Spanish name for the Diné, is at times also used by respondents.

At times I use the term *more-than-human world* in addition to the more common terms *nature* or *environment*. Ecologist and philosopher David Abram coined the phrase "more-than-human world" in 1996 in his book *Spell of the Sensuous: Perceptions and Language in a More-than-Human World* (Abram, 2012). Since then, other scholars and environmentalists have adopted the term instead of the words *nature* or *environment* to indicate that human culture is a subset within a larger "more-than-human-world" on which it depends.

FIGURE 0.3. *(opposite)* Diminishing snow levels due to climate change pose a growing threat to the vital role of snowmelt in replenishing the Colorado River. (Photograph by Janine Schipper)

VOICES

How do you use water?

Are there any restrictions on water use where you live?

Have you ever changed the way you use water?

We collect water off our roof and then I use that water. I take it in five-gallon buckets from outside and I use it to flush the toilet. When I'm taking a shower, I just save my shower water. If it's like really grungy gray-looking, then I'll use it to flush the toilet, and if it's not that bad then I'll do my handwashing in it.

—*Kaibab, fish restoration technician / social worker, Flagstaff, Arizona*

The girl at the forest service building would call and tell us that the trees were dying—huge cottonwood trees. Forest services depended on the wastewater to keep the trees alive. So sometimes we had to shut the water off to the golf courses, because the water waste treatment plant in this area gives 90 percent of the water to the golf courses. Working in wastewater and seeing how much a golf course uses has made me monitor and think about how much I use at home.

—*Dean, retired wastewater manager, Cornville, Arizona*

Conservation might not exactly be done for the right reasons in construction. It's being done to make a profit; however, it is being done.

—*Eric, construction project manager, Scottsdale, Arizona*

What inspired my efforts to conserve? Love. Love of this place, the community of relationships, that which gives me life. I'm using the word *love* in its full range of application, but it includes generosity, reciprocity, caring, and gratitude.

—*Cactus Ed, program director of a nonprofit environmental organization, Flagstaff, Arizona*

I didn't take a five-minute shower to lower the water bill. It was more just like me trying to be good.

—*Abby, College Republicans, Flagstaff, Arizona*

Agriculture in Imperial County has changed an awful lot in forty-something years. There are people now that grow more tons per acre of alfalfa than their fathers did thirty years ago, and they're using a fourth of the water. I mean think about that: they've cut it down to 25 percent and they're growing double the amount of tonnage. That's crazy, crazy good. And that's just through education and improvements in technology and people really embracing the proper use of water. And developing a disdain for misuse of it.

—*Parker, Native American farmer, Poway, California*

All of the conservation efforts add up to make a big difference. There's a lot of small efforts that all add up to help save water where we can. There are efforts to encourage people not to have the big lush green lawns that just soak in water, so changing your landscape to be more water-friendly. There are programs to convert old shower fixtures with low-flow fixtures . . . things like that.

—*Gomez, retired construction worker, Phoenix, Arizona*

Where I come from in Mexico, in Chihuahua, which is a dry state located in the desert part of the country, there are campaigns to conserve water. And at certain times the water is cut. So you have to be prepared to get what you need. You need to have containers; we call them *tinacos*, which is a big container that you keep in your roof to store water for when the water is cut. And then there's a reserve of water. The reserved water is used for your household, when there's no running water. When they cut it. So you have to have those containers in order for you to have access to water. Clean water.

Since I've been in the US, I've had periods of time when I was really busy. It was really easy for me to just grab a ready-to-go water bottle, instead of taking the time to fill my own bottle, taking, I don't know, one minute, of time to fill my water bottle from the sink. But then I was like, "what am I doing? This is totally wrong." I remembered my life in Mexico. And now, I just get water from the fountain.

—*Yaaxfin, mother and ecology student, Flagstaff, Arizona*

1
A Culture of Conservation

I'm sitting on a bench at Fountain Park, in Fountain Hills, Arizona, just north of Phoenix, watching water spraying over 300 feet high into the expansive blue sky (the fountain reaches its full height of 560 feet on special occasions). More than three times as high as Old Faithful Geyser in Yellowstone National Park, this fountain before me is the fourth largest in the world. Ducks swim around, gently gliding along on shimmering water. Green lawns roll out toward rocky desert mountains. A few people stroll around the park periphery. A cool late winter breeze mingles with hot desert sun.

It feels pleasant to be here, and I am lulled into a sense of well-being. There's a man with his son playing disc golf. Diners casually chat, sipping iced tea at the outdoor café with a view of the lake. At one o'clock in the afternoon, water surges into the sky. Three thirty-something women walk by, one with two poodles, another on a casual stroll, and another speed-walking past. The fountain is just a part of the background scenery for most. And what a scene it is! I stand in front of a small desert island, constructed to offer a taste of the desert, speckled with key Southwestern plants: mesquite, saguaro, agave, and barrel cactus, thoughtfully arranged.

Seeing all this water, we might forget that we are in the middle of the desert.

One week after my stroll around Fountain Hills, I'm walking on trails 150 miles north of Fountain Hills, on the Colorado Plateau, outside of my home near Flagstaff, Arizona. I'm walking out on mud bogs and melting snow trickling into streams. It wasn't like this last year. Last year the ground was dry and cracking. Thirsty. Last year it didn't rain for nine months straight, and neighbors worried and cleared their yards of every dry pine needle and browned aspen and oak leaf they could find, kindling for raging forest fires. They spoke about the future of water. They spoke about what we needed to do to change. This winter, the ground is wet. And there is less talk about our water future.

How soon we forget. Or do we?

How Do We Think about Water?

It might be easy to assume that many people living in the Southwest are willfully unaware that they live on arid lands during an ongoing drought. How is it possible for 60 million people to continue to live in places like Phoenix and Las Vegas with their fountains, human-made lakes, golf courses, and sidewalk café water spritzers, knowing that we receive less than fifteen inches of water per year? A close look at some of the respondent's attitudes about water provide some clues.

SOPHIE: "I FEEL A LOT OF GUILT."

Sophie, in her mid-forties, has lived in the Southwest her whole life. She identifies as New Mexican with a blend of Hispanic and European ancestry. Having majored in cultural anthropology, Sophie is committed to the well-being and integrity of this land and its peoples. When she thinks about her own water use, she admits, "I think I actually feel a lot of guilt through the course of the day."

Sophie goes on to explain that she's very water-conscious, yet any sense of wasting water leaves her feeling guilty and angry with herself:

> If I don't turn the water off real quick while brushing my teeth, I'm like "ahh, that's going away." And last night I was rinsing some produce and I turned the water on and then went to grab the produce and I was like "ahh!" and I turned it off and then went to grab the produce. So, I'm always kind of double-checking myself because I think that it's disappearing.

FIGURE 1.1. The fountain at Fountain Hills. (Michael Ellis, CC BY-SA 4.0)

Sophie shares how important it is to her to conserve water, explaining that as a child, she was never raised to think about water:

You remember the commercial with the Native American that walks through the stream and there's litter everywhere and he's crying and the message is "keep America beautiful"? That was the first environmental message ever, but no one was really saying, "we're going to run out of water," nobody ever thought about it. And so, we were kind of raised with these habits, like, do your laundry every week, and if you wear something once, its dirty. And now I'm pretty much infamous for a slightly pungent smell on my clothes. Not because I hate doing laundry but because I'm just aware of how much water we use just to live our lifestyle. And if everyone in the world did the same, where that would leave us?

Sophie, like many of those we interviewed, offsets her guilt by practicing water conservation and educating others about conservation, including her son:

I mean, I do feel a little bit of guilt for sure. But, you know, I try to be more mindful about it and I try to convey that to my son. With conservation teachings in his school and in his home, he's even more aware of it than I am probably, and you know, that's a good step. We're headed in the right direction if that's the case. You know?

Ultimately, Sophie justifies her water waste by explaining that she's doing her best: "I do feel a little guilt even though I don't think I'm particularly worse than the next person, and probably in a lot of ways better."

Practicing water conservation both in her home and at the botanical gardens where she works is the key way in which Sophie rationalizes living in the Southwest:

And so, the most water possible goes to the plants before it hits the storm drain at the bottom of the slope. In the gardens, we demonstrate how we planted all of the roses in T-beds that are kind of sunken, so all of the water runoff from the sidewalk flows into the T-beds. So again, we are harvesting that water and we're showing people that yeah, roses can be water-intensive, but this is how you can grow them in a mindful way.

While Sophie rationalizes her water use in an arid environment by highlighting how conservation strategies help reduce water use and serve as a model for how others can live and thrive even in an arid environment, others take a different approach.

GARY: "MY LAND HAS RIGHTS."

Gary, who holds a prominent position on the board of a large water aqueduct project, also mentions feeling guilty from time to time. However, Gary reasons that because of what he knows about how water is allocated, it doesn't make sense for him to conserve more than he already does:

> I have not made very many changes other than reducing some grass in my backyard as my kids have gotten older and don't play in the yard anymore. But I still do have a grass lawn, and part of the reason that I do is because of the [aqueduct] project. I know I am going to get a renewable supply every year. I don't have flood irrigation, but my land has rights to that water. So, if we have three acre-feet of water that we can use, then I don't have a problem using it. Because right now, there isn't any other way of doing anything with it. I am a water advocate. I would make even more efforts to conserve water if they would say, hey, you can conserve water if you'd like to, and you can choose what you do with that conserved water. You can leave it in the river, you can use it for your cabin, or whatever. If I had the ability to direct where my conserved water would go, I would probably conserve more water. But right now, I don't have a choice with what happens with my conserved water.

Because Gary knows that conserving any of the water allotted to him will not augment conservation efforts (since water conserved remains in a reservoir to be later consumed), Gary reasons that he may as well use that water himself. The guilt he feels is offset by his knowledge of how conservation works or, in this case, doesn't work.

PETUNIA: "THE ARTIFICIAL SNOW IS ALREADY THERE."

Petunia, a lead ski and snowboard instructor, rationalizes her job at the Arizona Snow Bowl, a controversial ski resort on the San Francisco Peaks outside of Flagstaff, Arizona. The Arizona Snowbowl is the first ski resort in the world to turn sewage effluent (the outflow from water treatment plants) into artificial snow so as to offset the effects of global warming and extend the ski season (Pela, 2016). In order to make this possible, the city of Flagstaff sells 1.5 million gallons of water a day during ski season to the Arizona Snowbowl. When asked how she feels about this, Petunia replies,

> I don't think about it because, the way I see it, the artificial snow is already there, there is nothing we can do now. I think I would feel bad if we made snow every day, that would be a complete waste. We just made some snow up there recently and they don't make snow every night, it's like maybe once or twice a week. With that being said, we are using it efficiently, to the most extent that we can.

Even while she expresses guilt about hauling water onto the San Francisco Peaks, for Petunia, the "efficient" use of water for snowmaking provides the justification she needs to continue working there.

Sophia's, Gary's, and Petunia's accounts exemplify a widespread mindset regarding water in the Southwest. People acknowledge the ongoing drought and place great emphasis on the necessity of conserving water and utilizing it in a more efficient manner. Some, like Gary, also acknowledge the inherent limitations of individual efforts and merely strive to make the best possible choices when living in a dry region. Despite the differences in their approaches, one common thread among all of these efforts is the emphasis on conservation. Additionally, despite experiencing differing degrees of guilt, they each rationalize their water usage through distinct conservation practices and perspectives.

AN INTRICATE WEB OF CHALLENGES AND TRADE-OFFS

Sophia, Gary, and Petunia's experiences serve as illustrations of the pervasive ecological anxiety gripping many living in the Southwest, particularly within the complicated context of water conservation. This anxiety is intertwined with the political and cultural framework of the region, where conservation has been placed at the forefront as the primary strategy for tackling the multifaceted challenges associated with water scarcity. Much like the individuals portrayed in Paul Robbins's *Lawn People*, who grapple with the maintenance of lawns, the use of toxic chemicals, and their concerns about global climate change, the ecological unease embodied by Sophia, Gary, and Petunia occurs within a broader political economy context (Robbins, 2007), which is challenging to navigate. Furthermore, in an individualistic society, there's a natural inclination to personalize problems, emphasizing individual solutions. However, this approach can lead to anxiety when individual choices alone prove insufficient in addressing issues of much larger scale, causing a sense of guilt and responsibility for problems that transcend personal actions. The complex landscape where these individual decisions unfold, encompassing political, economic, social, and cultural dimensions, further amplifies this anxiety.

There are issues of population growth versus water supply, with those living in the region being part of that population growth, which puts pressure on water resources, potentially leading to over-extraction of groundwater and conflicts over water allocation between urban areas and agriculture.

Additionally, allocating water between agriculture and urban use presents a trade-off, as agriculture, the largest consumer, uses 70 to 90 percent of the Southwest's supply. This requires balancing water for farming with the needs of growing urban populations. William deBuys highlights how economic interests, particularly agricultural, have played a pivotal role in shaping the region's water policies. In *A Great Aridness*, deBuys discusses how large-scale agricultural practices, supported by federal subsidies and incentives, have influenced water usage patterns. The book explores how the expansion of irrigated agriculture in arid regions has strained water resources and exacerbated ecological challenges (deBuys, 2013).

William deBuys also explores the historical development of water law and policy in the American West, with particular attention to the Colorado River Basin. He highlights the complex web of legal frameworks, such as prior appropriation, which allocates water rights based on "first in time, first in right." These legal structures have deep-rooted implications for water allocation, fostering competition among various users, including agricultural, industrial, and urban sectors.

There are also political hot-button issues to navigate like those elucidated by Andrew Ross, who illustrates how Arizona's legislature's skepticism toward science and the prioritization of unbridled economic growth often clash with sustainable choices (A. Ross, 2011). Economic growth, particularly in sectors like tourism and industry, often relies on water-intensive activities. Communities must weigh the economic benefits of such development against the need for water conservation and environmental protection. Protecting ecosystems and preserving natural habitats can also be at odds with water use for human purposes, where decisions about water allocation must consider the ecological health of rivers, wetlands, and wildlife habitats. As the region grapples with growing climate variability and droughts, the trade-offs between short-term water usage and long-term resilience become even more pronounced, demanding nuanced policy decisions.

These considerations, among others,[1] form the complex backdrop in which

---

[1] A multifaceted range of political, economic, social, and cultural issues collectively shape the backdrop within which attitudes toward water conservation develop. For readers who wish to delve deeper into these topics, here is a selection of books to consider: Mark Arax, *The Dreamt Land: Chasing Water and Dust across California* (2019); Robert Crifasi, *A Land Made from Water: Appropriation and the Evolution of Colorado's Landscape, Ditches, and Water Institutions* (2016); Patrick Dearen, *Bitter Waters: The Struggles of the Pecos River* (2016); Tershia d'Elgin, *The Man Who Thought He Owned Water: On the Brink with American Farms, Cities, and Food* (2016); Noris Hundley Jr., *Water and the West: The Colorado River Compact*

individuals navigate their water conservation decisions. In this context, people often find themselves navigating a landscape of limited choices, where they earnestly strive to make environmentally responsible decisions while contending with complex trade-offs, reflecting the complicated range of cultural norms, economic constraints, and environmental concerns that shape the Southwest's approach to water sustainability.

Cognitive Dissonance: Rationalizing Conservation

When I first came to live in the Southwest, I felt called to deepen my understanding of water. I had grown up in a water-rich region of the world, where water was completely taken for granted. Water was everywhere and we rarely had to consider conserving water, though I do have a few vague memories of being told the water reservoirs were low and we shouldn't water our lawns every day. Life in the Southwest is different, and people have an underlying awareness of the fact that water is limited. My awareness was growing, but I still sometimes took water for granted. When I first began devoting myself to water conservation, I found that, like Sophie, conservation alleviated some of my guilt. As I dove further into my research, I realized that conservation had become many people's go-to strategy for alleviating their discomfort and the dissonance they felt between valuing living in the Southwest, navigating the complex political and economic terrain as described above, and living amidst ever-increasing indications that the Southwest was heading toward water shortages and crisis.

Cognitive dissonance is what psychologists call the mental discomfort that arises when people maintain contradictory beliefs, values, or behaviors. In an effort to restore balance and reduce discomfort, we seek cognitive consistency and willingly alter one set of ideas or behaviors to accommodate the other set of contradictory ideas and behaviors. Leon Festinger introduced the notion of cognitive dissonance in 1957 after observing a cult whose members believed that a flood would destroy the Earth. Devotees attributed the absence of the great flood as evidence of the power of their faith, reasoning that had it not been for their faith and devotion to the cult, a flood would have destroyed the

---

and the Politics of Water in the American West (2009); Annette McGivney, *Resurrection: Glen Canyon and a New Vision for the American West* (2009); Andrew Needham, *Power Lines: Phoenix and the Making of the Modern Southwest* (2016); Marc Reisner, *Cadillac Desert: The American West and Its Disappearing Water* (1986/1993).

Earth. Rather than seeing the nonappearance of the flood as evidence that their beliefs were not aligned with reality, cult devotees reinterpreted the evidence to support their beliefs and reinforce their piety and zeal (Festinger, 1957)

Research has found that humans will justify their compliance with the status quo even in the most adverse conditions and under the most immoral policies. For example, Kristin Laurin and colleagues studied the extent to which people would rationalize their own political oppression. In three experiments, researchers found that restrictions on emigration lead to increased justification of the system that imposed the restrictions (Laurin, Shepherd, and Kay, 2010).

CONSERVING WATER IS BETTER THAN WASTING WATER

Like me, many participants grew up in water-rich regions where they never gave a thought to water conservation but rather perceived water as unlimited. They see their acquired water conservation values as a dramatic shift from one belief system (water is abundant and limitless) to another belief system (water is scarce and limited). Furthermore, they perceive themselves as dramatically shifting their behavior, from that of wasting water and taking water for granted to becoming more mindful about water through conservation.

Sally reflects on her shift in water values from childhood through adulthood:

> I think back then, and I was born in 1962, water wasn't the commodity it is now. I don't think we conserved it like we do now. Certainly, we didn't worry about running our sprinklers or of all of the things we do nowadays to conserve water. So, we took it for granted that we would always have it. It was always there for us; it was for recreation. And I don't ever remember ever being talked to about water issues and worrying about contaminants and things like that. That was never an issue. But you know, when I was a young girl, I always associated it with fun, and then when I was an older child, I feared it. Now as an older person, I have a different view of water, of conserving it.

The rationalization goes something like the following: now that we've woken up to our role in wasting water, we are doing the right thing by conserving water. As conservationists, we are no longer on the wrong side of history and we are not the bad guys. Conservation becomes a moral philosophy for many living in the Southwest, and as long as we align with a conservation ethos, we feel that we are living good and ethical lives.

PUBLIC SHAMING

If forced to adopt a behavior that is inconsistent with our beliefs or values, called "forced compliance," we tend to reevaluate our original attitudes so that we may better align with the behavior in which we are forced to partake. We see forced compliance at play through both social pressure and in acts of public shaming. Public shaming around water conservation reinforces this notion that we, the larger society, are trying to conserve, and those who don't conform to this greater value will face ridicule.

The *Santa Fe Reporter* publishes an annual *Water Guzzler's Report*. This report publicizes the top ten industrial and top ten residential water consumers. The intention of this list is to publicly shame people into complying with conservation measures. And it appears to work, at least temporarily. Jarold, a Santa Fe hotel owner and community organizer, explains,

> I think that it is very effective. . . . I don't know that in the long term that is the best strategy. It just makes people angry, but it seems to be effective in the short term. I think that two particular places, both with reputable positions in the community, have been at the top of the list over the years. And I think that because of the public shaming, they have done a lot of marketing and publicity over the last few years showing how they've cut down on their water use. So, they actually took that shaming and used it as a positive thing.

In some communities, the culture of conservation stigmatizes water waste. Public shaming persuades individuals to at least appear conservation-minded. A professor of physiology who calls himself "The Chief" explains,

> I don't want the neighbors to see me wasting water. It's funny how that works, but like I said, inside the house where the neighbors can't see, my shower is still long. It's a creature comfort. I kid myself; I turn it down as much as I can to get an extra few minutes, claiming I'll probably be using the same amount. But we all know better, I'm still wasting probably more water than I should.

Jarold, who leads various efforts to monitor and restore the Santa Fe National Forest, describes the impact public shaming has had on the culture of water conservation:

> I don't have a lawn. I don't water anything. I don't have a pool. I think, in this area, all of that is a waste. So that, you know, over time our culture's really

changed here in the Southwest. Especially in Santa Fe and Albuquerque, where it's like, okay, we don't really live in a place that sustains lawns and grass. Therefore, we're gonna go to xeriscaping, which is more natural, native grasses and native plants that don't require a lot. Either very little or no water at all.

The specter of public shame persuades community members either to put on a display of conservation behavior or hide their waste so as to appear conservation-minded, even when they don't maintain conservation values. Jarold continues:

I think that, in some ways, Santa Fe is a little bit hypocritical, where people talk the talk, where they say, "Yeah, it's bad to have water for the lawns," but they do. They tend to be able to hide that from other people. Like, they don't show it off. They hide it behind their fences or they hide it behind their gates where you can't actually see it. But most people here, you know, they're trying to honor the idea that we don't have a whole lot of water, and they're either not going to have lawns or they're going to be hiding their lawns.

THERE'S ONLY ONE ALTERNATIVE: CONSERVE

In an effort to assuage their feelings of discomfort, rooted in a sense of cognitive dissonance, people tend to increase the attractiveness of one alternative while decreasing the attractiveness of other alternatives. In the culture of conservation, there is only one alternative: conservation. Other approaches are not perceived as alternatives: the choices are to waste water or conserve water, so of course, most people, at least in the theory, choose water conservation.

As J. W., a camp manager in New Mexico, highlights, water conservation is the only choice when living in the Southwest: "I think most of the folks in our area are afraid that if their well goes dry, what's the alternative? And therefore, they have pretty much a conserving mindset."

Having only one choice, conservation, increases cognitive consistency. The choice is easy: conserve. The alternative, waste, is culturally, financially, and, for some, morally unacceptable. With only one option, the conservation message pervades the culture. Whether it be politicians, hydrologists, farmers, captains of industry, teachers, environmentalists, and so forth, all speak the language of conservation.

JUST KEEP CONSERVING

Festinger's cult devotees reinterpreted the information they received to align with their beliefs. By creating a scenario where they perceived their staunch faith as responsible for whether or not a flood arrived, they justified their continued devotion to the cult, even when the cult leader's premonition of impending doom did not manifest.

Many living in the Southwest interpret the appearance of rain after long droughts as a sign that things are not so bad after all. After all, after long periods of drought, it rains. They reason that as long as they continue to practice water conservation, all will be well in the long run.

For a nine-month period between fall 2017 and summer 2018, Flagstaff, Arizona, experienced less than half of its normal precipitation. The general mood was one of concern and unease as anticipation of forest fires grew. While the National Weather Service declared the rest of the country under "severe drought conditions," Northern Arizona was under "extreme drought conditions." During such spells, an unsettling reality sets in, and we wonder: How is it possible for us to continue to live in this region of the world?

And then, just when it seemed like grave danger was imminent, the monsoons arrived. Rain fell for days, weeks, and even months, and a huge sigh of relief was breathed. The concerns could be tabled for another time, conservation could be continued, and lives could be lived as usual.

Dave, an information technology consultant, remarks, "almost every monsoon season has been pretty significant, especially the last three or so, and then we've seen some major snowfall in the time that I've been here, so it's kind of different now. It's a little bit less immediate." Dave reasons that water conservation helps us ride out the harder times until the rains come. We ride the roller coaster of drought and rain, tabling our concerns for another season and reasoning that our efforts to conserve make an impact.

WE ARE ONLY HUMAN, AND SO . . .

Even in the face of cracks in conservation as a sustainable approach to water in the Southwest, many of us reassure ourselves that we are doing our best or conforming to societal expectations. At times, guilt arises as we acknowledge that there is always room to use less water. Occasionally, we are motivated to conserve due to external pressures or shame. Some individuals recognize that US conservation efforts pale in comparison to behaviors modeled in other parts of the world. However, ultimately, conservation becomes the primary means through which many rationalize and justify residing in this water-challenged region.

The Culture of Conservation

While Sophia, Gary, and Petunia, the three participants who open the chapter, have different approaches to how they manage their own engagement with water, they all are aware and making an effort. They appear to be "trying" not to waste water, trying to conserve in their own ways. This was a common theme among the ninety-five people we interviewed, who elaborated on what they sometimes perceived as extreme efforts to "do their part" in the quest to conserve.

Sometimes water conservation efforts happen not because people care or want to focus their energy on conservation but because messages about the importance of water conservation have pervaded the culture, even if sometimes in name alone. I think about a remark made by Jen, a biologist at the NOAA National Marine Sanctuaries, who shared the broad range of water conservation efforts her family engages in, when she admitted that sometimes people didn't take their efforts seriously enough: "I mean it became kinda cool, trendy, in California to write with your finger on dirty cars, 'doing my part, for the drought!'"

While people often use water conservation to rationalize living in a region with limited water supplies, the culture of conservation goes much deeper than that. The region has adopted an array of approaches to conserve water, spanning from personal lifestyle adjustments to governmental policies, water management practices, and scientific and technological advancements. As a result, water conservation has become an integral part of daily life, with individuals and communities alike making conscious efforts to minimize water consumption.

"DOING OUR PART" IN THE FACE OF DROUGHT

During the summer of 2019 and again in 2020, the torrential downpours that characterize monsoon season seemed to stall out. Weather forecasters called the lack of monsoon rains a "non-soon." The wildflowers, so vibrant and plentiful during other summers, grew in limited clusters, only the toughest able to survive in the dry, cracked land. The usual green grasses that blanket the meadows and hills turned yellow and brown. Water tanks, where grazing

> **BOX 1.1. A CULTURE OF WATER CONSERVATION:**
> **A SOCIOLOGICAL PERSPECTIVE**
>
> From a sociological perspective, the culture of water conservation encompasses the collective beliefs, values, norms, and practices that shape how individuals and communities interact with water and engage in efforts to preserve and sustain its availability. It involves examining the social and cultural factors that influence people's attitudes toward water, their behaviors related to water use and conservation, and the social dynamics that influence decision-making processes regarding water management. The culture of water conservation can vary across different societies and communities, influenced by factors such as historical traditions, local ecological conditions, socioeconomic contexts, and cultural beliefs about the value and significance of water. Sociologists analyze how cultural norms and social structures shape perceptions of water, create social expectations around its use, and influence collective actions and policies related to water. Furthermore, sociologists provide a critical perspective. They challenge our underlying beliefs and assumptions, shedding light on those unexamined convictions that shape our attitudes and behaviors.

cows come for a cool drink in the hot summer sun, shrank. Dry pastures meant leaner cattle, threatening ranchers' livelihoods. Cities, towns, villages, and reservations throughout the Southwest lived on edge, concerned that the drought conditions would lead to wildfires. The smallest spark can set the forests ablaze.

As the drought continued and demands on limited water supplies increased and water levels in Lake Mead fell to 35 percent of capacity, I found myself ever more conscious of my ways of relating with water, becoming even more concerned about wasting water. I began limiting shower time and giving up some of my treasured baths. My husband, Eliot, and I had always tried to be water-aware, turning water off while brushing teeth, avoiding water fun like running a sprinkler for our children, but now we had to up our game.

We intensified our efforts to conserve, and we worried about wasting water. I stopped reminding my children to take baths and showers, sometimes to my chagrin, as when I once realized they had not showered in three weeks. Eliot, my husband, discovered that he only really needed one shower a week to stay clean, and he seemed to find pleasure in taking as quick a shower as possible, sometimes making it in and out in thirty seconds. As for me, I had a lower threshold for feeling grimy but discovered the art of sponge bathing and also limited my showers to once a week (though I did take longer-than-thirty-second showers). If felt like our water conservation efforts were working.

THE FEDERAL GOVERNMENT STEPS IN

In July 2021, as my family and I were cutting back and trying to conserve, the US Department of the Interior took similar steps, announcing a "Tier I" shortage for operations on the Colorado River. With low water levels in Lake Mead, Lake Powell, and the entire Lower Colorado System, the Bureau of Reclamation (a federal agency under the Department of the Interior) announced an urgent call for action among the Colorado River Basin states.[2] Mexico's annual allotment will be cut by 5 percent, Nevada's by 7 percent, and Arizona's will take the largest cut, 18 percent, which amounts to 8 percent of the state's total water use (Carlowitz, 2021).

By April 2023, there was no consensus among the seven states on how to make the 2 million acre-feet of cuts called for by the Department of the Interior. As journalist for the *Nevada Independent* Daniel Rothberg writes, "Inevitably, every water user, from large irrigation districts to sprawling cities, has an argument for why it should not be cut" (2022). In May 2023, under increasing pressure and growing concerns about the declining water levels in Lake Mead and Lake Powell, the Biden administration facilitated an agreement with the Lower Basin states, namely Arizona, California, and Nevada. The states agreed to conserving a minimum of 3 million acre-feet of water by 2026. While this agreement represents a crucial step in averting an imminent crisis and potentially steers the states toward more sustainable water usage, it falls short of the conservation levels advocated by some scientists. They argue that far greater conservation efforts are necessary to address the ongoing drought and ensure the river's long-term sustainability (Bush, 2023).[3]

---

2 The Colorado River Basin States are a group of seven US states located in the southwestern part of the United States. These states share the Colorado River and its resources, making them integral players in the management and allocation of water from the river. The Upper Basin states consist of Colorado, New Mexico, Utah, and Wyoming. The Lower Basin states consist of Arizona, California, and Nevada.

3 As of March 2024, negotiations continued among seven Western states regarding future water allocations from the Colorado River. Despite improved conditions in 2023, concerns persist about long-term sustainability. Upper and Lower Basin states submitted

MAKING HARD CHOICES

The difficulties encountered by states in effectively regulating water usage should not come as a surprise. As the states struggle, household water conservation also requires making hard choices. There are trade-offs. One of the largest trade-offs for homeowners has been whether to maintain a green lawn, which uses a lot of water, or xeriscape, also known as wise landscaping or dry landscaping, which uses little to no water.

In the 1990s and early 2000s when xeriscaping was first introduced to the mainstream, many people associated it with austere landscaping. National Public Radio senior correspondent Ketzel Levine reports, "Good xeric gardens are wonderfully alive and abundant, but early on, they got a bad rep as being barren and plug ugly." Scott Varner, Executive Director, New Mexico Xeriscape Council, reflects on how homeowners in the Southwest reacted as though xeriscaping were a threat to their very way of life: "I was spit at, got hate mail, threatening letters." Many resisted water-saving approaches, holding onto promises that had been made to them by developers, who guaranteed an abundant supply of water and told them they would always be able to grow grass (Inskeep, 2007).

While the states are having to make hard choices, individuals have also struggled with embracing conservation measures. However, as water supplies are increasingly jeopardized, conservation measures at the state and individual levels have been seen as the answer.

Today, in the face of federal government water declarations and pressure on the states to make cuts, many Southwest cities and individual homeowners have embraced xeriscaping. Ten years after Varner began advocating for xeriscaping to an often hostile audience, he observed that even the affluent high-end developments no longer have any grass. Agencies like the Southern Nevada Water Authority incentivize xeriscaping, offering rebates to customers who replace grass lawns with desert landscaping. With no sign of the drought slowing down, conservation measures have become the go-to approach for addressing water issues in the Southwest.

---

contrasting proposals on how to distribute water cuts if levels continue to decline, highlighting disagreements over burden sharing. While the Upper Basin's plan suggests mandatory cuts for Lower Basin states, the Lower Basin's proposal advocates for a shared-responsibility approach across all seven states and Mexico. Negotiations continue amid calls for collaboration and compromise to secure the river's future.

RESPONDING TO THE CALL TO CONSERVE

The story that we collectively tell is that in order to adequately address the ongoing water crisis in the Southwest, we need to conserve water. Heeding the call to conserve, civic leaders advocate for "smart water use." Local government websites throughout the Southwest highlight the importance of lifestyle change and water conservation approaches. Scientists and government agencies caution that unless we increase conservation efforts, the region will become increasingly water stressed, leading to increases in threatened and endangered species (Marshall, 2010). Additionally, the public health and economic ramifications are unknown and unpredictable (Fuller, 2010).

The public has responded to these calls for conservation. Survey research indicates that a vast majority of Americans are "water-conscious," with 46 percent "water considerate" and 44 percent "water savvy conservationists" (Warner, 2017). A bipartisan conservation poll conducted in 2023 across Western states highlighted safeguarding drinking water as the most important conservation goal. The findings revealed that 86 percent of respondents considered this conservation goal to be of utmost significance, with an overwhelming 97 percent expressing its importance. The findings indicate strong support for various water conservation efforts in the West, stemming from concerns about water availability. Notably, 95 percent of respondents favor investing in water infrastructure to curb leaks and wastage, while 88 percent advocate for increasing the use of recycled water for residential and commercial purposes. Additionally, 87 percent support the requirement for local governments to assess water availability before approving new residential projects. Financial incentives for replacing lawns with water-saving landscaping are backed by 80 percent of respondents, and 62 percent support banning grass lawns in new developments. Finally, 54 percent endorse offering financial incentives to farmers to temporarily halt land cultivation during severe water shortages (Colorado College State of the Rockies Project, 2023).

Identifying water conservation efforts across the Southwest has been challenging, as there has been no centralized repository for such information until the recent development of the Water Adaptation Techniques Atlas (WATA). WATA has recorded hundreds of conservation efforts throughout the Southwest, whether they focus on decreasing water consumption, enhancing water availability, or altering the natural course of water across the terrain (USDA Southwest Climate Hub, n.d.). Here are a few examples that highlight a range of water conservation initiatives undertaken by Southwestern states.

The Conservation District of Southern Nevada's conservation measures have resulted in a 40 percent drop in water usage per person over the last twenty-five years. This district includes Las Vegas, a desert city known for its ostentatious displays of water, which is now touted as a model for conservation. However, Southern Nevada receives only a fraction of Colorado River water, with Las Vegas Valley heavily reliant on Lake Mead's resources. Wastewater from the city undergoes rigorous treatment to meet quality standards before being released into Las Vegas Wash, where it supports wildlife before returning to Lake Mead for reuse. This recycling process, totaling 200 million gallons per day (224,000 acre-feet annually), generates "return-flow credits," allowing Southern Nevada's water utilities to exceed the allocated 300,000 acre-feet from the Colorado River (USDA Southwest Climate Hub, 2023a).

In the 1980s, USDA researchers in Bushland, Texas, developed a "Limited Irrigation Dryland" (LID) system aimed at maximizing water-use efficiency, particularly in the Southern High Plains region, where fields are primarily irrigated by furrows. This system divides fields into sections with varying degrees of irrigation, effectively capturing and utilizing runoff water. Through this approach, the LID system significantly reduces water wastage compared to traditional irrigation methods, demonstrating remarkable water-use efficiency and promising agricultural yields while conserving water resources (USDA Southwest Climate Hub, 2023b).

While numerous examples of water conservation approaches exist in the Southwest, one final illustration highlights a distinct strategy. This approach centers on environmental water transactions, specifically targeting the support of riparian ecosystems along the Isleta Reach of the Rio Grande. These transactions entail voluntary agreements among various stakeholders, including Middle Rio Grande Pueblos, private water rights holders, municipalities, and conservation organizations like Audubon New Mexico. Through these transactions, water is allocated to mimic natural flood regimes and to provide essential moisture for existing and restored riparian areas, thus sustaining habitats for wildlife and promoting ecological restoration. Key elements of this approach include partnerships with water management agencies, stakeholder engagement, and coordination to facilitate the movement of water to target environmental flows. Lessons learned emphasize the importance of strong partnerships, community involvement, and public outreach in promoting sustainable water-management practices. Ongoing efforts involve continuing water-leasing initiatives and working collaboratively to strengthen the water transaction program (USDA Southwest Climate Hub, 2023c).

CONSERVATION VIA WATER MANAGEMENT

They say that water is the gold of the West. Like gold, water has been manipulated and fought over. Marie, a ranch owner in Northern Arizona, said it most vividly: "Oh, whiskey is for drinking, water is for fighting over in the West." Water is the fodder for endless policy debates, battles, agreements, and decisions. In the Southwest, water is at the root of conflict and cooperation across state, tribal, and international borders. The politics of water in the Southwest is about who can control this increasingly rare resource. And as Marc Reisner observes, control over water has driven "politicians of every stripe [to sacrifice] their most sacred principles on the altar of water development" (Reisner, 1986/1993, p. 12). It is within this political climate that water conservation and the culture of conservation has grown. Water management has become the main way that conservation has become institutionalized and integrated into the larger society.

Listening to the participants, I hear a kind of hopefulness in their efforts to conserve. While experts in water management have different viewpoints about what is needed, many express what can sound like hopefulness as well. Water management, as we'll explore in chapter 3, has always been at the root of conservation efforts to save water in the Southwest. Even today, some continue to view water management as the means through which to maximize water efficiency for economic development, despite ongoing environmental issues.

In his report "Water Management in the American Southwest: Lessons for an Age of Climate Change," Andrew Holland, former security officer for the nonpartisan American Security Project, emphasizes the role of water management for economic development:

> The American Southwest is seeing the worst span of drought in a generation, lasting since 2000 in some regions. However, this has not held back economic development. This paper argues that key adaptations, including dams, legal title, and effective regulations, have allowed the region to thrive even in the face of water shortages. (2014, p. 1)

From Holland's perspective, not only may the Southwest thrive amidst prolonged drought, but also "the lessons from the American Southwest can prove to be a model for the rest of the world, as climate change makes the world's drylands more prone to drought and unpredictable precipitation" (2014, p. 1).

Regulatory frameworks, legal systems, and infrastructure for water utilization compose the core of water management. For example, there is a long

BOX 1.2. THE CENTRAL ARIZONA PROJECT: "A VISION FOR ARIZONA"

The Central Arizona Project (CAP) diverts 1.5 million acre-feet of water, covering 336 miles and lifting water over 2,900 vertical feet, delivering Colorado River water to central and southern Arizona and serving 80 percent of the state's population. The system includes fourteen pumping stations, one hydroelectric pump and generating plant, one storage reservoir, and dozens of radial gate structures and turnouts to control the flow and delivery of water.

The CAP was designed to provide water until the year 2000, but no new sources of water have been developed, The CAP's vision remains centered on the integration of conservation practices with highly controlled management strategies. To manage the water supply, the CAP employs conservation measures, such as the Intentionally Created Surplus (ICS), which incentivizes water conservation and new contributions to Lake Mead.

According to the CAP website, the ICS "is an innovative—some say visionary—way for water managers to create incentives for water conservation and new contributions to Lake Mead" (Person, 2020). CAP incentives include investing in and paying users to develop high efficiency irrigation; develop non–Colorado River water supplies, including desalinization technology; and in the case of agriculture, to keep fields fallow. Touting ICS as an innovative conservation tool for water managers, ICS leaders outline several types of conservation projects, even calling one of them "Extraordinary Conservation," defined as conservation that "[saves] Colorado River water that would have otherwise been used" (Person, 2020).

The CAP is representative of other large-scale water management efforts throughout the Southwest, and conservation at all levels has been predicated on efficiency and reducing water use. Despite claims of effective water-system adjustment and adaptation to water shortages, the question remains whether such efforts can protect the water resources of the state of Arizona and the Colorado River system overall.

history of regulations and efforts to manage the Colorado River as a resource, including a complex hodgepodge of agreements and guidelines first established in 1922 with the Colorado River Compact. Readers looking for more

FIGURE 1.2. A Central Arizona Project canal (Photograph by Sam Minkler)

information on this history can refer to textbox 3.1 "1922 Colorado River Compact and Overallocation" in chapter 3.

The example of the Central Arizona Project (CAP) provides a lens through which to examine water management within the context of water conservation. The CAP is a canal system in Arizona that brings water from the Colorado River to the central and southern regions of the state. As such, it is a crucial piece of infrastructure for water management in Arizona, and it provides an excellent example of how water conservation is integrated into water management practices.

LOOKING TO SCIENCE FOR SOLUTIONS

My family was trying our best to conserve water, but it didn't feel like reduced showers, watering our garden less, limiting our tree watering to leftover water in our cups, and installing low-flow showers and toilets were enough. So, we turned to science, thinking that scientific research might help us find our way into a more developed approach to water conservation. Looking at the research on household water conservation, we learned that, despite our efforts, our water footprint was still quite large. While, as vegetarians, we consumed a lot less water per day than meat eaters—1,000 to 2,000 liters of water in the process of making and transporting our food, as compared to meat eaters, who indirectly consume approximately 5,000 liters of water per day—we learned that a plant-based diet could cut our water footprint yet further. We became vegans.

Yet our food was not sourced locally; it's hard to do that in Northern Arizona, where the growing season is limited to a couple of summer months. Our food gets shipped from other areas around the Southwest, and gasoline production is one of the largest consumers of water. So, even as vegans, we indirectly consume a lot of water through the transportation of our food. I don't mean to give the impression that we are a one-issue family focused exclusively on water consumption, just that we took our role as conservationists seriously. We wanted to be good conservationists, and we were hoping that learning more about the science of conservation could help us.

CONSERVATION SCIENCE

Turning to science seemed like a good way for us to learn more about how we could conserve water. After all, the Southwest is home to numerous water conservation and ecological restoration projects. Environmental organizations, both large and small, have established specialized science and water divisions dedicated exclusively to advancing water conservation initiatives. These divisions play a vital role in the region's sustainability by generating scientific data, which in turn supports the political endeavors aimed at promoting water conservation practices.

Conservation science strongly influences policy decisions. Whenever large-scale projects are proposed, whether they pertain to housing developments, agriculture, or mining operations, comprehensive ecological impact assessments are required. This ensures that potential environmental consequences, especially those affecting waterways, are thoroughly evaluated. Scientific research serves as the backbone of such assessments, exposing the potential ecological ramifications of these projects.

In essence, water conservation science casts a wide net across the Southwest, exerting its influence on multiple fronts. It shapes public perceptions of the water-related challenges faced by the region, informs policy decisions that carry long-term ecological implications, and drives approaches to water conservation. However, scientific evidence of ecological issues does not necessarily halt such projects, though it may slow them down or alter plans so as to reduce impact. Nevertheless, the science of water conservation extends throughout the Southwest, impacting perceptions, policy, and approaches to conservation.

THE HOPE OF HIGH TECH

Technological innovations also seek to address water scarcity. High-tech solutions include water desalinization plants, pipelines, importing water, and groundwater treatment plants. With shrinking snowpack in the Sierra Nevada, California has increased investments in desalinization plants. While desalinization is costly and energy inefficient, many consider it a necessary evil.

Towns and cities scattered throughout the Southwest are weighing their options as they plan for continued population growth. Many are looking to build large-scale pipelines. However, pipelines are expensive and time-consuming, and while they may temporarily alleviate water scarcity, they also have other environmental consequences. Southern Nevada Water Authority (SNWA) has been in court for the past decade over a three-hundred-mile pipeline that would transport 7.8 billion gallons of water per year from desert groundwater basins located on public lands in eastern Nevada to supply water for swimming pools and golf courses in Las Vegas. However, due to opposition from White Pinal County and the Great Basin Water Network (a coalition of environmentalists, tribes, ranchers, rural communities, and local governments) the SNWA announced in 2020 that it would not appeal a court ruling that denied water rights for the pipeline project. Pipelines are time-consuming and often wracked with legal issues such as negotiations and settlements and years of environmental assessments and feasibility analyses. Take the example of Flagstaff's purchase of Red Gap Ranch near Winslow, Arizona, in 2005. The intention was to build a forty-mile pipeline to deliver water to Flagstaff; however, by 2024, they were still entangled in environmental impact and feasibility studies.

In an effort to manage the Colorado River's uncertain future, federal agencies and researchers are employing advanced modeling techniques to simulate thousands of potential scenarios, incorporating past extremes and projected climate shifts. Traditional forecasting methods based on historical data have proven insufficient as the river faces unprecedented stresses. The new approach aims to test various management strategies to navigate uncertainties, with the goal of ensuring the river's sustainability for millions of people. Despite optimism, some scientists advocate for simpler solutions, emphasizing the need to plan for reduced water flows in the face of escalating risks (Partlow, 2024).

...AND LOW-TECH STRATEGIES

In response to drought and ecological threats to the Ogalla Aquifer, some New Mexican ranchers are turning to Criollo cattle, a resilient breed capable of thriving in arid conditions, according to research by the US Department of Agriculture (Moreno, 2017). Similarly, Dennis and Deb Moroney, owners of a ranch in Cochise County, Arizona, have incorporated Criollo cattle into their ranching practices as part of their commitment to ecosystem restoration and sustainable agriculture. Criollo cattle, well-suited to arid environments, require minimal food and water compared to British breeds, and their grazing habits promote natural ecosystem regeneration. Despite the ecological benefits, marketing Criollo beef poses challenges due to a lack of processing facilities designed for smaller-framed animals (Good Food Finder, 2023).

In Colorado's drought-stricken San Luis Valley, Rocky Farms plants "crop cover," a mixture of crops that decompose and enrich the land, creating more nutrient-rich soil, which needs less water. Yet crop cover is expensive and time-consuming and is only used on 1 to 4 percent of cropland throughout the Southwest (Zulauf and Brown, July 24, 2019). Crop cover requires part of the land to go out of production each year, resulting in less revenue. Furthermore, it often takes years before farmers see the soil benefits. While crop cover is seen more regularly on the East Coast, agricultural economists Carl Zulauf and Ben Brown suggest that since cash crops require conservation of moisture, farmers are unlikely to use this approach widely in drier climates.

The perception of science and technology as beneficial motivates the pursuit of scientific and technological remedies to imminent water crises. My family and I had developed a devotion to conservation. We were trying our best to conserve. However, the more we learned about the science and technology of conservation, the more we began to wonder if conservation might be too narrow a path. Still, we believed and continued to believe that conservation is good. But we were starting to question just how far individual and collective conservation efforts could bring us.

CONSERVATION: THE GO-TO STRATEGY

Conservation, whether through individual efforts in homes or large-scale actions by government and institutions, has become a clarion call for action and a way of coping. Xeriscaping yards, installing low-flow appliances, and creating water restriction policies are common actions taken. However, water levels in reservoirs continue to drop, despite these technological wonders that have enabled large-scale agriculture and population growth. Long periods without precipitation are followed by hopeful relief when rains finally arrive. It's important to believe that everyone is doing their part, and so sacrifices are made such as replacing grass with desert vegetation, taking shorter showers, cleaning cars less often, and collecting rainwater to water gardens.

And every now and then, those of us who can afford it indulge in a little guilty pleasure, enjoying a spray of fine cool mist while sitting beneath great palms, sipping on iced tea, or taking trips to Las Vegas and marveling at how the now iconic Fountains of Bellagio, spanning over 1,000 feet and spouting water 460 feet into the air, will "romance your senses" with "thoughtfully interwoven water, music and light designed to mesmerize its admirers." We "fall in love with this unprecedented aquatic accomplishment as (we) enjoy an enchanting concert of opera, classical, Broadway and pop tunes" (Bellagio MGM Resorts, 2018).

What about individuals who choose to avoid such indulgences? Some may adopt a vegan diet, which can reduce their daily water consumption by 1,100 gallons simply by switching from animal-based to plant-based foods (Vegan Calculator, n.d.). Others may explore new and more efficient water-conservation methods using science and technology. Nevertheless, we live in the arid Southwest and continue to depend on limited water sources in order to survive.

The longer I lived in the Southwest, the deeper my connection to these lands became and the greater my internalization of the values of conservation, what I call a "conservation ethos," became. However, my family and I had done everything we thought we could do to become better at conserving water. As I dove yet further into this research, I began to see how I, like others, had come to rely on conservation to justify my lifestyle and continuing to live in this region of the world. For many participants, as well as myself, conservation transcended being a mere justification for living in the Southwest; it became an intrinsic part of the culture and an embedded core value system. With limited water resources available in the Southwest, the adoption of conservation practices was thought of as not just a choice but a necessity for many participants, including myself. What else could we do? Move to a wetter region of the world? How would living somewhere else potentially negatively impact that area? I began wondering: Can conservation ultimately be enough—perhaps if we do it better, do it more? The more I dove into these questions, both through my own reflections and through my research, the more I began to see drawbacks to conservation, especially in the face of the water issues we face. We will look at the inherent limitations of conservation in chapter 2.

A Culture of Water Conservation: Unexamined Assumptions

As we delve into this exploration of water conservation culture, it becomes evident that it has pervaded our society, with conservation often being hailed as the ultimate solution. The opening quotes from Sofie, Gary, and Petunia, the examples of guilt, the cognitive dissonance highlighted in many of the respondents' efforts to rationalize living in the Southwest through conserving water, my family's own struggles to make a difference through conservation, and the communal struggles at various levels of governance all reflect the prevailing belief that water conservation is the primary approach necessary for addressing water issues in the region. This assumption is deeply embedded in our cultural psyche. From federal government initiatives to state, regional, and local water-management strategies, as well as advancements in science and technology, down to individual efforts, the prevailing notion is that we must conserve more effectively.

However, it is essential to understand that conservation, as it stands today, did not emerge in isolation. Rather, it evolved from a specific historical and political context, leaving a lasting imprint on our collective consciousness and social structures. To truly grasp the nuances of our water conservation culture, as we will explore in chapter 2, it's imperative to delve beneath the surface and unveil the prevailing assumptions that have been widely embraced. We must also examine the historical and political context from which a culture of conservation emerged. The roots of conservation culture are entwined with a history of colonization, resource exploitation, and a quest for dominance over land and water resources. To fully comprehend our culture of water conservation, we must confront these historical and political undercurrents that continue to shape our approach to water in the arid Southwest, a topic we will delve into in chapter 3. Only then can we embark on a journey of greater understanding and transformation.

FIGURE 1.3. Kachina Wetlands Preserve. Human-created wetlands, often originating from wastewater treatment facilities, have proliferated across the country and play a role in conservation efforts and habitat restoration. They offer sanctuary to diverse flora and fauna while mitigating the impacts of habitat loss and environmental degradation. (Photograph by Janine Schipper)

VOICES

Do you think there are shortages in the Southwest? Who is responsible?

The way that we run ag[riculture] in Arizona is a major problem. And because of our water rights laws, there are very perverse incentives. People are afraid they are going to lose their water rights. The people who have them try to use them as much as possible. There is pretty much no incentive at all to doing dry land ag or any sort of intelligent effort to take water into account in farming.
—*Minerva, sustainability specialist, Flagstaff, Arizona*

As a species we are just not thinking clearly about what's ahead, seven generations ahead, and more than that. It's just nuts. We have too many people living in arid environments that shouldn't have lots of people living in them. Phoenix is a great example of a city that shouldn't be there. The way we think we can move water around—it's that whole humans-over-nature conquest mentality—that to me is pretty crazy.
—*Darrah, Community Program Coodinator, Ridgeway, Colorado*

As time progresses, Mother Nature is finding it harder and harder to keep all of its babies, all of its life-forms, alive and healthy, and that is because of water shortages. And who is there to blame? Well, us, of course, the humans! The select few people making environmental decisions for the vast majority are filled with greed and materialistic values. These governors and politicians are the ones who dictate what happens with our water, and, unfortunately, they are motivated by money and power, leaving the environment and water security at a dead end.
—*Mark, retired chair of the board and CEO for an electrical services company, Paradise Valley, Arizona*

I agree that it's the younger generation's responsibility, but I also think that it sucks that older people say this. The drought isn't a new thing. The water shortage isn't a new thing. Climate change isn't that new of a thing. And yet, now it's all on our (young people's) shoulders.
—*Florence, GIS and aerial photography technician for USGS, Flagstaff, Arizona*

Overpopulation is the main problem. It's not agriculture, it's not development, it's children and bigger families, and more families. It's just people. And yeah, we're gonna dry up our rivers. And so, what we do is we blame ag, 'cause it's a big water user, it's easy to blame ag. So, we get rid of ag. And then we cover land with houses but we still have water problems. And we haven't solved the water problems. So, then we look down the road and blame the next guy, and so forth.
—*Marie, ranch owner, Mormon Lake, Arizona*

We have built our economy on a myth of infinite water. Look at Phoenix, where I was born. That's not sustainable. We are pumping that water uphill, a lot of it from the Colorado River, which is using coal and which feeds back into climate change. This myth around which we have constructed an economy has built into it its own collapse by virtue of its dependence on coal.
—*Cactus Ed, program director at a nonprofit environmental organization, Flagstaff, Arizona*

2

The Limits of the Conservation Ethos

I should have been encouraged. Wasn't it a good thing to find through my research that people throughout the region are generally conscious of how much water they consume? Clearly, descendants of Europeans had internalized the lessons of conservation that only one hundred years earlier were considered novel and innovative, lessons that made living in the desert Southwest even possible. Over the years of living in the region, I too had come to internalize these values. It felt good to conserve, to feel like I was doing my part in reducing my water footprint and to be part of a community that values conservation.

However, as I delved deeper into my research, I started to uncover cracks within the conservation paradigm that the dominant culture[1] continues to ardently embrace. As with any paradigm or worldview, a set of taken-for-granted values underlies conservation. Values delineate what we care about

---

1 By "dominant culture" I refer to the attitudes, values, beliefs, and worldview of the cultural group that wields political and economic power. In the United States, the dominant culture is composed of white, Protestant, and middle- and upper-class people of northern European descent. Dominant cultural values are not limited to the cultural group from which they derive but become incorporated throughout the society and are experienced as the "norms" of that society.

and prioritize. They guide how we make decisions and how we act. Yet the more I explored the values underlying conservation, the more I began to see gaps—ironies, paradoxes, and outright problems—within approaches to conservation.

The internalization of a conservation ethos has reached such a profound level that altering our course or determining a new direction becomes a formidable task. In this chapter, the focus is on unveiling the underlying values of conservation and examining their limitations and challenges. By identifying these values and recognizing the problematic consequences they have led us to, we can start gaining insight into the necessary changes that lie ahead.

Valuing Resources

> We value water for the nonrenewable consumptive resource that it is.
> —*Andrea, hydrologist, from Sedona, Arizona*

The language of water as a "resource" pervades literature, scientific discourse, news accounts of drought and water scarcity, politics, and the interviews that we conducted. What does it mean to talk about, write about, study, and relate with water as a resource? For one thing, it means perceiving water as a noun, an object. Resources are objects to be utilized, generally to generate wealth, as in the etymology of the term *resource*, which referred to "a country's wealth," as first recorded in 1779. Let's pause a moment to consider what objects are. They are things; as such, we can do what we want with them. Perhaps we worry about whether they will last or, as is often the case in the dominant culture, we may mindlessly accumulate them and treat them with indifference, as they will not protest. We tend to take care of objects only when we need to, only when we perceive that our own welfare is at risk.

As an object, water may be moved, taken, quantified, and transferred from one place to another. It is collected in reservoirs and moved through technologically sophisticated storage and conveyance systems. As Henry Vaux Jr., emeritus professor of resource economics at University of California, Berkeley, expounds, "the result is that one of the prominent characteristics of today's western waterscape is a vast maze of dams and canals. Parts of this maze are so imposing physically that they can be seen from outer space" (Vaux, 2005, p. 5).

Water resource managers make a living by moving water around from areas that have it to areas that need it, or, in the case of highly populated or

FIGURE 2.1. Central Arizona Project pumping station during construction in 1980. (Central Arizona Project)

agriculturally developed places in the Southwest, areas that demand it. Craig Childs, a well-known environmental writer in the Southwest, notes that the hydraulic infrastructure of the region captures and diverts the majority of incoming river water, blending it with redirected Colorado River water pumped from a distance of three hundred miles. Childs writes,

> Sustaining this number of human beings has become a careful, daily balancing act, control rooms glowing with batteries of monitors where people called "water masters" monitor every twist and turn, their fingers dancing on keyboards to open and close head gates. When chains of upstream storage reservoirs dip below their desired capacity as snowpack and runoff dwindle from the mountains, the city turns from surface storage to groundwater. Switches are thrown so pumps can haul aquifer water from beneath the city up into the daylight. (Childs and Darby 2015)

When we think about water as a thing to be used, all of our efforts to conserve are by definition utilitarian. The result is that water conservation takes

> **BOX 2.1. HISTORY OF CONSERVATION AND UTILITARIANISM IN THE SOUTHWEST**
>
> President Theodore Roosevelt established the US Reclamation Service in 1902, which aimed to manage Western rivers' flow to conserve unused water for irrigation and settlement. John Wesley Powell, an explorer and geologist, warned against this utilitarian approach to water conservation and advocated for river management based on the flow of the river itself. However, the utilitarian approach prevailed, driven by a desire to develop industry, agriculture, and settlement. This sentiment was epitomized by Herbert Hoover, who believed that "every drop of water that runs to the sea without yielding its full commercial returns to the nation is an economic waste." (Owen, 2018, p. 258). Water conservation became economically beneficial, and families began recycling water through various domestic uses. Journalist David Owen summarized the burgeoning utilitarian conservation ethic as follows: "In the 1920s 'conserving' river water meant extracting as much profit from it as possible before it flowed into the sea" (Owen, 2018, p. 21).

on a utilitarian drive, the drive to measure, collect, move, and ultimately use water. Utilitarianism itself is not bad. As an ethical model, utilitarianism strives to produce resources to provide the most benefit for the most people while creating the least amount of suffering. The problem with treating water as a resource to be used is that it keeps the focus on allocating a decreasing amount of water to an ever-growing population while supporting an agricultural system that faces serious problems, as discussed later in the chapter. Ultimately, utilitarianism's focus on human well-being, by elevating human needs, has the paradoxical effect of removing us humans from the larger environment that sustains us. The underlying assumption is that conservation will provide humans with water resources to meet all of their needs and desires without tipping us over into environmental devastation.

RESOURCE MANAGEMENT

While having broadened their focus to include preserving land, water, habitats, and, recently, the biome for ethical and aesthetic reasons, the notion that nature is a "resource" that may be effectively managed to serve human purposes continues to shape conservation work.

There are a number of problems with this orientation. Effective resource management is complex. There is a certain amount of human and cultural hubris built into the notion that natural resource management will provide just the right recipe for success—and with that, continued unrelenting use. Typically, conservation projects focus on managing individual resources like water, land, or agriculture, yet overlook connectivity and "how different habitats . . . complement each other" (Sneed, 2019). The end result is that many conservation projects do not adequately address the problems they seek to address. Furthermore, while successes exist, they are often short-lived, due to continued population growth, resource exploitation, inadequate funding, and excluding local communities and failing to consider their needs, which results in a lack of local buy-in (Dasgupta, 2016).

Valuing Water as a Commodity: Save Water, Save Money

> We've done really well with water. We conserve that commodity and that resource really well.
> —Sally, superior court clerk in a small town in Arizona

When I first arrived in Arizona, I was struck by how people talked about water using phrases like "Water is the gold of the West," "Water runs uphill toward money," and "Our next major war will be a water war." But perhaps the most common way that I heard water spoken about was as a "precious resource," and as such one that needed "to be conserved." So it's not surprising that a major approach to conservation is treating water as a commodity, with its value expressed in dollars.

Putting a price on water at the individual, household, and institutional levels monetizes conservation. As Sally puts it, "people conserve water when it hits them in their pocketbooks."

INCENTIVIZING CONSERVATION AND OVERUSE

Indeed, the interviews were replete with examples of how individuals conserve water in order to save money. As Evan, who works with federal labor-law enforcement, says, "I decided very quickly that I didn't want to pay unbelievable water bills for the pleasure of having green grass." Evan began to xeriscape in order to reduce his water bill and saw his bills decline dramatically.

Respondents discussed how their respect for the value of water developed when the costs of water were higher. Such was the case for Joshua, a businessperson and city council member for a small Southwestern city, who grew up in Israel. Joshua described how hauling water as a child helped him value water, remarking, "You feel the value of water when you don't have the money to pay for it."

When water is monetized, there is a risk of inadvertently incentivizing overuse, even without any intention to do so. The question arises: What happens when there is no obligation to make payments for water? As one of the participants, Thea, an undergraduate environmental science major, remarked, "I know people that will sit in the shower here on campus for two hours because we're not paying for the water bills."

Perhaps even more dramatic, notes Mason, director of sustainability for a resort, is when those visiting the Southwest are economically incentivized to waste water. For hotel and resort vacationers, water is often seen as something one has already paid for and therefore should consume. When guests paying $350 a night see a sign in the bathroom explaining how the hotel reuses their toilet water, many are appalled. "They can't believe that we use toilet water on the flowers," Mason explains. Mason's job exists because of the economic model of conservation. Explaining that "everything is driven by numbers and profit," Mason reflects on the company's approach to "champion sustainability and water conservation through every one of our properties. This is our number one concern right now." The concern is not simply about saving water to lower prices; The concern is about conserving water so that there will be enough water to continue to run resorts in the desert.

"WATER FOR MONEY"

At a larger scale, economic strategies have been devised to incentivize water conservation among farmers. "Water for money" strategies have become increasingly popular. Planning for a hotter, drier Southwest, water conservation managers seek ways to adapt in the face of what many consider byzantine water laws, through implementing voluntary conservation programs with economic incentives. Through "water for money" strategies, state and local governments pay farmers to conserve water by leaving some of their land fallow for a growing season. As water becomes scarcer, these economic incentives constitute a significant portion of the annual revenue for many farmers.

For example, in 2006, facing an overtaxed water basin and shrinking water tables, the Rio Grande Water District in San Luis Valley in Southern Colorado created a state-mandated plan to charge $75 per acre-foot for pumping groundwater. They used the money earned to then pay farmers to leave their fields fallow. By 2012, the district began seeing a rebound in the aquifer, recovering approximately 250,000 acre-feet of water. This initial success encouraged proponents of the plan to view the "money for water" approach as a model conservation effort and template for other arid agricultural communities facing the economic uncertainty of prolonged drought. The problem here is not that these efforts don't result in less water use but that, because they can be effective in the short term, they have become a go-to strategy for dealing with a diminishing supply of water. However, as water becomes scarcer, these economic incentives will constitute an increasingly significant portion of annual revenues for many farmers turning "not using water" into a kind of business in itself. Will "money for water" strategies be a first step in developing a conservation ethos with greater connections to water, as some argue, or will they further undermine the relationship with water as it becomes a bargaining chip for farmers? (Tory, 2017).

BLOCK PRICING, WATER FOR THOSE WHO CAN PAY

Through block pricing, "essential water," such as that used for washing clothes, drinking water, bathing, and cooking, costs less; while "additional water" or "nonessential water," such as water used for landscaping, costs more. Yet equity issues arise. Higher prices for "nonessentials" mean that lower-income families bear the burden for water conservation, while higher-income families have the privilege of deciding when and how they wish to practice conservation. Some, for example, pay to use rather than conserve water, opting for green lawns and swimming pools. To address the economic inequality fueled by block pricing, some cities (like Las Vegas) and states (like California) have banned it, promoting conservation through other means like incentivizing xeriscaping and installing low-flow appliances, and creating and enforcing water restriction policies.

The problem with commodifying and monetizing water is that the primary relationship to it becomes economic rather than lived. Water is life. It sustains us. Yet the more we think of it in terms of money, the more alienated we are from this vital and central truth, something further explored in chapter 5. Ultimately, valuing water primarily as an economic resource has not brought us to a sustainable place.

Valuing Ownership and the Rights to Water

> I often wonder, who's going to own the water? In the old West, if you owned the water rights, you controlled everything. You controlled your neighbors, you controlled whether they could eat, drink, sleep. Is it going to be that way again?
> —The Chief, professor of physiology, Flagstaff, Arizona

The notion that water should be managed via rights and ownership is deeply ingrained in Western[2] practices and attitudes. Sally expressed pride around how her community's water rights were secured:

> Our fore-founders were actually very smart about water rights and securing water rights for the community and county. A lot of other counties weren't as smart as we were, even though we're kind of at the bottom of the food chain as far as the Colorado River allocation goes. Now a lot of them ask for water from us.

Indeed, many participants highlighted how water rights is a key bargaining chip in the desert Southwest. As Sophie explained, "water is hugely political. People have been shot over water rights, you know? I think water in the West is one of the most contentious things—who owns it and how is it used."

In order to use, buy, and sell water, someone must own the water. However, since water moves, changes form, and cannot be counted and distributed in the same way as land, ownership is based on the *rights* to use water. Conservation depends on this sense of ownership to "save" water for future use.

WHEN CONSERVATION CONFLICTS WITH WATER RIGHTS

One day Eliot and I visited our good friends Rob and Cara in their new home in a small town in southwestern Colorado. They used to live in our neighborhood

---

2 By "Western" I refer to countries and parts of countries whose cultures are rooted in a Western European worldview.

> **BOX 2.2. WATER RIGHTS AND THE LAW OF THE RIVER**
>
> Water allocation along the Colorado River is highly valued and contested. In 1922, the Colorado River Compact was established to govern the river, with Upper Basin states concerned about Lower Basin states' growing dependence on its water. Mexico and Indigenous American Nations were left out of the negotiations, despite having prior rights to the water. The Law of the River, of which the 1922 Colorado River Compact is a part, and which comprises numerous rules, provisions, regulations, and court decisions, is so complex and ambiguous that there is no one set of clear guidelines to administer it. According to Greg Hobbs Jr., a prominent authority on Colorado water law, there are fifteen compacts, agreements, acts, treaties, and guidelines that compose the Law of the River, along with conservation and recovery plans, Indigenous American agreements, and water rights. Commenting on the complexities of water rights and the Law of the River, Hobbs concludes, "What an arrangement of federalism interlaces the relationships formed around this river!" (Hobbs, 2005, p. 2).

but had bought land in Colorado that bordered a creek and spent the next decade traveling back and forth between Arizona and Colorado while they built their dreams over there. While visiting them in their new home, we experienced some monsoon rains and together watched as large drops came splashing down into the running creek.

We had always admired Rob and Cara's rain harvesting system at their Flagstaff home: three barrels that would catch the rain as it poured off of their roof and funneled through a cistern system and into their gardens. Now, watching the rain pouring off their new roof and dispersing into the yard, we wondered about their plans for rain harvesting and water conservation. Would they use the same simple but effective barrel system, or did they have other ideas? They had worked with an architect to design a sustainable home, thoughtfully integrating water- and energy-saving features into their architectural plans, so we assumed they had a plan for the rainwater. Rob shook his head and, with disappointment in his voice, remarked that they cannot collect rainwater from the roof. He explained to us that it was illegal to collect rainwater, because it was considered "stealing" water that belonged to downstream owners, primarily to farmers to irrigate the Uncompahgre Valley.

Who owns water? The laws we and our friends bumped up against made it clear that property rights don't necessarily confer water rights. And perhaps this is as it should be. But these laws also make it clear that someone else owns the rights to the water. In any one city or county, the answer can be different depending on a complex set of water rights laws.

Rainwater harvesting at first glance seems a thoughtful alternative to the culture that is preoccupied with water abundance even while facing water scarcity. Rainwater harvesting involves collecting and storing rainwater for domestic use rather than allowing rainwater to run off. Ironically, however, rainwater harvesting conflicts with the ownership of water rights policies throughout the Southwest. In some states, there are strict rainwater harvesting rules. That is, catching rainwater and collecting it in a barrel to use for landscaping is essentially considered "stealing" another area's first-priority water rights. In California, collecting rainwater for landscaping purposes requires a permit. In Colorado and Nevada, it used to be illegal to collect rainwater. Texas and Utah both also have fairly strict rules for rainwater harvesting. However recent legislation has loosened the restrictions allowing for some water catchment on residents' own properties and for specific uses.

The problem comes back to seeing water as an object, not only to be used but also to be owned. Water has been monetized, leading to the establishment of a complex system of rights and laws that restricts our perspective of water to a narrow framework. In some cases, we don't even have the water rights to conserve water.

WATER RIGHTS PARADOXES

Water laws and water rights play a crucial role in shaping conservation efforts in the US Southwest. As illustrated by the case of Gary, a board member of an aqueduct project mentioned in chapter 1, conserving water is often dependent on an intricate web of water laws and rights. It is valuable to dedicate some time to untangling these intricacies and delving into the paradoxes they entail, as they can pose challenges to conservation efforts.

One of the most ironic aspects of water rights in this region is the "use it or lose it" principle embedded within Western US water law. According to the doctrine of prior appropriation, individuals and communities must demonstrate that they put water to "beneficial use" to maintain their rights to it. When this principle was first enshrined in Western states' laws, it served a purpose—the sparsely populated West lacked the necessary water infrastructure for land settlement and resource development. Those who invested in water infrastructure were rewarded with water rights. However, over the years, changing priorities have raised doubts about the suitability of prior appropriation. The era of Western expansion has concluded, and continued population growth comes at significant social and environmental costs. Many water rights holders now find themselves in a conundrum. Economic development and conservation often mean that they do not wish to fully utilize their allocated water. Yet, they are often compelled to do so, or they risk forfeiting their rights.

As highlighted by Richmond and colleagues in the *National Law Review*, this conflict, between the need for water right-holders to demonstrate continuing beneficial use and the imperative to conserve water, creates a disincentive for water right-holders to engage in conservation practices, as they fear losing their right to unused water (Richmond, Mandell-Rice, and Lipinski, February 19, 2022). While some states have adapted their "use it or lose it" laws to address climate change and the importance of water conservation, the doctrine of prior appropriation remains the guiding force behind Western water rights. Consequently, the tension between conservation and water rights continues to persist.

Another paradoxical issue is the allocation of more water rights than there is actual water available. As outlined in textbox 3.1 in chapter 3, the 1922 Colorado River Compact allocated more water to the Colorado River Basin states than the river could supply. In the years leading up to the 2000 drought, Lake Mead and Lake Powell were close to full capacity. However, two decades later, they have dwindled to below 30 percent of their capacity. Officials issue warnings that if reservoir levels continue to drop, revealing the turbines responsible for generating electricity across the region, rolling blackouts may become a reality, as intermittent wind and solar energy sources cannot compensate for the region's heavy reliance on hydroelectric power.

Over the past decade, water consumption has exceeded supply by over 1.1 million acre-feet per year, depleting the reservoir system. Industries and infrastructure built around the 1922 compact's allocations have been resistant to renegotiating the compact, as they fear losing their allocations. As pointed out by Shawn Regan of PERC Reports, this scenario is replicated throughout the American West—there are more water rights on paper than actual water to fulfill them, and stakeholders are embroiled in legal battles to safeguard their interests (Regan, 2022). To avert a major water crisis, Bureau of Reclamation commissioner Camille Touton stated in a Senate hearing in June 2022 that the Colorado River Basin states will need to conserve between 2 and 4 million acre-feet of water in 2023.

Ironically, another water conservation paradox may offer a solution. John Fleck has observed that some of the Southwest's largest growing cities, including Albuquerque, Las Vegas, and Phoenix, have conserved more water in the twenty-first century, even as their populations have expanded (Fleck, 2019). Yet, while impressive conservation efforts may temporarily delay the depletion of reservoirs, the water crisis will persist as long as snowmelt and the Colorado River's flow continue to diminish. Furthermore, water efficiency leads to other unintended negative consequences, as described later in this chapter.

For Indigenous nations, one of the most profound ironies lies in the fact that while the Western water system rewards those who were the first to put water to productive use, many tribes who were forerunners in utilizing water for productive purposes lack legal first rights to the water. Among the thirty federally recognized tribes in the Colorado River Basin, twelve still grapple with unresolved water claims. As legal battles for securing first rights become protracted and costly, many Indigenous nations have opted for water settlements, forfeiting their first rights to secure timely access to water. Journalist Kalen Goodluck highlights the difficulty of navigating the legal process, stating,

> It can take years, sometimes decades, for tribal nations to navigate the legal maze negotiating their rights within the massive tangle of other users staking claims. . . . A majority of tribes . . . have resolved water claims that are moving at a glacial speed through the courts. . . . With the oldest one filed in 1966 [in New Mexico]. (Goodluck, 2022)

Furthermore, even tribes that have secured Colorado River water rights face challenges in managing their water resources. Former chairman Dennis Patch of the Colorado River Indian Tribes (CRIT) notes the struggle to "claim our own destiny with our land and our water" (James, 2020). Although CRIT holds rights to 20 percent of Arizona's water, they face legal limitations that prevent them from leasing water to growing metropolitan areas. An antiquated 1790s law restricts tribes' ability to lease water without congressional approval. In essence, CRIT, the largest first-priority-rights holder in Arizona, lacks the authority to determine how they allocate their water resources. For more information on Indigenous water rights and water settlements, see the section "The Colonial Legacy in Tribal-State Water Conflicts" in chapter 3.

Valuing Efficiency

> I think our irrigation techniques today are so much more efficient than they were one hundred years ago. And I think, fifty years from now, our techniques will be even more efficient. So even though our water tables may be dropping, we're increasing our efficiency, and that will hopefully save us from running into big water shortages.
> —Danielle, co-owner of a potato farm, New Mexico

Anyone driving through farmland, playing golf, or walking through an industrial park or shopping mall—that is, any human-built landscape that requires irrigation—may come upon this sign: "irrigated by reclaimed water." When I've seen these signs, I've often felt a flash of relief, maybe even pride. Yes, I think to myself, we are being efficient with our water use. We are not taking it for granted. We are using it well. And I would be right to have such thoughts and at the same time, I would be wrong.

UNINTENDED CONSEQUENCES OF RECLAIMED WATER

Let's look at agriculture, which stands as the largest consumer of water in the Southwest, accounting for approximately 70 to 90 percent of water usage. Certainly, efforts to increase efficiency in how farmland is irrigated would result in substantial water savings. But this isn't necessarily the case. For example, farmers often point to their use of recycled water to irrigate fields as evidence of their conservation efforts. However, as researchers have discovered, and as W. Cheng and colleagues explain, irrigating with recycled water is tricky because of the high salt content (Cheng et al., 2013). In order to offset the high salt content, which can destroy crops, farmers have to irrigate more heavily, ultimately undermining conservation efforts. Furthermore, declining water flow from conservation efficiencies increases salinity, too toxic for most crops to grow and thrive in (Scott et al., 2014). Water efficiency and the resulting increased salinity can compromise soil quality and resiliency.

> **BOX 2.3. AGRICULTURE IN THE SOUTHWEST**
>
> The United States Geological Survey (USGS) reports that irrigated agricultural land consumes approximately 85 percent of the Colorado River Basin withdrawals (Maupin, 2018). As Pro Publica's Naveena Sadasivam writes, "Farmers profit from crops that can't be sustained by the river's natural flow" (Sadasivam, May 27, 2015). Throughout the Southwest with its limited water supply, farmers grow rice, cotton, and alfalfa, three of the most water-intensive crops in the world, in order to turn a profit. Often native plants that require far less water are also far less lucrative, and water-intensive crops are planted in order to economically sustain farms. Government subsidies that encourage cultivation of water-thirsty crops or that place few or no limits on water consumption facilitate these high levels of agricultural water consumption. Furthermore, because irrigators were some of the first to put the water from the basin to "beneficial use," they have some of the oldest water rights in the region.
>
> Ironically, while agriculture constitutes the highest consumption of water in the Southwest, most public campaigns to conserve water focus not on shifts in agricultural water consumption but rather on lifestyle changes. Perhaps we can best understand the support of agriculture in the region when we consider that the rest of the country relies on Southwestern agriculture. Southwestern agriculture produces approximately 15 percent of the nation's crops, 90 percent of the nation's winter crops, and more than half of the nation's "high value specialty crops" such as crops coming from fruit- and nut-bearing trees (USDA Southwest Climate Hub, 2021).

THE EFFICIENCY PARADOX

As the title of a research article from the U.S. National Academy of Sciences reads, "Water Conservation in Irrigation Can Increase Water Use" (Ward and Pulido-Velazquez, 2008), and another from *Science* reads, "The Paradox of Irrigation Efficiency" (Grafton et al., 2018), agricultural water conservation is not only not enough, it often results in more water consumption, not less. UNESCO chair in water economics R. Quentin Grafton and colleagues write, "substantial scientific evidence has long shown that increased IE [Irrigation Efficiency] rarely delivers the presumed public-good benefits of increased water availability" (Grafton et al., 2018). For example, adoption of technologies that increase irrigation efficiency also limit "return flows," which recharge aquifers. As Grafton and colleagues note, the decrease in water recharging aquifers adds to the water crisis (Grafton et al., 2018). This is because the groundwater from aquifers is "the lifeblood of the rural Southwest" (Nilsen, November 27, 2022). Aquifers act as natural underground reservoirs for the fresh water necessary for drinking water, irrigation, industry, and power generation. However, the aquifers are rapidly declining due to overuse including pumping out more water than can be replenished.

Ward and Pulido-Velazquez's research also demonstrates that increased public subsidies of drip irrigation, while acting to conserve water on specific irrigated lands, lead to increases in overall water use. This is because introducing additional drip irrigation allows for more total acreage to be put into production, thus requiring more water (Ward and Pulido-Velazquez, 2008). In a boom-bust society, where all growth is considered good (described later in the chapter), when more acreage becomes available for production, it is put into production.

WHEN EFFICIENCY LEADS TO GROWTH, NOT SAVINGS

Because California agriculture produces half of the nation's fruits and vegetables, it was given access through the 1922 Colorado River Compact to an abundant water supply (approximately 30 percent of Colorado River water is allocated to California, a larger allocation than any other state). Yet because of the abundant supply of land in the state, there will always be more land available to be put into production than water available to supply that production. Doug Parker and Faith Kearns, leaders of the California Institute for Water Resources, highlight that increased water efficiency leads to increased water supply, which leads to

> more agricultural lands being brought into production, more water available for cities to grow, and more water to remain in streams to ensure a healthy environment. But, eventually, we will face a new drought, and water supplies will again be inadequate to meet the new, higher levels of demand. (Parker and Kearns, 2015)

In other words, as Parker and Kearns write, "enough water will never be enough." Nevertheless, modern water conservation efforts value improved water efficiency. This seems a significant improvement from last century's conservation ethos focused on building dams to "save" scarce water resources of the West from being "wasted" by running into the ocean (see textbox 2.1, "History of Conservation and Utilitarianism in the Southwest," for more about twentieth-century approaches to water conservation). However, as journalist Matt Jenkins writes, "instead of vanquishing the demons of aridity, efficiency has only chased them into the dark. And it has now run up against the quintessential problem of the West" (Jenkins, 2007). The pursuit to expand and grow the West overlooked the real costs of living in the West.

Some of the ironies of improving water efficiency in urbanized areas of the region are fairly straightforward, if unexpected. Improved water efficiency frequently goes hand in hand with increased consumption. Efficiency leads to more value per gallon of water, lowering the price of water and, ironically, increasing the consumption of water as economic incentive to conserve water shrinks. As journalist David Owen puts it, "we almost always reinvest our savings in additional consumption" (Owen, 2018, p. 63).

WASTE NOT, WANT NOT

The conservation ethos exhorts us not to waste water. It is precious, after all, and watching it run off into the roads from car washing or sprinkler systems can feel like a travesty. Isn't it our job to make good use of it? However, conserving water by making systems more efficient sometimes leads to unintended negative consequences.

As the drought progressed in the early 2000s and levels in reservoirs began to fall, US cities sought ways to recapture water and keep it from "running wasted into the sea" (Jenkins, 2007). Jenkins explains that avoiding such waste "is frequently seen as a way to conjure more water out of thin air" (2007). But efforts not to "waste" water are complicated, leading to unforeseen adverse consequences, as in the case of the All-American Canal.

If you drive along the relatively flat land of California Highway 98, you might notice yourself crossing over what looks like a large stream. If you flew above, you could follow this stream as it zigzags, first running west from the Colorado River through Calexico, California, then south, and then west along the California-Mexico border, crossing fourteen miles of sand dunes and running through agricultural and rural lands. This is the All-American Canal, which travels eighty miles from the Imperial Dam on the California-Arizona border, carrying Colorado River water to the Imperial Valley and nine cities in southeastern California.

Since it was built in the 1940s, it has posed a problem to the people managing the water. A full 22 billion gallons of water was lost every year because the canal wasn't watertight. This leakage made its way into the groundwater rather than to the people and farms where the canal irrigates 630,000 acres of cropland in the Imperial Valley. The answer was obvious to many. In order to conserve water, they needed to fix the canal. In the late 1990s, as part of California's Colorado River Water Use Plan, an effort called the All-American Canal Lining Project began, with the goal of increasing efficiency and preventing seepage.

However, since the late 1940s, Mexicali Valley farmers (just south of the California-Mexico border) had been relying on the water that leaked out of the All-American Canal every year and entered Mexico. The leaked water percolated underground and reemerged in the Mexicali Valley, creating fertile land where there was once only desert brush.

The city of Mexicali, home now to 180 maquiladoras, also came to depend on the water from the leakage. The double irony here is that the Mexicali Economic Development Council (EDC) that represents numerous maquiladoras (which are notoriously rife with hazardous worker and environmental conditions) because of their dependence on the seepage, became the leading group to promote economic and quality-of-life issues in the city. They led the fight against lining the All-American Canal to make it more efficient.

In 2006 the All-American Canal Lining Project was canceled. Mexicali business and civic organizations launched a lawsuit that maintained that by preventing the continued seepage, the canal violated Mexican water rights. The lawsuit was joined by two California environmental nonprofit organizations that argued that fixing the seepage also negatively impacted the Andrade Mesa Wetlands. Rather than fight the lawsuits, the Imperial Irrigation District completed the building of a new and efficient canal parallel to the All-American Canal, thus preventing further water leakage. Importantly, the Colorado River Delta, which had turned into a cracked barren desert, largely due to the impacts of damming the river, had also benefited from the seepage. Water seepage from the All-American Canal into the Delta had revitalized the Delta, and wildlife that once found home there, such as herons, pelicans, and cranes, had returned.

Mexicali identified alternative water sources, including sources depending on the Mexicali aquifer and the Morelos Dam, which diverts Colorado River water to the region. However, the drought is hitting Mexico hard, and these water sources are maxed out. Binational efforts to restore the Colorado River Delta have resulted in securing approximately 8,000 acre-feet of water, with a pledge of an additional 210,000 acre-feet through 2026 for habitat restoration, a far cry from the 2 million acre-feet that once led Aldo Leopold to remark about the Delta, "The river was everywhere and nowhere" (Isakowitz, July 31, 2019).

Ultimately, the effort to make the All-American Canal "waste"-free, and the negative impacts this had on the Mexicali Valley as well as the Andrade Mesa Wetlands and the Colorado River Delta, highlights the complex and interdependent web of relations, both human and environmental, that can get disrupted in the name of efficiency and conservation.

Valuing Individualism and Lifestyle

While conducting research on suburban sprawl, I met up with Dana, a real estate agent in Cave Creek, Arizona. She showed me around her property, pointing out the cacti and other native plants that she took care to preserve when building on the land. Cave Creek runs through her backyard, and she explained that a land trust wanted to purchase, and so protect, that section of the creek. Dana's demeanor changed, and with a sense of frustration, she commented,

> I'm perfectly capable of maintaining it as well as they are. I don't build on it and nobody in their right mind would, because the next flood would take it all out . . . I don't believe you can tell me how to use my land because you like a desert view so I can't build a house here. And I'm just as capable as the next person of taking care of this creek. (Schipper, 2008, p. 69)

Like Dana, many living in the Southwest believe they are personally better suited to care for the waterways than governmental entities, conservation groups, water boards, and other collectives that influence water policy. An individualistic mentality pervades the dominant culture and manifests itself in individual conservation efforts.

Individualism is the idea that individuals, rather than the collective (state or community), should have the freedom to make decisions that impact individuals' lives. In the Southwest, this individualistic approach is especially strong and has come to be known as "rugged individualism." As Wendell Berry writes, "the tragic version of rugged individualism is the presumptive 'right' of individuals to do as they please, as if there were no community, no neighbors and no posterity" (Berry, 2006).

In the case of water conservation, many throughout the Southwest believe they exclusively have the right to make their own choices about what, how, and when they wish to conserve. Any efforts by groups to guide that effort are seen as impositions on personal freedom and are considered anathema to the rights of the individual. This was vividly illustrated by a story I wrote about in *Disappearing Desert* about a Las Vegas Valley Water District investigator who confronted a homeowner about his illegal sprinkler. "He got so angry," the investigator said, "he poked me in the chest and said, 'Man, with all these new rules, you people are trying to turn this place into a desert'" (Schipper, 2008, p. 77).

The idea that we are separate individuals who can succeed on our own falters in the face of water scarcity. Our dependence on water for biological and social existence challenges the mythos of the rugged individual, demonstrating that we are not separate individuals who may make decisions for ourselves alone without creating harmful repercussions for ourselves and others. Nevertheless, many living throughout the Southwest value rugged individualism and uphold the idea that water is an individual right and water conservation is an individual choice.

The notion that we as individuals are better suited to care for the waterways that sustain entire communities permeates the mindset of those living throughout the region. We see this in the way that cities and states emphasize the importance of individual domestic conservation efforts in the form of minor lifestyle adjustments. For example, Utah's Division of Water Resources homepage links to numerous conservation organizations that promote lifestyle changes. Click on "Slow the Flow" and you will learn about water-saving tips like "Seasonal Reminder: Turn Off Your Sprinklers" and "Quickly Fix Leaks: A Leaky Faucet Can Waste Thousands of Gallons of Water and Add Costs to Your Water Bill" (Slow the Flow, 2023). Select "Utah Water Savers," and you'll find a prominent heading in bold font stating "Earn Money for Saving Utah's Water," which promotes incentives for engaging in water-saving initiatives, such as water-smart landscaping, toilet replacement, and smart sprinkler-controller installation, as part of Utah's water conservation endeavors (Utah Water Savers, n.d.).

Environmental Protection Agency fact sheets for six out of the seven Southwest states (Utah is not included) all point to household water conservation efforts as evidence of what each state's residents are doing to address water issues (EPA, 2017). These examples highlight the emphasis placed on household water conservation efforts by states in their promotional materials.

Many people rationalize their decision to live in the Southwest through making minimal adjustments to their lifestyles. It is easier to focus on lifestyle adjustments than to make substantial structural and cultural changes—so many take shorter showers, wash cars less, xeriscape, and so forth and assure themselves that they are doing their part.

Because we are connected to each other, individual efforts can make a difference, but they can also be futile unless they are coordinated. Conservation efforts that center on lifestyle changes and promote an individualistic mindset are ultimately contrary to the goal of cultivating a truly healthy relationship with water, as we will explore further in chapter 5.

Valuing Growth: Conserving to Grow

In 1996 I began conducting research on suburban sprawl in the Phoenix metropolitan area. I was new to the region and intrigued by a place so different from what I had been used to in the Northeast. I was astonished to learn that the Phoenix metropolitan area was growing at a rate of one acre per hour during the housing boom of the early 2000s. I flew above the city in a Cessna airplane to gain a bird's-eye view of the growth and felt a growing sense of concern as I noticed the distinct lines where housing developments met desert. I imagined the line moving outward hour by hour as housing developments slowly but steadily swallowed up the desert.

I was perplexed by the rapid rate of growth in the desert region, as it receives less than fifteen inches of water per year. I wondered how such growth could be sustained and where the necessary water would come from. During my research, I discovered that the 1980 Groundwater Management Act mandates that developers demonstrate a one-hundred-year supply of water. One way they achieve this is by contributing funds to the Central Arizona Groundwater Replenishment District, which promises to recharge the Colorado River water to replace the groundwater being pumped out by developers, albeit not necessarily in the same location. However, despite these measures, groundwater is still over-pumped, and the groundwater tables are dropping, indicating the urgent need for alternative water sources or different approaches to water use in the region (Ferris and Porter, 2021).

Since the 2000 housing boom, the rate of growth has slowed down. Nonetheless, Southwestern cities, facing drought and escalating water scarcity, remain among the nation's fastest-growing urban centers. From 2010 to 2020, all seven Colorado River states experienced substantial population growth, solidifying the Southwest's status as one of the country's most rapidly expanding regions (National Association of Counties, 2022). The Integrated Climate and Land Use Scenarios (ICLUS), employed by the US Environmental Protection Agency for forecasting decadal population trends up to 2100, suggest a persistent and steady rise in population despite prevailing drought conditions and heightened water concerns. One projection anticipates a stabilization of the population by 2090, while the alternate scenario predicts a continual upward trajectory in population figures (EPA, February 13, 2024).

In the case of Phoenix, the days of unlimited growth may be drawing to a close. In June 2023, Arizona state officials suspended the establishment of certain new residential communities within the Phoenix Active Management Area due to growing apprehensions regarding excessive water consumption and the diminishing groundwater reservoirs. It's important to note that existing building permits remain unaffected by this decision. Instead, the state intends to enact water conservation measures and explore alternative water sources to sustain the housing projects that have already gained approval. Despite this shift in policy, Governor Katie Hobbs asserted, "We're committed to effectively managing this situation . . . We have confidence that our water supply is not in immediate jeopardy" (Flavelle and Healy, 2023).

As journalist Keith Schneider reports, in order to be successful, developers will need to create more innovative conservation designs that save fresh water and recycle wastewater. And while this is challenging, developers are finding ways. Schneider (2022) highlights several new developments like Teravalis, a sprawling development planned on 37,000 acres of desert land west of Phoenix, that will need access to enough water to house a projected 300,000 residents. Teravalis and other Southwest developments will need to install expensive water-saving infrastructure. Some developments may get stalled or need to downgrade their original plans; nevertheless growth continues based on the notion that saving water will make it possible.

While developers may not be able to "grow and grow on these far-flung lands and put industries anywhere you want," said Kathleen Ferris, former director of the Arizona Department of Water Resources, they will find ways of "being smarter," which means conserving more in order to continue building more (Schneider, 2022). Maximizing water conservation efforts is essential to development efforts and ultimately facilitates continued economic and population growth of the Southwest.

ENABLING GROWTH VIA CONSERVATION

Justifying growth via efforts to conserve acts much the same way as enabling someone with an addiction. As family therapist Kyle King explains, enabling is a process "wherein the family members excuse, justify, ignore, deny, and smooth over the addiction. This notoriously allows the addicted person to avoid facing the full consequences of his or her addiction, and the addiction is able to continue" (King, 2013). It may be argued that the insatiable thirst for growth acts as a collective addiction. Conservation, in this metaphor, acts as a drug, promising prosperity (a high), while numbing us to the deep wounds that continue to fester beneath the surface. The wounds include both economic inequality and less access to water resources, as explored further in textbox 2.4, "Economic Disparity and the Growth Model." Economic, social, and political systems are set up to feed the addiction to growth, and dominant cultural narratives support it. There is a collective belief that functioning in any other way is not possible.

In broader terms, conservation supports the economic status quo. Modern neoliberal economic systems with their focus on free-market capitalism, privatization, deregulation, globalization, and free trade view growth as essential to a working economy. However, as economist Douglas Brown (2001) has written in *Insatiable Is Not Sustainable*, the obsession for more, fueled by the neoliberal model of continual economic growth, is no longer viable and has ultimately become a threat to all life on the planet, including humanity. Conservation does not challenge the growth model; rather it advocates for adjustments within the growth model, so that no matter how much growth is achieved, water will be available for more growth.

Ultimately, these conservation values and the contradictions, problems, and paradoxes inherent within them reveal profound cracks in the conservation model. Water is valued as a resource, essential for supporting population growth and agricultural production. It is commodified and assigned a price. Conservation is pursued to save money. However, treating water, a vital element for all life, as a mere object to be conserved, bought, sold, and used

BOX 2.4. ECONOMIC DISPARITY AND THE GROWTH MODEL

Ironically, conservation efforts that propel continued growth and economic prosperity also undermine economic security. Poverty and income inequality tend to increase in areas of rapid population growth (Mather and Jarosz, 2014). The boom-bust cycle that characterizes the American West, including the Southwest region, undermines economic security for vast sectors of the population (Limerick, Travis, and Scoggin, 2010).

Journalist, author, and musician Rubén Martínez characterizes the boom-bust cycle this way:

> Call it the ethics of boom and bust, the dialectic of the American dream in which there truly is no failure like success—in which boom is predicated on bust. The desert knows this process intimately, having been conquered and colonized over and again. The gap in income inequality has grown steadily over several generations—during times of growth and recession. (Martínez, 2012, p. 326)

While the growth model claims to create economic prosperity for all, the reality is often increased economic disparity with more pressure to access already beleaguered water sources. Take the example of the Salt River Pima-Maricopa Indian Community, located east of Phoenix. The Salt River once snaked through the community, providing water for the Salt River Community's agricultural lands. However, in 1906 the Salt River Project diverted the water in order to manage and ensure a regular flow of water for the growth of Phoenix. A new irrigation system was built for the community; however, by the early 1940s, Salt River Community residents could no longer afford to pay for the water to farm the land. While they still identify as agricultural people, they have leased their land out to non-Pima agribusinesses who can afford to pay the higher water costs to farm the land.

raises concerns. The monetization of water perpetuates an economic relationship with it. Furthermore, valuing ownership necessitates intricate rights and laws to allocate a limited water supply. Paradoxically, ownership can undermine conservation efforts, as evident in the case of rainwater harvesting.

Efficiency is another underlying value of conservation. The goal is to avoid water wastage, leading to the development of efficient systems to maximize water capture. However, this pursuit often results in unintended negative consequences, such as those seen in the All-American Canal. Furthermore, improved irrigation efficiency frequently leads to increased water consumption. Municipal water efficiencies save us money, which tends to be reinvested in higher water usage.

The cherished notion of rugged individualism often leads individuals in the Southwest to perceive their own conservation efforts as sufficient and their individual rights to make decisions about water usage or conservation as inviolable. Unfortunately, the "every person for themselves" approach is ineffective in the face of water scarcity. Shifting gears toward a more water-sustainable future necessitates collective action aligned with the ways of water.

Lastly, the Southwest thrives due to the value that propelled its growth: the belief that growth is desirable. Conservation has been employed to reinforce and sustain the growth model rather than challenge it. However, continued growth and water scarcity are fundamentally at odds. Conservation is not enough. We will need to find another way.

Reflecting on the problems underlying conservation, a graduate student who had read an earlier draft of this book remarked:

> The section on the Colorado River Delta hit me hard; I never knew that it was once lush and green. I thought it had always been this way (dry). We humans make assumptions such as "this is just the way it is. It's always been this way," and so we believe water conservation *is* enough. If we continue to allow these areas to be deprived of water for our own use, if we do not do something, future generations may never know that this area here was once a conifer forest.

The intensifying water crisis in the Southwest and the problems with conservation outlined in this chapter, along with the arguments made throughout this book, should compel us to seek new ways of relating with and understanding water—a new water ethos. However, as we will explore in chapter 5, the new approaches must be rooted in a shift in perspective. We will need to think outside of the conservation ethos. But first let's look at where the values underlying conservation came from. For in order to explore new possibilities, head in new directions, and avoid repeating mistakes, it is important to understand the roots and patterns that have gotten us to where we are now.

VOICES

What do you think water looked like one hundred years ago?

There used to be a lot of water for being in a desert. The Verde River still flowed. It's been flooded, but it hasn't flowed as a natural river for a long time. And the Colorado used to be murky and have coloration to it. Colorado translates to "color red." Now it's completely clear and very much lower.
—*Florence, GIS and aerial photography technician for USGS, Flagstaff, Arizona*

The Rio Grande is a poster child for a Dead River. And a lot of it is because of dams. A lot of the channels on the Rio Grande use to be wider and flatter. The streams would braid back and forth within wide channels. And now that the vegetation has encroached, with invasive vegetation such as tamarisk, the water now is forced to stay in a narrower channel.
—*Wupatki, natural resource specialist for National Park Services, Northern Arizona*

A hundred years ago, there were buffalo roaming in the Southwest. How did the buffalo contribute to water preservation? Well, they liked to roll around in the dirt and create these little pits, and the water would congregate and sink into aquifers. And believe it or not, that is why aquifers are as extensive as they are today. But we wiped out the buffalos and we put in roads. Now there's no place for the water to gather and naturally filter down into the aquifers.
—*Evan, federal labor law enforcer, Phoenix, Arizona*

One hundred years ago, there was a river in my hometown, the Santa Clara River. Now we call it "the wash." It is where all the homeless people hang out and it is dry. You would not even guess there use to be a massive river there. An eighty-year-old man once told me that he remembered being on a boat and swimming in the river as a child. At one point, people used to go there and take baths.
—*Petunia, lead ski and snowboard instructor at Arizona Snowbowl, Flagstaff, Arizona*

I remember reading about the first Spanish that came into the area. They said that there were rivers flowing and that they had trouble crossing them, they were so deep. There were periods of drought and dryness in this area. There were periods when there were forest fires and grass fires, because it was dry. There was a lot more water back then than there is today. The aquifers were high. People used to dig down, you know, three to six feet and there would be water in that pit, and that's not the case today.
—*James, retired teacher, Albuquerque, New Mexico*

People talk about how the West was won. Well, it was won with groundwater. The water tables have gone down pretty much everywhere. A hundred years ago, everybody who settled in these Western towns had a backyard well. I'm sure those all ran dry. When you pave over something, you drain the water away. If you think about how it was developed and settled, there was little surface water, so everyone relied on the groundwater, especially for agriculture.
—*Billy, landscape architect and planner, Denver, Colorado*

3

The Origins of the Conservation Ethos

Roxanne Dunbar-Ortiz begins *An Indigenous Peoples' History of the United States* by sharing a simple exercise that she does with students. She asks students to draw a rough outline of the United States after independence. Although students know that the map should only include the thirteen British colonies that ran along the Atlantic coastline, Dunbar-Ortiz points out, the results of this exercise are consistently the same: students draw an approximation of the shape of the United States as it currently exists. Dunbar-Ortiz concludes that students internalize the "'manifest destiny' embedded in the minds of nearly everyone in the United States and around the world" (Dunbar-Ortiz, 2015, p. 2).

Dunbar-Ortiz's observation is interesting because it points out that whether we realize it or not, most of us to some extent have internalized the values of Manifest Destiny. When examining water conservation approaches closely, it's apparent that these values have become infused in them as well.

The Colonial Mentality: Roots of the Conservation Ethos

The origins of contemporary conservation values arise from a long and complex history of European settler colonialism (abbreviated as colonial mentality) that spawned Manifest Destiny and the idea that European Americans had the God-given rights and responsibility to expand across, inhabit, develop, and use the land. This meant modeling arid Western lands in the image of the agrarian lands of the East Coast. It also meant that a Eurocentric worldview based on Western values such as individualism, competition, ethnic superiority, domination of nature, and Judeo-Christian beliefs, to name a few, shaped the way in which US society in general, and the Southwest in particular, was formed. Here is a brief history of what these values looked like in relationship to water in the Southwest.

The Hohokam people created an intricate irrigation system around 700 BCE. They successfully utilized it for many centuries, and their descendants, the Tohono O'odham, still reside in the area today. Anthropologists are still grappling with the reasons why the Hohokam irrigation system ceased to be utilized by the Hohokam people during the fourteenth and fifteenth centuries. However, in the late 1860s, a group of settlers constructed canals on the former Hohokam irrigation system and founded a colony, which they ironically named "Phoenix," suggesting a city emerging from the ashes of its predecessors.

While European settlers may have continued an agricultural tradition that had already existed on the arid lands and waters of the Southwest since the time of the Hohokam, their resulting water systems, agricultural systems, and cities have had a dramatic impact on the region. From the settler point of view, wild rivers needed to be tamed, controlled, and put to human use in a way and on a scale never before seen in the history of the region.

The 1922 Colorado River Compact marked the beginning of a series of laws and infrastructure projects[1] designed to tame and put to use the waters of the Colorado River. Therein followed a series of compacts and federally funded

---

1 These federal water compacts and resulting water infrastructure projects include the Boulder Canyon Project Act of 1928, authorizing construction of the Hoover Dam and All-American Canal; the 1956 Colorado River Storage Project Act, authorizing Glen Canyon Dam, Flaming Gorge Dam, and Navajo Dam; the 1968 Colorado River Basin Project, authorizing the Central Arizona Project and other projects along the Colorado River; the 1944 Treaty with Mexico, promising annual allocation of Colorado River water of 1.5 million acre-feet; and other acts and projects designed to deliver water to Denver, Albuquerque, and Salt Lake City.

The Origins of the Conservation Ethos | 81

FIGURE 3.1. Glen Canyon Dam. (Photograph by Janine Schipper)

water projects, all designed to divert water out of the Colorado to enable growth of cities to serve the politically powerful Anglo population. As law professor Jason Robinson and colleagues note, "during this period of intense water development, tribes had virtually no voice or input, and as a result, virtually no water" (Robinson et al., 2018, p. 865). Revealingly, the 1948 Upper

Basin Compact, designed to equitably apportion the 7.5 million acre-feet among the Upper Basin states, included a disclaimer that the water was to be apportioned to the Upper Basin states, not the Upper Basin tribes. Robinson and colleagues conclude,

> what came to be called the "Law of the River" generally coalesced during this period into a political-legal framework for diverting water away from Indian reservations and to non-Indian farms, power plants, and cities, largely funded by the federal government and built by the Bureau of Reclamation. (Robinson et al., 2018, pp. 865–66)

Ultimately, over a period of one hundred years, the once wild Colorado, along which John Wesley Powell apprehensively traveled with the first US expedition, a journey he described as three months of "pain and gloom and terror" (Ross, 2018), is now tamed, regulated, manipulated, and overused to such a degree that in 2015 it was deemed as the United States' most endangered river (American Rivers, 2015). Furthermore, Indigenous people became a "forgotten people," provided no voice in the development of compacts and projects that allocated and redistributed Colorado River water. As emphasized by scholars such as Kyle Whyte (Potawatomi), settler colonial domination constituted a violent disruption of intricate human-environment relationships, endangering the adaptive capacity of Indigenous communities and ecosystems (Whyte, 2018).

Taming the "Uncivilized Wilderness"

Environmental historian William Cronon examines the European idea of wilderness as "uncivilized" and morally vacuous. The colonists brought to the "new world" a view of undeveloped and unsettled land as "desolate," "barren," and a "waste." Furthermore, human contact with wilderness evoked "'bewilderment'—or terror" (Cronon, 1996, p. 70). Cronon traces the colonial mentality back to associations evoked by the King James version of the Bible, whereupon "untamed" land led to depraved perceptions, "where it is all too easy to lose oneself in moral confusion and despair" (Cronon, 1996, p. 70). The wilderness needed to be subdued, brought under control by the "civilizing forces" of Europeans, and turned into a garden of Eden so that it could be "'reclaimed' and turned toward human ends. . . . In its raw state, it had little or nothing to offer civilized men and women" (Cronon, 1996, p. 71). In

BOX 3.1. 1922 COLORADO RIVER COMPACT AND OVERALLOCATION

The Colorado River is managed by federal laws and compacts, with the 1922 Colorado River Compact at the center. This agreement among seven states governs the use of the river and distribution of its water, with half of the allotted water per year going to the Upper Basin states and half to the Lower Basin states. However, the river is overallocated, with an average of 16 million acre-feet per year allocated to Western states from 1906 to 2018, 2 million acre-feet higher than the long-term average.

The common assumption and mythology that grew up around this overallocation was that the 1922 Colorado River Compact had been negotiated around a false reading of average water flow from 1905 to 1922, which turned out to be a period of abnormally high precipitation. However, Eric Kuhn, a former general manager of the Colorado River Water Conservation District, and John Fleck, director of the University of New Mexico Water Resources Program, have recently contended that studies conducted in the 1920s based on US Geological Survey data demonstrate that policymakers knew that the Colorado's flow was significantly lower than the 17.5 million acre-feet the compact allotted. This overallocation was not due to a false reading of water flow during a period of abnormally high precipitation, but rather it was based on political and economic interests. The Southwest was developing at a rapid pace, and Congress, invested in development of the West, sought to ensure enough water to continue that development (Kuhn and Fleck, 2019). As *New Yorker* staff writer and author of *Where the Water Goes: Life and Death along the Colorado River* David Owen states, "Water issues are never only about water" (Owen, 2018, p. 105).

Furthermore, the 1922 compact did not account for surface evaporation from Lake Mead and Lake Powell, nor did it allocate any water for Mexico nor a share for the tribes. To meet the high demand, states have historically not withdrawn their full allocation and relied on reservoir storage capacity. However, with declining reservoir levels, a Colorado River Drought Contingency Plan was passed in 2019 to implement conservation measures.

short, the European settlers saw it as their moral imperative to control, tame, and appropriate wilderness to protect humanity and meet the settlers' objectives. Furthermore, setting themselves in opposition to those indigenous to the land was an integral part of the European need to tame nature. As Robert A. Williams Jr. (Lumbee Tribe of North Carolina) examines in *Savage Anxieties*, Western civilization invented itself in opposition to the "savage," who they perceived to live in a state of untamed nature (Williams, 2012). Ultimately, Western attitudes toward water are steeped in a fear of untamed nature.

European colonizers normalized these values of undomesticated wilderness through the idea of *terra nullius*, the idea that "wild" land or "land belonging to no one" would be made available to the first settler. This set the stage for privatization of land and prior-appropriation water rights laws—whoever first puts the water to "beneficial use" has the first rights to that water. The colonial mentality is essentially a series of attitudes, values, behaviors, and norms that have served to justify appropriating and turning nature into a resource to be used by the settlers. From these original ideas emerged notions that drive laws, regulations, and attitudes today.

Prior Appropriation: A History of Water Ownership

The Southwestern United States established prior appropriation laws that govern the entire Southwest to this day and distinguish water law in the Southwest from other parts of the country. The doctrine of prior appropriation evolved during the California Gold Rush of 1849, when large amounts of water were needed to sluice or extract gold. New claims made upstream reduced water supply for older claims made downstream. The eastern "riparian water laws," which gave landowners adjoining waterways "reasonable use" of the water, was infeasible during the gold rush.

Although slightly different by state, the laws based on the doctrine of prior appropriation hold that those who first use water for "beneficial use" have the right to continue to use that water. Built into the laws is an approach to conservation: since water is sparse throughout the region, focus is placed on beneficial use. Ultimately, prior appropriation laws are based on productivity; are specifically designed to support agricultural, domestic, and industrial uses; and reinforce an ethos of ownership—that is, prior appropriation laws determine who has the rights to the water.

It is important to consider the ways in which an ethos of ownership is built into prior appropriation laws. Prior to colonization, ownership was antithetical to the lifeways of Indigenous peoples living throughout the Southwest. In Indigenous worldviews, nature is not an object to be owned but rather a living being who has intrinsic value and with whom human beings form relationships. Through the doctrine of prior appropriation a European worldview—control over nature—was codified into law. Now individuals owned "rights" to water.

Indigenous American water rights today are also based on the "prior appropriation system," as demonstrated by the two US Supreme Court rulings *Winters v. United States* (1908) and *Arizona v. California* (1963). In *Winters v. United States*, non-Indigenous settlers attempted to divert the Milk River, bordering the Fort Belknap Indian Reservation in Montana, claiming that they made use of the water after the reservation was created and before the Nakoda and A'aninin tribes began putting it to "beneficial use" for themselves. The Court ruled in favor of the tribes, saying that the creation of a reservation implied the capacity for those living on the reservation to be self-sufficient and have the capacity to make the land habitable.

Whereas *Winters* ruled that the establishment of a reservation implied the water to make the land habitable, *Arizona v. California* ruled on the amount of water to which tribes had rights. In *Arizona* the Court ruled Indigenous American water allotments should not be limited to their population size but rather should be based on the capacity to irrigate all "practically irrigable acreage on the reservations" (Arizona v. California, 1962), making it possible, even for those Indigenous communities with small population sizes, to cultivate the land.

Most of those living in the Southwest are unfamiliar with the ins and outs of water rights; however, they are aware that tribal nations have "first rights"— rights to water based on their presence on the land prior to settlement. Yet, as explained in chapter 2 and later in this chapter, for a number of reasons, many Indigenous communities do not have access to their water, despite their first priority rights.

FIGHTING OVER WATER: "IN A FIGHT FOR OUR LIVES"

As we discovered in our research, this notion of first rights, grown out of the idea that water can be owned, promotes an us-versus-them mentality that, for some, results in resentment.

BOX 3.2. COLONIAL ROOTS OF GOVERNMENT-INDIGENOUS RELATIONSHIPS

Colonialism, a prevailing force in shaping modern nation-states, significantly molded the complex dynamics between federal and state governments and Indigenous communities. Throughout history, as European colonial powers expanded their empires, they imposed structures of governance that inevitably integrated Indigenous peoples into these political systems.

Colonialism established distinct hierarchies of power. European colonizers, driven by imperial ambitions, exerted authority over Indigenous lands and peoples. This power imbalance laid the foundation for federal and state governments to assume a dominant role in shaping the lives of Indigenous communities. These colonial powers aimed to control not only the land but also the cultures, economies, and legal systems of Indigenous nations.

Additionally, Indigenous communities became subjects of empire. Colonial regimes often subjected Indigenous peoples to assimilation policies, forcibly erasing their traditional cultures and imposing European customs and values. This process of cultural assimilation and subjugation fundamentally transformed the social fabric of Indigenous societies. It established colonial authority, rendering Indigenous peoples politically subordinate.

In the American Southwest, Indigenous communities were forcibly integrated into political systems imposed by colonial powers. As the US government expanded westward, it established territories and states, often encroaching on Indigenous lands through military force, land grabs, and broken treaties. These actions led to significant territorial disputes and the outright seizure of Indigenous lands. The creation of reservations further marginalized Indigenous peoples, stripping them of autonomy and control over their ancestral territories. Through treaties like the Treaty of Guadalupe Hidalgo and federal policies like the Dawes Act, Indigenous nations were pushed under US jurisdiction, severely curtailing their sovereignty and subjecting them to the legal authority of federal and state governments.

As a consequence of such treaties or agreements limiting their sovereignty and placing them under federal and state jurisdiction, the ongoing struggle for Indigenous self-determination and recognition remains an essential aspect of addressing the historical injustices wrought by colonialism.

Jarold, a community organizer and hotel owner in Santa Fe, New Mexico, claims, for example, that these rights enable Indigenous people to "do what they want":

> I find it incredibly wasteful. So, you don't find as many golf courses here per capita as places like in Arizona. But what you see is that a lot of these golf courses around Santa Fe are not in Santa Fe, the city limits, they're on what's called "native land." So it's Native American tribes that have golf courses, lots of them. The Tesuque Pueblo is one example, but they all have golf courses.

Sophie, curator for a botanical garden in New Mexico, says people ask, "Why are we being restricted when Pueblos have so much water for a golf course? Why are we being restricted when Native Americans are irrigating their alfalfa?" Yet, as Sophie points out, these water-intensive crops "are part of our culture now." Alfalfa, imported from Mexico from the early missionaries, is now considered a traditional New Mexican crop, even though it was first introduced during World War II as an easy and lucrative crop to cultivate.

Chris, a farmer, veteran, and former state legislator, articulates a common attitude:

> The couple of tribes that own land should profit from it and should pay taxes and do what everyone else does. If they pay like the rest of us, then by all means the land is theirs. Make full-blooded American citizens out of them.

It is unfortunate that the misconception that Indigenous Americans do not pay taxes and are not considered real citizens of the United States is so widespread. However, it is important to refute this myth, as it is entirely false. Furthermore, the resentment around tribal uses of water in what is considered a wasteful and unsustainable manner evokes a subtle form of the colonial mentality. Thomas, a Diné artist, reflects on the resentment around Indigenous water rights:

> Why do so many Bilagáanas [White Americans] care about Native water rights? If a tribe takes advantage of the system for economic gain, how is this any different from any town and community throughout the United States who abuse water for economic gain? Building a ski resort on our holy mountain and spraying pee water on the Peaks so they can have a little fun [referring to reclaimed water and the Snowbowl controversy]? They don't

fight against this, but they critique tribes for growing hay. Some tribes grow alfalfa. Some waste water and lose their traditional ways. We're in a catch-22. The system is rigged. We don't have much access to economic resources. If we have to use water to grow crops, build a golf course or a casino . . . This is about survival. We are in a fight for our lives.

THE COLONIAL LEGACY IN TRIBAL-STATE WATER CONFLICTS

A growing tension exists between the tribes and states as Colorado River water continues to decline. While the tribes hold senior water rights, they were excluded from the 1922 Colorado River Compact. "Tribal water use is taken out of state allocations," report journalists Anna V. Smith and colleagues, "meaning the more water tribes use, the less states have" (Smith, Blaeser, and Lee, 2022, p. 7). Historically, water negotiations between the states and tribes have been a combative "zero-sum game," says Jay Weiner, water counsel for the Quenchan Indian Tribe and the Tonto Apache Tribe. This combative approach, Weiner explains, "is something that seems to be deeply embedded in the fabric of Arizona and how it approaches Indian water rights settlements" (Smith, Blaeser, and Lee, 2022, p. 8).[2]

In Arizona today, an adversarial approach to water negotiations prevails, as highlighted in a comprehensive investigative report jointly authored by Anna V. Smith of *High Country News* and Mark Olalde and Umar Farooq of *ProPublica* (Smith, Olalde, and Farooq, 2023). This approach has had significant detrimental effects on tribal communities, resulting in prolonged delays in granting them access to essential water resources, which, in turn, hampers their economic development prospects.

One of the most pressing challenges faced by tribal nations revolves around their struggle to secure a sufficient water supply to support economic development and critical infrastructure, such as hospitals. This challenge extends to meeting basic hygiene needs, as underscored during the COVID-19 pandemic, when access to clean water for handwashing became critical. In May 2020, the Navajo Nation, grappling with the nation's highest COVID-19 infection rate, faced the stark reality that limited access to clean water exacerbated the virus's spread within the reservation. This scarcity of water resources not

---

2 For additional insight into Indigenous water rights and the political dynamics within colonial settler states, consider exploring Curley (2021), O'Donnell (2023), and Wilson et al. (2021).

only hinders economic growth but also compromises the ability to respond effectively to public health crises.

Furthermore, in 2020, Arizona legislators attempted to pass legislation that would have denied tribes gaming licenses if they were entangled in unresolved water-rights disputes with the state. Such legislation posed a severe threat to the economic well-being of numerous tribal nations, illustrating how negotiations can be wielded as a tool to pressure tribes into accepting unfavorable terms.

Additionally, water settlement agreements in Arizona often impose constraints on the volume of water tribes can utilize or market for various purposes. This frequently results in unused water being redirected downstream to non-Indigenous communities, further exacerbating the water-related challenges faced by tribal nations. Moreover, tribes are sometimes compelled to make concessions regarding the priority of their water rights. During water scarcity periods, tribes may bear the brunt of supply reductions, while non-Indigenous communities maintain more secure access to water resources.

Furthermore, Smith and her colleagues (Smith, Olalde, and Farooq, 2023) shed light on how private interests benefit from tribal water settlements, gaining access to water resources, securing water contracts, and obtaining protection from future litigation. Mining companies, for instance, have benefited from at least six out of fourteen tribes' water settlements in Arizona, accessing water resources for various purposes, including mining operations.

In some instances, these settlements force tribes into protracted negotiations with corporations, utilities, and other nongovernmental entities to acquire the water they are legally entitled to. The Navajo-Hopi settlement of 2012 serves as an example, where reservation drinking-water access was linked to renewing land and operational leases for a Peabody Western Coal Company mine and the Salt River Project's power plant, contributing to the settlement's failure and further delaying tribal access to water resources.

Tribes also find themselves pressured into making concessions during water negotiations, including dropping objections against mining companies and forfeiting their right to engage in future litigation. This effectively allows corporations to continue their activities without the looming threat of legal challenges from tribes. In the San Xavier Apache Tribe's settlement, for instance, mining company Phelps Dodge secured right-of-way permit extensions through 2090, enabling its operations without legal disputes from the tribe.

Settlement terms frequently guarantee water contracts for the companies involved, as exemplified in the Hualapai Tribe's 2022 settlement, where

Freeport-McMoRan negotiated the transfer of water rights to supply its mining operations. Private interests often align against tribes in legal cases related to water rights, as seen in the *Arizona v. Navajo Nation* case, where business interests joined forces with the state to oppose the Navajo Nation, arguing against a ruling favoring the tribe, citing adverse consequences for the state and its businesses.

As Andrew Curley (Diné) writes, water agreements with Indigenous communities represent a continuation of colonial practices, rooted in legal traditions that sustain the dispossession of Indigenous lands despite the 1908 Supreme Court ruling in *Winters v. United States* that affirms the inherent right to water for reservations. These agreements, like ones forged by the the Navajo-Hopi Little Colorado River Settlement and the San Juan River Settlement, permit non-Indigenous users to access and use any unquantified Indigenous water rights, ultimately serving the interests of continued colonial-capitalist expansion in the western states (Curley, 2019).

Smith and colleagues highlight the most recent example of this modern colonial expansion movement, the case of the Hopi Tribes' quest for water rights. In examining the Hopi case, a court proceeding in September 2020 revealed how their water needs were jeopardized due to Arizona's unique water-allocation method, which required tribes to quantify and justify every drop of water they requested. During the months-long court battle, experts examined the Hopi population throughout history, water usage for crops and livestock, fertility rates of Hopi women, and economic projects.

Ultimately, the court awarded the Hopi Tribe less than a third of the water they sought. This decision has been described as "modern-day genocide" by Chairman Timothy Nuvangyaoma, as it withholds crucial water resources from the Hopi, impacting their ability to thrive and foster economic development.

This case sets a precedent for other Colorado River Basin tribes in Arizona with pending water claims, subjecting them to similar scrutiny of their way of life and economic plans. Such conflicts between tribes and states over limited water resources could shape future water law in the United States, profoundly affecting Indigenous American tribes (Smith, Olalde, and Farooq, 2023).

Tribal access to water is undergoing modest shifts, albeit within the context of substantial barriers, as described above. In February 2022, the federal government allocated $1.7 billion to tribes for water settlements due to unresolved water-rights issues affecting twelve tribes within the Colorado River Basin.

Communities and tribes are also beginning to create agreements to work together for equitable distribution of water. Examples include the collaboration between the Pascua Yaqui Tribe and the city of Tucson, Arizona, to build infrastructure to deliver water to the tribe, and the federal Navajo-Gallup Water Supply Project, a $123 million infrastructure project designed to deliver water to the Navajo Nation, the Jicarilla Apache Nation, and the city of Gallup, New Mexico (Smith, Blaeser, and Lee, 2022). Nevertheless, tribes continue to lack direct governance of Colorado River water, and tribal water rights don't always align with outcomes that directly benefit the tribes, as highlighted by a landmark 5-4 Supreme Court ruling on June 22, 2023, in the case of *Arizona v. Navajo Nation*, which determined that the United States holds no "affirmative duty" to secure water for the tribe.

Despite facing obstacles in resolving water rights issues, the Navajo Nation persists in working with individual states. In Arizona, Navajo leaders are actively engaged in addressing water claims. The Northeastern Arizona Indian Water Rights Settlement Agreement seeks to officially recognize and quantify the nation's water rights within the state while also securing financial support for constructing essential water delivery infrastructure for Navajo Nation residences.

Conserving in Order to Use

"We conserve in order to use," a value expressed by many of the participants, can also be clearly traced to the settlers. This value was originally articulated as early as 1662, in the first published conservation paper, "Sylva: Or a Discourse of Forest-Trees and the Propagation of Timber," written by John Evelyn. In raising concerns over the destruction of trees throughout England, Evelyn's focus was squarely on the central concern of how depletion of England's forests impacted the timber industry. The solution was to create a conservation program to fell trees at a "sustainable rate," cutting down only so much as could be replenished for further use. While timber overexploitation continued into the eighteenth and nineteenth centuries, conservation became the means to ensure continued timber availability throughout Central Europe.

EARLY US CONSERVATION MOVEMENT

The settlers brought with them this European approach to conservation, and by the late nineteenth century, President Theodore Roosevelt and George Bird

Grinnell spearheaded the early US Conservation Movement (1890–1920). Big game hunters, Roosevelt and Grinnell were concerned with how the devastation of large areas of land through reliance on laissez-faire market forces placed the species they hunted at the edge of extinction. Their interest in conservation soon took on an economic imperative as Roosevelt and Grinnell recognized the long-term economic benefits of conserving natural resources. In 1887 they formed the Boone and Crockett Club, a group of national experts devoted to creating policy to protect large swaths of North America in order to protect big game and stimulate economic production. Gifford Pinchot, appointed in 1905 by Roosevelt as the first chief of the United States Forest Service, further developed this view that management over natural resources was profitable and therefore necessary. Pinchot's approach is summed up by his resolve "to make the forest produce the largest amount of whatever crop or service will be most useful, and keep on producing it for generation after generation of men and trees" (Pinchot, 1947, p. 32). Over 230 million acres of land were placed under federal protection under Roosevelt, yet this was accomplished through marginalizing and displacing Indigenous people. Roosevelt's famous line, "The only good Indians are dead Indians," illustrated and reinforced a colonial mentality that viewed Indigenous people with extreme animosity and hearkens back to Williams Jr.'s idea of Indigenous peoples as a symbolic stand-in for wild, untamed nature that needed to be subdued.

THE CONSERVATION MOVEMENT TODAY

The modern Conservation Movement maintains vestiges of its colonial past. Some conservation groups have begun to grapple with their history of perpetuating Indigenous oppression and social injustices and have made efforts to collaborate on conservation projects with local Indigenous communities. But it is a slow process, perhaps necessarily so. As one conservation manager shared with me, "relationships with the tribes move with the speed of trust." Many conservation groups, however, have not considered how their practices are rooted in a colonial past. As Nicole Cuaz has written,

> without critically challenging the dominant narrative, the conservation movement carries its exclusive and unjust historical roots with it today. Because those who maintain power in conservation today shape the dominant narrative, they continue to overlook the stories, perspectives, and voices of those outside of dominant groups, and thus center conservation's agenda around the dominant group's perspectives and voices. (Cuaz, 2020, p. 5)

Indeed, Cuaz's observations of a conservation group on the Arizona-Mexico border point to the core argument of this chapter: the extensive history of conservation spanning over a century, along with the various approaches that have arisen during this time, has been profoundly influenced by the settler colonial mentality. This mentality shapes the way in which water is perceived and the ways in which water issues are addressed today.

Erasing Indigenous Water Wisdom

The approaches to water brought to this country by European settlers have prevailed. Concepts of owning nature and taming it for human use, and the notion that this is a God-given right, have resulted in not only domination of the land and water but the eclipsing of Indigenous ways of knowing and worldviews, effectively relegating them out of view.

A FIGHT OVER IDEAS ABOUT "THIS EARTHLY PLACE"

Dr. Rena Swentzell of the Tewa-speaking Santa Clara Pueblo writes about the cultural history of the Pueblo people. In tracing missionary colonization—the effort by Spanish invaders to force Christianity upon the Pueblo people—Swentzell reveals how missionaries imposed their ways of knowing and being on the Pueblo people through the building of churches in the middle of Pueblo villages. These structures "dominated the landscape with the purpose of turning the minds of the Pueblo people toward an abstract heaven away from this earthly place whose character was dictated by sun, wind, and water patterns" (Loeffler and Loeffler, 2012, p. 35).

The conflict over "this earthly place," which eventually evolved into a dispute over water rights, initially represented a struggle against these foreign Spanish approaches to land ownership. As a result, Spanish influence began to shape the way in which the Pueblo people interacted with the land. Swetzell explains,

> As the political and military branch of the Spanish colonization strengthened, lines in the ground were drawn from the front door of those mission structures defining boundaries of ownership. The Pueblo people were contained within alien boundaries. No longer could communities of Pueblo people move through the valleys and over mesas as they had always done, imitating the water, the clouds, and the wind. (Loeffler and Loeffler, 2012, p. 35)

The idea that humans could own land or water was an entirely foreign and inimical concept to the Pueblo people. Swetzell continues,

> But it was the idea of human ownership of pieces of the Earth that was such a huge, disruptive concept. How could any person own any part of the Earth, the mother, who gave birth to the people? How could any person own part of a flowing entity such as a stream or a river? These continue to be earth-shattering concepts. (Loeffler and Loeffler, 2012, p. 35)

Prior to European colonization, the deep connections to land and water were a living reality, "encoded in the songs and prayers of the Pueblo world" (Loeffler and Loeffler, 2012, p. 34). However, this shifted as a colonial mentality of land ownership shaped the way Pueblo people could interact with water.

Land and water appeared plentiful to the European occupiers. We can see how the roots of growth, waste, and overconsumption emerge from this period. Lord Dartmouth, the Governor of Virginia, noted in 1774 that the Americans "forever imagine the Lands further off are still better than those upon which they are already settled." Furthermore, "if they attained Paradise, they would move on if they heard of a better place farther west" (Olmstead, 1997, p. 219).

LOST TO A "CORPORATE WAY OF LIFE"

Subjugation of Indigenous American ways of relating with water continues today. In 2015 Arizona Senator McCain added a last-minute Southeast Arizona Land Exchange bill into the must-pass National Defense Authorization Act, providing no time for surrounding communities to discuss and debate the bill. This bill gives Resolution Copper, a multinational mining company, 2,000 acres of Tonto Forest Service land in Oak Flat—land sacred to the San Carlos Apache tribe and from which they were forcibly removed in the 1870s—in exchange for 5,000 acres of land currently owned by the mine across Arizona. The mine plans to use an approach called "block caving" to extract ore beginning at 7,000 feet below ground. Block caving will cause the land to cave in and the surface to collapse and is expected to create a drain in the groundwater aquifer.

Dr. Wendsler Nosie Sr., former chairman and councilman of the San Carlos Apache Tribe and a prominent voice in the movement to protect Oak Flat, reflects on the colonial and capitalist dimensions of the land exchange:

What I see is that people don't understand colonization. Colonization comes from capitalism so it puts us in a corporate way of life. It takes away all the family values. It takes away everything from you. As Indian people we see . . . Mother Earth . . . take[s] care of us. So we're all intertwined together. What the corporate world does is take that apart. And then it starts to eliminate things, to where you don't have the strength of that intertwine with Mother Earth anymore. (Poor People's Campaign, n.d.)

ADOPTING THE VALUES OF ECONOMIC DEVELOPMENT

The colonial mentality has influenced the thinking and behavior of some tribal officials who elevate economic development at the expense of cultural preservation and environmental stewardship. Historian Sonia Dickey reflects on the decades of coal extraction (which requires a large consumption of water) from Black Mesa on the Navajo Reservation:

Native leaders seemed *just as responsible* for the environmental degradation of their homeland as federal officials orchestrating the entire deal. Although Nakai advocated tribal sovereignty and Navajo self-determination during his election campaign in the early 1960s, his resolve to industrialize Diné Bike'yah in an effort to generate much-needed revenue on the reservation helped tighten the bond between water reclamation and Navajo colonization. (Loeffler and Loeffler, 2012, p. 84)

Caught in a catch-22, a number of tribes have accepted and created employment opportunities for their people in resource extraction, tourism, and golf courses, all of which threaten traditional Indigenous culture and approaches to land and water sustainability. As Vine Deloria Jr. (Lakota) writes,

tribal governments, attempting to serve the remnant of the tribe on the reservations, have had to devote an increasing percentage of the tribe's natural resources to creating an income for social service programs, thereby turning some reservations into an economic resource rather than a homeland. (Deloria, 1988, p. xii)

The focus on economic development dominates many tribal decisions. Diné artist Roy Kady remarks,

Now we're in this time when we're dominated by sort of the technological culture, and we're dominated by economics rather than other things that we could be dominated by. One of the things that's come through to me loud and clear is that I have never known an Indigenous person who's still traditional who doesn't have a deep regard for the sacred quality of homeland. (Loeffler and Loeffler, 2012, p. 111)

Sarah, a Diné water activist, reflects on how the "colonial mentality" has filtered into tribal politics and decision-making:

We (Diné) are so ingrained with the colonialism thinking that we've got to provide for our economy, and we're just so ingrained with "let's listen to what D.C. is thinking of" and "they know what's right." But we need to change that thinking and see the effects that it's doing to us and our land, the air we breathe in, and within ourselves.

"WE'RE PLAYING ON THE WESTERN FIELD OF LAW AND SCIENCE."

Working to protect their most sacred sites, and act as stewards of the Earth and water protectors within the dominant society, often means playing by the dominant culture's rules. This is powerfully illustrated in the case of the Hopi people and Sípàapu, a sacred spring and the Hopi place of emergence. Sípàapu is traditionally considered the Hopi umbilical cord, connecting contemporary Hopis to the Old World. Sípàapu is regarded as a passageway through which the Hopi people emerged from the Third to the Fourth World. However, water no longer bubbles up from Sípàapu. To many Hopis this is an indication that Sípàapu is dying: "Sípàapu is the heart of Mother Earth.... The heartbeat is weakening. Water no longer comes in and out of the mound. It is dying" (Masayesva, n.d.).

Vernon Masayesva, former chair of the Hopi tribal council and founder of Black Mesa Trust, reflects,

In Western science water is a commodity, a thing you own, trade, and make. In Hopi, water is not a commodity. It is life. It is a spiritual thing, a flow of water, a flow of life. Sípàapu. They want scientific evidence, proof. Fighting everything using Western law. There's no other playing field for the Hopi. We're playing on the Western field of law and science. (Ellis, 2019)

In order to stop water from being pumped from the surrounding aquifers that feed Sípàapu, the Hopi must use quantitative data to prove precisely how the water, extracted to support coal mining on Black Mesa, impacts Sípàapu. Masayesva throws up his arms in frustration, "We are at a complete disadvantage. How do we prove that it's diminishing our water? Why can't *you* prove it—prove it's not harming us?" (Ellis, 2019)

As an educator and Hopi leader, Masayesva seeks to raise awareness, opening eyes and hearts to reveal how the colonial mentality and dominant social structures function to subjugate not only the Hopi people but people everywhere:

> Hopis have a message to tell the world. Hopis have a huge burden. Children of all colors; we care for all races, all children. We pray in six directions for children everywhere. We suffer because children suffer everywhere. This is the Hopi concern. (Ellis, 2019)

The example of the Hopi and Sípàapu demonstrates how Indigenous values of the sacred—respect and reverence, primordial connections to the land ("Sípàapu is the heart of Mother Earth"), teachings of the elders, generational and place-based knowledge, all themes discussed in the next chapter—are all deemed inconsequential by those in positions of power to affect water policy.

A SEAT AT THE TABLE

The colonial mentality permeates conservation management, as decisions about watersheds across the Southwest have often been made by federal, state, and city governments and by nonprofit organizations without consulting or involving Indigenous communities in the decision-making process. Phoebe Suina of the Pueblos of San Felipe and Cochiti, reflects on the problems underlying water management systems in New Mexico as community leadership endeavors to plan for the future of the San Juan and Rio Grande basins in the face of diminishing water supplies:

> The current system is based on assumptions from back in the early-1900s with their interstate stream compacts and the other water agreements that didn't have the breadth of understanding or the expertise or the knowledge or wisdom of Indigenous peoples at the table to help the decision-makers create a framework. So if it was deficient in that, how can it be a sustainable system, a sustainable framework, a sustainable way to go forward? (Goodluck, 2022, p. 15)

The United States has nearly 3,000 conservation districts, with over 17,000 citizens working on conservation district boards to promote and conserve healthy land, water, forests, and wildlife. While demographic data is not available regarding board composition, it is fairly clear that Indigenous people receive little to no representation. As Masayesva states,

> tribes need to be on equal playing field and serve on water boards.... Because the tribes have first rights, 50 percent of the CAP (Central Arizona Project) goes to Natives, but Natives have no voice. They are not even invited to speak. The CAP views water as a property right. Water can be bought and sold whether there is any water there or not. Shouldn't we have priorities for water? Shouldn't Natives have a voice in these priorities? (ITKI and UNESCO, 2016)

Hydrologist Karletta Chief (Diné) echoes Masayesva's concern: "Tribes have not been at the table and when they are, their voices are not always recognized" (ITKI and UNESCO, 2016). Few consider this oversight. In an opinion piece titled "Now, More than Ever, We Need Tribes at the Water Negotiating Table," published in the *Arizona Republic*, Dennis Patch, former chairman of the Colorado River Indian Tribes, and Ted Kowalski, who leads the Colorado River Initiative for the Walton Family Foundation, write,

> We need each other if we are going to protect and save the life of the Colorado River that supports us all.... Tribal nations have historically been left out of planning and negotiations that develop river management across the Colorado River Basin. (Patch and Kowalski, 2020)

Patch and Kowalski write that "meaningful tribal inclusion going forward," while not an easy task, is essential "in the face of one of the most severe droughts in over a century." Ultimately, they conclude, "it is time for each of us to recommit to what connects all of us—and what it means to conserve and live in a responsible, sustainable way, together" (Patch and Kowalski, 2020).

Journalist Ian James reports for the *Los Angeles Times* that leaders from multiple tribes within the Colorado River Basin express ongoing exclusion from crucial discussions between state and federal authorities. They insist on participation as the Biden administration embarks on formulating new regulations to address water shortages post-2026, when existing rules are due to lapse. Governor Stephen Roe Lewis of the Gila River Indian Community in Arizona emphasizes the need for inclusive dialogue regarding the post-2026 plan, stating, "it's no longer acceptable for the U.S. to meet with seven basin states separately, and then come to basin tribes, after the fact." Reflecting on historical exclusion, Jordan Joaquin, president of the Quechan Tribe of the Fort Yuma Indian Reservation, notes, "A century ago, we weren't at the table. We weren't even U.S. citizens at the time. But now we are." He stresses the importance of tribal involvement in future discussions, asserting, "Tribes should be at the table . . . It's meaningful to us. It's the right thing to do." Nora McDowell of the Fort Mojave Indian Tribe speaks about the urgency of protecting the river, stating,

> If that river could speak today, what would it say? "You guys pretty much screwed up." We have to be here to speak for it. And I know it would say, "Respect me. Take care of me. Let me heal. . . . Don't let me die."

McDowell emphasized the necessity of rethinking river management for sustainability, stating, "We have to think about sustainability in different ways. We all have a place and a voice that needs to be heard, that needs to be taken into consideration, that needs to be a part of the solution" (James, 2023).

Reporting on the increasing pressure on the states to address the tribes' senior water rights, Smith and colleagues write, "A fundamental shift in how the river is governed—to a system that acknowledges tribes' sovereignty and gives them a greater say—will be key to sustainably and equitably distributing water in the years to come" (Smith, Blaeser, and Lee, 2022, pp. 7–8)

INTERNALIZING A COLONIAL MENTALITY

Even those non-Indigenous Americans who are sensitized to these issues, myself included, maintain subtle forms of the colonial mentality. As I read over the first draft of this chapter, I identified some subtle colonial assumptions that pervaded my writing. For example, in the first draft of this chapter, I wrote, "To understand how a modern-day colonial mentality persists, it is necessary to briefly review water rights granted to Indigenous Americans." At first glance, this sentence may appear benign; however, notice the assumption embedded in the use of the term "granted." This presumes that Indigenous Americans don't have rights and that non-Indigenous policy bodies must give rights to Indigenous Americans. Furthermore, the term presupposes that tribes are not sovereign nations and are dependent upon, and ultimately *less than*, the more powerful nation, the US federal government, who must grant (which also assumes a level of generosity) rights to this less powerful (perhaps this assumes, less important) group.

In another area, I wrote: "The refusal to acknowledge and accept the rights and processes that have been created to protect Indigenous communities and cultures is a subtle form of the colonial mentality." The assumption that rights and processes have been created to *protect* Indigenous communities implies a type of paternalism whereby those in power view themselves as responsible to support the "best interests" of the subordinate group—both reinforcing the group's subordination and dependence and presuming that the dominant authority knows what is in the best interests of those less powerful groups. The underlying assumption is that the subordinate group is unable to take care of themselves.

Numerous participants had internalized the colonial mentality, often expressing this mindset in similarly subtle ways as described above. Tim, an earth science lecturer who has collaborated with various tribes in the Southwest for many years, exemplifies this subtle colonial mentality in his discussions about Hopi culture. Tim explains,

> Look at the Hopi, they have created a culture that is based on dryland farming and finding just the right genetic mix in a corn kernel to grow this type of corn off of the landscape that they not only depend on but they created religions around.

Once more, at a cursory glance, this statement may seem sympathetic and appreciative of the Hopi religion being rooted in their homeland. However, a closer examination reveals underlying assumptions. It's worth considering whether the Hopis themselves would concur that they constructed religions centered on the landscape. Perhaps from a Hopi perspective, the land, corn, water, and all interacting elements provide wisdom and guidance to the Hopi people.

These subtle forms of colonial mentality assume knowledge and overlook Indigenous ways of thinking, perceiving, knowing, and relating with the land. Furthermore, because primarily non-Indigenous people are in positions of power and influence, especially around land and water rights discussions in the US, how we write about and talk about Indigenous Americans has real and potentially dangerous consequences. Deloria Jr. (Lakota) writes in his now classic book, *Custer Died for Your Sins*, that his central message is "that Indians are alive, have certain dreams of their own, and are being overrun by the ignorance and the mistaken, misdirected efforts of those who would help them" (Deloria, 1988, p. xiii). I view this as a cautionary message: individuals like myself from the dominant society, who may have "good intentions," have experienced collaborating with tribes, or even have intermarried and share their lives with Indigenous partners and children, can inadvertently uphold attitudes that prove ultimately harmful to those we seek to understand, learn from, and support.

Decolonization

How may we resist the colonial mentality and avoid reproducing cultural imperialism while learning from Indigenous ways of knowing? How may Indigenous voices be included in decisions about the future of water in the Southwest? These questions do not have simple answers.

Indigenous activists and scholars advocate for the practice of *decolonization*, a term that has gained prominence over the past thirty years. Decolonization involves dismantling the colonial legacy from systems, institutions, and mindsets. It goes beyond historical independence movements aimed at liberating colonies from global colonial empires. As articulated by E. Belfi and N. Sandiford of the Community-Based Global Learning Collaborative:

> Decolonization is work that belongs to all of us, everywhere. It asks us to think about our relationship with Indigenous lands that colonizers have unjustly claimed, re-defined, and repurposed all over the world. It asks us to embrace responsibility as opposed to accepting fault. Lastly, decolonization is a path forward to creating systems that are just and equitable, addressing inequality through education, dialogue, communication, and action. (Belfi and Sandiford, 2021)

However, José Antonio Arellano's examination of decolonization efforts in states formerly colonized by Spain, such as New Mexico and California, reveals potential limitations of the decolonization paradigm. It may not adequately address issues of economic exploitation and poverty, as it often focuses on cultural identity and representation, potentially overlooking structural and systemic factors contributing to inequality. Arellano emphasizes the importance of considering the broader economic and political context when discussing decolonization and its implications for social justice (Arellano, August 10, 2021).

In the context of decolonization efforts in the Colorado River and the broader Southwest region, Melanie K. Yazzie (Diné) explores the actions of Diné resisters who actively oppose capitalism and development while critiquing resource-extraction practices, which consume large amounts of water and significantly impact water availability. These activities have profound effects on the Navajo Nation. Drawing on insights from Indigenous feminists, Native studies scholars, and Diné land defenders, Yazzie shows that development, particularly in the form of resource extraction, embodies a colonialist and violent expression of capitalism that threatens Diné livelihoods. In response to this destructive aspect, Diné resisters have developed a political stance centered on interconnected life, with the aim of challenging and resisting development and capitalist practices that perpetuate harm in their communities (Yazzie, 2018). See chapter 4 for more on Indigenous leadership and Indigenous-led water justice movements.

Melanie K. Yazzie (Diné) and Cutcha Risling Baldy (Hupa, Yurok, and Karuk) maintain that decolonization is a collective endeavor that emphasizes our interconnectedness and shared responsibilities, something that Yazzie and Risling Baldy call "radical relationality," which extends into politics as well as how we understand the world (Yazzie and Risling Baldy, 2018).

It's crucial to recognize that *decolonization* is a complex term that warrants careful consideration. As Eve Tuck and K. Wayne Yang discuss in their seminal article, "Decolonization Is Not a Metaphor," the term can be offered too easily as a solution for white guilt, complicity, and white saviorism. It can become a way to "take action without effectively dismantling racist systems and ideologies ingrained in Western culture" (Tuck and Yang, 2021).

I believe, as this chapter attempts to do, that a first crucial step is to learn about and acknowledge how the colonial mentality is infused throughout institutional and cultural frameworks, driving water conservation policies, ways of relating with water, and ways of relating with Indigenous peoples of the Southwest, who offer dramatically different approaches to water and living sustainably on these arid lands. Please see textbox 4.1 in chapter 4 to become further educated and involved in the work of decolonization and Indigenous water justice in the Southwest.

This chapter explored how the conservation ethos—with its values of utilitarianism, commodification, ownership, efficiency, waste, individualism, and growth—emerged out of a colonial mentality. Yet, scattered throughout the Southwest are Indigenous communities with cultures that model resiliency not only in their ability to survive in these arid regions for thousands of years but also their capacity to survive even amidst the violent efforts to displace them. There are other ways of living within this arid region of the world that have worked. However, in the mainstream conservation ethos with its utilitarian ideals, Indigenous approaches to living sustainably in the arid Southwest are continuously overlooked. Let's now look at traditional Indigenous values and examine how they contrast with what has prevailed and shaped contemporary approaches to water in the Southwest.

FIGURE 3.2. Colorado River at Grand Canyon National Park, Marble Canyon.

VOICES

The following quotes come from speakers at the 2016 ITKI and UNESCO City of Gastronomy conference, "Food and Water in Arid Lands: Dialogues across Contemporary and Traditional Knowledge."

Water is life. It is also fundamental to Spirit and afterlife. Water is the first to come, then the baby. Water is the lifeblood of Mother Earth, like the arteries in the veins of our body. Rivers are like the waterways of the human body. Water is a treasure, and a gift from the Creator. Water was our first medicine and has the capacity to heal on a physical and spiritual level.
—*Darlene Sanderson, RN, MA, PhD, Cree with roots from northern Manitoba and Russian descent, British Columbia, Canada*

We need to be thinking like the Hopi. Hopis have been building gabions to catch water for centuries. The land becomes a sponge if you work with it. Native plants catch the rain. Gabions do the same thing. Land behind the gabions gathers and forms a huge sponge, and water seeps into the land slowly. Gabions capture the water and keep it soaking into the ground.
—*Anna Valer Clark, Waterock, L3C, and the Hopi Raincatchers, Pearce, Arizona*

We started TOCA (Tohono O'odham Community Action) twenty years ago. Our people have been dying because of what we're eating. We've planted 20,000 acres of traditional crops and are training a new generation of O'odham farmers. We're getting young people back into farming. The elders bring the knowledge to the young people. All generations are part of the planning, sharing, and knowledge.
—*Terrol Johnson, director and cofounder of Tohono O'odham Community Action (TOCA)*

Hopi agriculture redefines water conservation. We start with the traditional and add science. The best science is what works. Culturally based agriculture includes generational knowledge which gets passed down. Growing corn in arid regions represents resiliency. Years of knowledge passed down generation to generation.
—*Michael Kotutwa Johnson, Hopi farmer, PhD in natural resources*

What makes knowledge traditional? If elders are not with us, it is not traditional knowledge. What are we willing to do for our lands and waters? There are people who speak with thunder, who can see into the womb. This can't be found in a workshop. This knowledge is intangible knowledge.
—*Patrisia Gonzales, Kickapoo, Comanche, and Macehual; traditional healer and midwife; and professor of Mexican American studies and American Indian studies at the University of Arizona*

4

Indigenous Water Relationships

A yearning to connect with, perhaps even honor, the Earth exists for many; however, as the conservation ethos described in previous chapters indicates, mainstream dominant culture may not have the language and tools to forge these connections. When asked to name three adjectives to describe water, many respondents say "respect." Yet, when asked what respect means to them, we see a concern that suggests little connection to the water itself; rather, respect means not polluting the water. In the words of Dan, owner of a sustainable farm in northern Arizona, respect means "looking at water and not treating it as our toilet bowl." Similarly, "love" means loving water enough not to pollute it. Both Andrea, a hydrologist, and Becky, an environmental and policy graduate student, talk about "loving our rivers to death." By this they mean we enjoy our rivers so much that our presence unintentionally compromises the water quality of the rivers.

This all seems quite positive. After all, isn't *not* polluting the water a good thing? But just how far does this sense of respect take us? What else is needed besides keeping water clean or reducing everyday water consumption in order to build a sustainable water future?

FIGURE 4.1. Image of Grand Falls of the Little Colorado on the Navajo Reservation. (Photograph by Phil Konstantin)

An Indigenous water ethos looks quite different from the conservation efforts, programs, and values held by the dominant culture. Hopi farmer and scholar Michael Kotutwa Johnson sums up an Indigenous relationship with water like this: "Water is the spiritual essence of who we are as a people." This offers a radically different way of knowing, relating to, seeing, and experiencing water. An Indigenous water ethos may be understood, in part, as a relationship with the sacred. As Darlene Sanderson (Cree, with roots from northern Manitoba, and Russian), secretariat for the Indigenous World Forum on Water and Peace, explains, "water connects us all. The ocean is the sacred mat." Indeed, within an Indigenous water ethos, water is not reduced to a mere resource or commodity; rather, it is acknowledged as a living relative with whom humans share deep and intrinsic connections. Yazzie (Diné) and Risling Baldy (Hupa, Yurok, and Karuk) highlight the significance of an Indigenous feminist perspective wherein water becomes a central axis of relationality. This perspective transcends the conventional view of water, challenging its commodification and exploitation while emphasizing the fundamental values of respect and interdependence (Yazzie and Risling Baldy, 2018).

In chapter 2, we considered the values underlying the water conservation ethos of what I'm calling the dominant culture. In this chapter, I outline some of the values and assumptions underlying some key components of an Indigenous water ethos.

Before diving in, I wish to acknowledge that this exploration into an Indigenous water ethos is preliminary. It is based on interviews with Indigenous Americans from various tribes throughout the Southwest, as well as texts focused on Indigenous ways of knowing.[1] This should not be considered a comprehensive nor definitive account. The purpose here is to shed light on a water ethos and not address every way that it might be expressed or communicated in Indigenous cultures.

Furthermore, this exploration is filtered through the lens of a non-Indigenous person. Sharing the thoughts and ideas of people from cultures other than one's own is always a precarious venture. Mistakes and misplacements of emphasis are bound to happen. Many subtle and nuanced dimensions of another's culture are invariably overlooked no matter how much familiarity or time one spends embedded in a culture different from one's own.

In my case, I was married for ten years to a Diné man and spent considerable time over that decade among Diné and Hopi families. My oldest daughter is Diné and Jewish. Still, it would be a grave mistake to assume that my experiences with these families provide me with the type of deep cultural knowing that one born and raised within a culture has.

Indigenous peoples have lived on these lands for hundreds of generations, and in spite of the limitations of my knowledge, I feel it is critical to include their voices and learn as much as we can about the thinking and practices that have served their communities for so long. With this in mind and with a sense of humility and gratitude, I make this offering—my initial interpretation of an Indigenous water ethos.

---

1 I relied heavily on three sources for Indigenous water narratives of the Southwest: (1) participants in the research who had tribal affiliation; (2) Jack Loeffler and Celestia Loeffler's *Thinking Like a Watershed: Voices from the West*—an anthology of essays by and interviews of people from varied cultural backgrounds about their relationship with water and land; and (3) presentations given at Food and Water in Arid Lands, the ITKI UNESCO City of Gastronomy Conference in November 2016. Since Loeffler and Loeffler's book and the 2016 Food and Water in Arid Lands conference were both public venues, I included the full names of participants when quoting them.

A Way of Knowing

While acknowledging the diversity of thought, language, ways of knowing and being, beliefs, and perception from diverse tribal perspectives (there are 574 federally recognized tribes in the United States), it's important to also acknowledge that there are some deeply embedded values that connect Indigenous peoples. As historian and author Donald Fixico (Shawnee, Sac and Fox, Muscogee Creek, and Seminole) explains, "An Indian way of 'seeing' exists, according to a native perspective about all things" (Fixico, 2003, p. 17).

In the late 1970s, rancher and anthropologist Keith Basso set out to understand the Western Apache sense of place and how this sense of place shaped values, identity, and community. In *Wisdom Sits in Places*, Basso describes his work with tribal elders to construct a map of Apacheland. "Not whitemen's maps," explains Charles Henry, an Apache elder, "we've got plenty of them, but Apache maps with Apache places and names. We could use them. Find out something about how we know our country" (Basso, 1996, p. xv).

From his travels throughout Apache land with Henry, Basso gets trained in an entirely new way of experiencing and relating with the land and waters. Basso laments that already on their second day out, he runs into what he at first perceives as a rather insignificant communication problem. After four attempts, he keeps mispronouncing the Apache name of the boggy hollow they see before them.

"I'm sorry," Basso says to the translator, Morely Cromwell, "I can't get it. I'll work on it later. . . . It doesn't matter" (Basso, 1996, p. 10).

Henry responds to Basso, telling him it matters. Then he turns to Cromwell and in Western Apache says,

> What he's doing isn't right. It's not good. He seems to be in a hurry. Why is he in a hurry? It's disrespectful. Our ancestors made this name. They made it just as it is. They made it for a reason. *They spoke it first, a long time ago!* He's repeating the speech of our ancestors. He doesn't know that. Tell him he's repeating the speech of our ancestors! (Basso, 1996, p. 10)

Cromwell translates Henry's words to Basso without removing their sharpness, challenging Basso to reevaluate his own ways of knowing. Henry's words highlight a Western Apache way of knowing that, while in many ways is particular to the Apache, shares underlying values with other Indigenous peoples throughout the Southwest. The emphasis on respect, ancestral history, and the power of language offers an introduction to Indigenous ways of thinking and knowing and, while not obvious at first, offers insights into Indigenous approaches to water sustainability.

Respecting and Revering Water, in Contrast to Valuing Efficiency

Why is he in a hurry? It's disrespectful, Henry had rebuked Basso. Nineteenth-century sociologist and political economist Max Weber observed that the West's bureaucratic forms of organization were designed during the Industrial Revolution to maximize efficiency to ensure economic effectiveness. Efficient forms of organization would maximize production through creating time-saving means for workers to accomplish their tasks. We saw in chapter 2 how efficiency also became integral to conserving water for future use. For many Indigenous groups, the fast-paced society that emerged from these bureaucratic forms of organization conflicts with core values: respect and reverence. Respect means admiring the qualities of and honoring the more-than-human world. Reverence includes great respect as well as developing and cultivating relationships, which take time. An Indigenous water ethic honors the development and unfolding of relationships with the more-than-human-world over time.

Lyle Balenquah, Hopi archeologist and a member of the Greasewood Clan from the Village of Bacavi, offers a detailed description of the ways in which connection is valued above efficiency as he describes Hopi dry farming techniques. The planting process is all done by hand. Each step of the process connects farmer to earth and to valuable ecological lessons. Balenqua reflects,

> To the outside world (i.e., non-Hopi), this [Hopi farming techniques] may seem inefficient, but it has a deeper meaning that relates to the concept of remaining connected to our natural landscapes. Though the process is back-breaking and monotonous, it reminds the farmer of one of the Hopi tenets: hard work is necessary to achieve something good for one's family. This leads to another Hopi truth: farming requires one to have a healthy and positive caregiver connection with his family and children, both human and plant forms. (Loeffler and Loeffler, 2012, p. 62)

Valuing Water as Life, Not Only as a Way to Stay Alive or as a Commodity

Tó Nizhóní Ání.
—Diné for "beautiful water speaks"

Among respondents from a wide variety of backgrounds, from environmentalists, to hydrologists, to ranchers and farmers, those from Indigenous and non-Indigenous cultures consistently express that "water is life." At first glance, it appears that a deep appreciation for water has filtered into the dominant culture; however, when we look at the sentiment carefully, we see there are very different layers of meaning and value behind these words.

When non-Indigenous respondents express that "water is life," they typically imply, water keeps us alive. We can't live without water, so we must take care of the water. This emphasizes a utilitarian perspective that, as we saw in chapter 2, pervades water conservation. We take care of water because we need water.

Mirana, a Cuban American community organizer, contextualizes the prevailing conservation philosophy within a utilitarian framework, highlighting the distinction from Indigenous perspectives on water. She states,

> The conservation movement was led by a couple white guys who wanted to preserve stuff. Conservation was really for white people, and they really didn't have an understanding of how, for years before white men came to this continent, the native folks had a different philosophy and a different mindset that wasn't a utilitarian mindset about water.

In contrast, the expression "water is life" seems to mean something quite different to Indigenous respondents. When Indigenous respondents say, "water is life," they often draw on teachings from past generations who perceived water as a living being, as a form of life itself. Water is considered a being whom we need to treat with respect, reverence, and care, not only because our lives depend upon water but for the very well-being of the water itself. As chair of the Colorado River Indian Tribes, Amilia Flores says, "The river's a person. The river can't speak for itself. And we as stewards need to step up and protect the river" (Krol, 2023).

In an Indigenous worldview, "water is life" also means water is alive. Roy Kady, Diné from the Teec Nos Pos Chapter, a weaver and fiber artist, highlights this thinking of water as a living sentient being, when he refers to the rivers' feelings: "We can't just pray for it and disrespect it. . . . when they [the rivers] feel like they're being neglected and disrespected, they have every means to cease for a short moment, or for a long moment. It's really up to them" (Loeffler and Loeffler, 2012, p. 107).

This sense of water as a being has important real-world implications. Kady explains what happens when water isn't respected and revered:

> Anything in nature, you capture it and you enslave it, you give it a different intention, you disharmonize the process. The whole cycle of life gets out of whack . . . But to capture anything and to deprive it from its natural ability to be a part of its community is something that to us is not only disrespectful but also can backfire in many ways. And I hear a lot of my elders talk how without the water's permission some of our offering places that were very sacred to us are now underwater. It's like drowning yourself. We've drowned the sacred places where we did our offerings. (Loeffler and Loeffler, 2012, p. 124)

Indigenous water ethics are not only about respecting water because water keeps us alive; they are also about revering water as a living sentient being who exercises its own will, works for its own survival, and responds in its own way to threats. Roy Kady explains:

> The Water People have life just like we do. . . . What they resort to is just like what we as humans resort to—it's really not any different—to survive. . . . There's offerings that are not made there anymore. The usage of it is not respectful. They're for commercial purposes and wasteful intentions. And they [the waters] know that. They have their own set of values and feelings. So that's how naturally they go back to sleep. . . . We've captured rivers without their permission. (Loeffler and Loeffler, 2012, p. 124)

Water is a living being and as such is not a commodity to be bought and sold. William, a tribal council member of the Laguna Pueblo, views placing monetary value on water as a "non-Native concept." He explains that even though now there is a fee for water in his community,

> there never used to be that [fee], because part of our beliefs was that water is not for sale. We don't create it, and it was given to us as a gift from the Creator. For us, water is life and cannot be bought or sold.

Valuing Place-Based Ancestral Knowledge and Practices in Addition to Science and Technology

"Without generational knowledge we lose sustainability," explains Michael Kotutwa Johnson, who traces his farming lineage back through two hundred generations of Hopi farmers. In an arid region of northeast Arizona that receives between six to ten inches of rainfall a year, a place that seems like it would be highly unfavorable to corn, Hopi agriculture relies upon generational knowledge. For the Hopi, Johnson explains, growing corn on the arid mesas represents resiliency: "Those who pass down the knowledge will still be there. Those who don't adapt will disappear" (ITKI and UNESCO, 2016).

Indigenous participants in this research discuss learning from the wisdom of their ancestors as they reflect upon water. Patrisia Gonzales (Kickapoo, Comanche, and Macehual) associate professor in Mexican American studies at the University of Arizona, talks about the importance of honoring her ancestors, "peoples who traverse many different waters and lands." When thinking of water, she evokes the memory of the generations who came before her:

> When I think of water, I think of the water that my grandmother gathered for washing, cooking, healing, ceremony. I think of the different waterways that my people were part of. My ancestors were the last guardians of Trinity River. I think of amniotic fluid, blood, semen, tears, breast milk that also carries heavy metals and toxins. (ITKI and UNESCO, 2016)

Ancestral and multigenerational water knowledge holds a profound significance in the context of Indigenous cultures worldwide. As reflected in the experiences of Darlene Sanderson, who received traditional wisdom from three Cree elders, including one who had lived to the remarkable age of 110, this knowledge transcends generations, embodying the collective wisdom of Indigenous communities. Sanderson explains, "Every place in the world has Indigenous elders who understand Mother Earth has a life of her own," a holistic perspective that sees water not merely as a resource but as a living entity intricately connected to all life. However, this wisdom is not a concern solely for contemporary Indigenous people. Sanderson thoughtfully asks, "Where are your sacred waters of origin? Trace your heritage back five hundred years," encouraging everyone to embark on an exploration of the historical and ancestral bonds that all cultures share with specific bodies of water (ITKI and UNESCO, 2016).

The traditional knowledge of elders offers guidance on how to care for and value water in these arid lands. Sarah, Diné water activist and organizer, shares stories of how her grandmother reprimanded her and her siblings as children for playing with water: "I remember my grandma yelling at me and saying, 'Don't be playing with water. It's, you know, it's not something you play with.'" Now it is Sarah's mother who reprimands Sarah's children for playing with water. The role of the elders in passing down these lessons remains crucial.

HIGH-CONTEXT KNOWLEDGE

Teresa Newberry, a science instructor at Tohono O'odham Community College, calls the place-based ancestral knowledge passed down through generations "high-context knowledge." For the Apache, high-context knowledge is a means by which history enters the present:

> For the place-maker's main objective is to speak the past into being, to summon it with words and give it dramatic form, to *produce* experience by forging ancestral worlds in which others can participate and readily lose themselves. . . . Thus performed and dramatized, Western Apache place-making becomes a form of narrative art, a type of historical theater in which the "pastness" of the past is summarily stripped away and long-elapsed events are made to unfold before one's eyes. (Basso, 1996, p. 33)

This narrative approach to bringing ancestral knowledge into present-day teachings is demonstrated by Henry as he stands with Basso at the edge of a circular swale one early spring morning in 1979. Standing upon Goshtl'ish Tu' Bil Sikane (Water Lies with Mud in an Open Container), Henry begins, "They came to this country long ago, our ancestors did. . . . They were very poor. They had few possessions and surviving was difficult for them. They were looking for a good place to settle, a safe place without enemies" (Basso, 1996, p. 11). Henry's description of what his ancestors must have gone through becomes more vivid as, through his narrative, ancestors themselves begin to take form:

> None of these places had names then . . . and as the people went about they thought about this. "How shall we speak about this land?" They said, "How shall we speak about where we have been and where we want to go?" (Basso, 1996, pp. 11–12)

The narrative continues as the ancestors get excited about the hunting possibilities in this place and a leader discusses the importance of settling in the area and giving it a name.

What happens when this place-based generational knowledge disappears? There is a high cost, says Lyle Balenquah, a Hopi archeologist:

> In many cases, they [ancestors] lived close to their resource bases of rivers, springs, forests, and hunting and gathering areas. In essence, they lived literally among the resources that sustained them from day to day. This is of course a far cry from today's modern existence, where most people never see their food before it is served to them or arrives at the grocery store. In that sense, many of our humankind have definitely lost some part of the connection to our ancestral lifeways. How many of us continue to view our natural world with eyes that not only see the landscapes, but sense the inherent energies that still exist there? We seem cut off from the greater forces that have shaped our lives for thousands of years. (Loeffler and Loeffler, 2012, p. 50)

NAMING AND PLACE-BASED KNOWLEDGE

Consider what gets lost when the language changes. Newberry explains that language encodes traditional ecological knowledge. Knowing the names establishes relationships with the land, water, animals, and plants. Karletta Chief, a Diné hydrologist, has asked elders what has changed in the environment. The elders offer a map of environmental change over decades: "Elders said there were beavers. There are new plants that have no names. That's indicative of invasive species" (ITKI and UNESCO, 2016). The names of plants forged a connection with those lands so that when plants with no names appeared, elders recognized them as foreign, unconnected to those lands.

Basso learns that sprinkled throughout Apache Country are places named for sources of water: springs, seeps, bogs, and seasonal pools at the bases of canyon walls. However, now these places are permanently dry. Because these places have water names, Henry concludes that Apache land was wetter and greener during the time of his ancestors. Henry explains, "The names do not lie. They show what is different and what is still the same" (Basso, 1996, p. 16).

Yet is there a place for high-context deep generational knowledge in today's approaches to water conservation? Jesus Garcia, education specialist at the Arizona–Sonora Desert Museum, considers the ways that mestizo (Mexican of Spanish and Indigenous descent) culture has been influenced by generational knowledge from both European and Indigenous American traditions. Garcia reflects, "Three hundred years ago something happened to the Sonoran Desert. Two worlds collided, or we could say, came to be as one. Missionaries arrived. At the beginning, Germans, then Spanish" (ITKI and UNESCO, 2016). Missionaries brought trees and cultivated them using traditional European practices. Indigenous American knowledge fused with European practices to produce a mestizo culture rich in wisdom about how to cultivate and care for the lands and waterways. This fusion of European and Indigenous approaches has gotten passed on generationally through mestizo culture.

Garcia warns, "When elders with generational knowledge die, their knowledge disappears. We see our water tables are dropping. Rivers are drying up. Populations are growing. And delicious white pomegranates are disappearing. Many only exist now in *abuelitas'* backyards."

Garcia asks, "What are you doing to keep traditional knowledge alive?" He suggests that we dig into our ideas about the question "What is heritage?" and uncover the eternal wisdom that "could just be a flower in your childhood. This is part of traditional knowledge: knowing when to harvest it, how to prepare it, how to eat it." Many of us may not be able to trace our generational knowledge two hundred generations back as some Hopi farmers, like Johnson do; however, Garcia suggests that we can look to the more-than-human world for wisdom and guidance: "Saguaro and native vegetation are also heritage for some" (ITKI and UNESCO, 2016).

Mirana asserts that for effective water policy, the adoption of an Indigenous seven-generation approach, is imperative. The seven generations principle, drawn from Haudenosaunee (Iroquois) philosophy, urges the current generation to make decisions that will lead to sustainable outcomes seven generations into the future. "I can't speak for all Native traditions" Mirana says, "but my sense is that when many traditions talk about conservation, it was for the next seven generations and they see themselves as the ancestors. They already are ancestors of the children who are unborn." In this way, high-context generational knowledge not only includes generations of the past but also includes present and future generations.

Valuing Interdependence and Connection with Water in Contrast to Individual Rights to Own and Dominate

Historian and author Rina Swentzell, a Tewa-speaking woman from the Santa Clara Pueblo in New Mexico, explains that in the Pueblo world, "community and watershed are synonymous. A watershed is an interwoven web of life energies from clouds to rivers to streams, springs—and tears" (Loeffler and Loeffler, 2012, p. 29). Contrast this with the conventional definition of a watershed as an area of land which bodies of water drain off of. In the Pueblo world, human beings, their tears and their lives, are deeply connected with the life of the entire watershed, whereas the non-Indigenous view of a watershed does not include human life.

What emerges here is an ethos based on relationship and communication with water. These relationships "are honored in ceremony, song, story, and life" writes Winona LaDuke (Ojibwe) (LaDuke, 1999, p. 2). LaDuke expresses that for many Indigenous Americans, the interaction with water is reciprocal: as they communicate with water, water communicates with them. One San Felipe Pueblo woman, interviewed by Swentzell, observes, for example, "Water can talk with water" (Loeffler and Loeffler, 2012, p. 29). Swentzell explains that, since we are made of water, we have the ability to communicate through water. "We too can communicate with the clouds through our songs, dances, and thoughts. There is fast water and there is slow water." Swentzell adds, "they must be treated and talked with differently" (Loeffler and Loeffler, 2012, p. 30)

The relationship to water requires great care, which is expressed in the way water is named and referred to. For example, Roy Katy says that using the Diné name for water is critical for communicating with water:

> To' (water) is as important as the sound that it makes . . . the word is sacred for water, and powerful. . . . In my community there are several natural springs where the to' comes out in a natural form to come greet us, to remind us that you "take care of me, and I can take care of you." (Loeffler and Loeffler, 2012, p. 106)

Nor is water a distant relative who may only be remembered from time to time. Marks in the Sand, a high school advisor to Indigenous American students in Flagstaff, Arizona explains,

> Water is very integral to our culture and plays a huge part into who we are. So, like, for my clan, Zuni Edgewater, my people already come from water,

and that's where our existence and our beginnings and our emergences come from.

For the Zuni Edgewater clan and for many other Indigenous Americans, water is the very essence of who they are as a people. Many of the clan names throughout the Southwestern tribes reinforce the spiritual relationships the people have with the water. For example, the Diné who belong to the Tó dích'íinii, Bitter Water Clan, trace their heritage back to their origin story and the bitter water that sprang from a hole dug by a spiritual man.

A deep sense of interconnectedness characterizes Indigenous American ways of relating with water. LaDuke writes, "These are our older relatives—the ones who came before us and taught us how to live" (LaDuke, 1999, p. 2). Camillus Lopez of the Tohono O'odham Nation expresses: "When you live as part of an environment, I guess you become it, and everybody else around you is it" (Loeffler and Loeffler, 2012, p. 137). Water is intricately intertwined with all existence and, for Bernadette Adley Santa-Maria, cannot be thought of as separate from the rest of life:

> My late maternal grandmother, Mary Velasquez Riley, used to tell us about water—how *tu hadazlii'* (springs and little creeks) form below *Dzil Ligai Si'an*. She said *tu* (water) is a sacred element, along with the land, environment, weather, fire, and natural resources. All are related and interconnected. It doesn't make sense to an elder Apache to only talk about water. (Riggs, November 2, 2021)

In this cosmology of interconnectedness, frogs are not merely amphibians with long hind legs that leap, but rather their songs are, in Lopez's words, the "magic that brought the rain." And mountains are not just a rise in the earth's surface, for they "make the clouds" (Loeffler and Loeffler, 2012, p. 135). Rina Swentzell (Santa Clara Pueblo) tells of a Tesuque Pueblo woman who speaks about springs as "being the opening into the womb of Mother Earth." And Roy Kady says, "Corn is our embodiment" (Loeffler and Loeffler, 2012, p. 113).

CEREMONY SUPPORTS CONNECTION

One of the ways Indigenous communities maintain connection with all relations and all elements of Mother Earth is through prayer and ceremony. Swetzell explains that ceremonial life for Pueblo people was important to express acknowledgment of energies that flowed through the land, the sky, and the waters. Prayer and songs are talking with those energies. Dances and shrine visits are an act of becoming one with those energies (Loeffler and Loeffler, 2012, pp. 32–33).

Ceremony facilitates a close relationship with the water world, Swetzell shares:

> Since all waterways are connected to lakes, hills, and mountains, "it is essential that we spend a lot of time up in the foothills, all around the communities," noted the Tesuque Pueblo man. Visiting these places on an almost daily basis made the entire region intimate. The rocks, animals, and plants were all familiar. How the water flowed from mountains and into valleys was intensely known. Where the fish found harbor and which plants grew alongside the waterways was information needed for survival. (Loeffler and Loeffler, 2012, p. 33)

During ceremony, Swetzell says, "the human, in the dance place, is the connector of Earth and sky. And it is all about water. Pueblo dances and songs are about collecting water from the skies" (Loeffler and Loeffler, 2012, p. 32).

Michael Kotutwa Johnson (Hopi) explains, "All ceremonies are about rain" (ITKI and UNESCO, 2016). William of the Laguna Pueblo tribe explains that ceremony involves making requests to the Creator, with respect and humility:

> Most of the ceremonies that we do are requests for water, and that's the reason why I have always been of the belief that, since water is not created by us, that we ask for it. Water ethics for me is participating in ceremonies that help us to ask for the water, and when the ceremonies are done correctly, then, usually, we do get water.

WE ARE ALL GOURDS...

This recognition of interconnectedness extends to the water cycles themselves. Vernon Masayesva explains that in the Hopi way, "we are an important part of the hydro cycle." Since water cannot be destroyed and only "changes faces," death is not viewed as an end to life. Masayesva continues,

> We are all water gourds. Our body is the gourd; inside is the water. Our heart moves water through every part of our body. Shell [of the gourd] disintegrates in the ground. Water is released and goes to the Cloud People.

Masayesva continues the teaching: "Water has memory. We are taught when first rain comes: thank you for the memory. Water has memory, you cannot destroy water. We are still part of cycle, being taken care of by Ocean Mother." Masayesva's lesson also contains a warning: "But we are abusing the Mother. We are making her sick. She is crying out" (ITKI and UNESCO, 2016).

Professor of Indigenous geography Michelle Daigle (Mushkegowuk) writes about the importance of nurturing relationships with the water, emphasizing that being on and with bodies of water is a means to reactivate a deep-seated consciousness among her people, the Mushkegowuk Cree First Nation people. For them, these water connections transcend mere geographical boundaries and form an integral part of their cultural and political identity (Daigle, 2018).

An Indigenous water ethos recognizes the vital importance of nurturing connections with water and embracing the intricate web of interdependence that binds us and water together. For without recognizing and honoring "all our relations," we become imbalanced and eventually sick. As Fixico explains,

> everything in life is connected. Learn to understand the bonds between humans, spirit, and nature. Realize that our illness and our healing alike come from maintaining strong and healthy relationships in every aspect of our lives. In my culture—the Navajo culture—medicine is performed by a *hataalii*, someone who sees a person not simply as a body but as a whole being. Body, mind, and spirit are seen as connected to other people, to families, to communities, and even to the planet and universe. All of these relationships need to be in harmony in order to be healthy. (Fixico, 2003, p. 63)

Valuing Storytelling: Sharing a Water Ethos, Not Just a Water Problem

Interpretations of and stories about why the water went away also reveal a Western Apache way of thinking, knowing, and relating with the land and water. They are ways of communicating and sharing a particular water ethos. Looking upon the dry land with water names, Henry describes how the people must have acted in a disrespectful manner to the water. "Maybe," Henry says,

> the people were greedy, taking from springs and streams more water than they needed; maybe they were wasteful, throwing water away they should have been careful to save; or maybe they ceased doing everything correctly, neglecting in haste or forgetfulness to give repeated thanks to Water for giving of itself. (Basso, 1996, pp. 16–17)

As Henry explores why the water dried up, he shares his interpretation in the form of a story. Henry recounts what must have happened as their thirsty ancestors first discovered the dry springs at Snake's Water:

> The people came again to get water and saw that there was none . . . now they are walking away, thirsty and shaking with fear. . . . They are wailing as if a relative has died. . . . They say, "Our holy people must help us by making amends to water. . . . They must ask Water to take pity on us! What if this happened everywhere." (Basso, 1996, p. 17)

Fixico explains that storytelling serves multiple roles for Indigenous groups. Stories are the fabric that holds groups together. They impart important messages and lessons about ethical conduct and cultural action. While stories are also told to entertain, they often do more: "The story has power and energy, and it brings the past into the present" (Fixico, 2003, pp. 36–37). Through Henry's accounts, we see the power of the story to bring the lessons of the past into a vivid rendering of lessons to be learned and experienced in the present. Lyle Balenquah also explains that, many times, stories are told not only to teach an important lesson but to remember: "To remember to remain connected to the landscape and the history contained within" (Loeffler and Loeffler, 2012, p. 48).

Sometimes stories are told as warnings of what can happen if respect is not offered and greed takes over. Balenquah shares, "I also heard stories of great calamities and misfortune that befell my ancestors due to their own greed, corruption of power, and forgetting their spiritual and earthly connection to their natural world" (Loeffler and Loeffler, 2012, p. 48). In addition, Balenquah explains that Hopi children are warned of beings like the Water Serpent, who if they get too close to a spring might poke his head out and take them back to his underworld home with him: "it was a powerful method of teaching us kids about the immense physical and spiritual energy that water contains" (Loeffler and Loeffler, 2012, p. 56).

By attentively heeding the messages conveyed by the Earth, we can nurture what Daniel R. Wildcat (Yuchi and Muscogee) refers to as "respectful attentiveness." This state invites us to listen with care to the unfolding narrative of the natural world. It encourages us to craft fresh stories, develop new techniques, compose new songs, adopt transformative practices, and even engage in ceremonies that enhance our connection to life (Wildcat, 2009).

Storytelling is used as a way of teaching not only the mind but also the heart. Introducing himself at the Food and Water on Arid Lands Conference,

Vernon Masayesva begins, "I don't do PowerPoint or use computers. I tell stories. It's very personal. Storytellers have heart" (ITKI and UNESCO, 2016).

To engage in cultural revitalization projects with the younger generation, Tohono O'odham Community Action (TOCA) employs traditional storytelling with modern digital methods, creating a form of "digital storytelling." In one project, O'odham interns put together a video called *Attack of the Junk Food Zombies* (TOCA, 2012). In this video, a young woman narrates how the youth are learning how to use traditional ways to survive. They are learning dry farming techniques and how to harvest traditional foods. A scene of youth harvesting vegetables cuts to a "junk food zombie," a young man stuffing chips from a Cheetos bag into his mouth. When the day is over and the youth feast on their small harvest, a zombie tries to attack the group with his large bag of Cheetos. However, before the zombie can wage his attack, one of the youths shoves a traditional melon into the zombie's mouth. The narrator concludes, "We discovered that a traditional melon cured the junk food zombie," who is now seen devouring the melon feast before him.

The narration in *Attack of the Junk Food Zombies* draws on oral tradition, unique to Indigenous identity, where lessons, speeches, even jokes are shared orally. Fixico explains:

> To the American Indian, history is better explained as the importance of "experience." People recall an experience in greater detail because of the emotions involved, vivid colors, familiar sounds described, and the people and/or beings involved. When retold, the experience comes alive again recreating the experience by evoking the emotions of the listeners, transcending past-present-future. Time does not imprison the story. The vehicle for transmitting this same reality of past and present is the oral tradition, which differs from oral history. Oral tradition is the process; oral history is an event told orally. Orality is the way of the American Indian mind. (Fixico, 2003, p. 22)

Indigenous Leadership and Indigenous-Led Water Justice Movements

An Indigenous water ethos, intertwined with values of respect and reverence, ancestral knowledge, interdependence, storytelling, and ceremony, serves as the foundation upon which Indigenous leadership and Indigenous-led water justice movements have been growing. As discussed in chapter 3, Indigenous voices and wisdom have historically been sidelined in decision-making processes and policies concerning water. However, the tide is turning. Jason Robinson and colleagues highlight a series of political victories where Indigenous communities have successfully advanced their legal and political perspectives, particularly with regard to water (Robinson et al., 2018).[2]

By the late 1970s, after a series of cost-ineffective water projects, a sense prevailed that the major US rivers had maximized their damming capacity, with over 80,000 dams and what many widely considered Bureau of Reclamation overreach, and so the age of massive water projects appeared to be coming to an end. Concurrently, a series of tribal political victories opened the way for "the settlement era" whereby eighty-nine settlements, agreements, and compacts were signed adjudicating water rights to tribes. To date, twenty-two tribes have rights to 3.2 million acre-feet of Colorado River water annually. Twelve tribes have unresolved water claims (Water and Tribes Initiative, 2022). Should these tribes' water claims also get settled, "the amount of water that could potentially be claimed by these tribes is enormous" (Robinson et al., 2018, p. 869).

Tribal influence on the waters of the Southwest has continued to grow. In 1992 ten Colorado Basin tribes formed the Ten Tribes Partnership with the purposes of "embrac[ing] and own[ing] the stewardship of the Colorado River and lead[ing] from a spiritual mandate to ensure that this sacred water will always be protected, available and sufficient" (Ten Tribes Partnership, 2022). The Colorado River Tribes, as they are commonly called, have rights to approximately 20 percent of the Colorado River water flow, with outstanding claims existing.

Ironically, the Bureau of Reclamation, who served non-Indigenous interests exclusively for the better part of a century, has begun shifting focus. They have been facilitating tribal water rights settlements, including helping to resolve or partially resolve claims for ten tribes in Arizona. They have also made efforts to study water rights from a tribal perspective.

The Bureau of Reclamation together with the US Department of the Interior and the Ten Tribes Partnership undertook a comprehensive, Basin-wide analysis of Colorado River water that "allows each of the tribes to provide, from their own perspective, their views on the challenges and opportunities

---

2 Indigenous political victories that advanced Indigenous political and legal perspectives include the 1908 *Winters v. United States* Supreme Court decision; the 1924 Indian Citizenship Act; the 1934 Indian Reorganization Act; the National Congress of American Indians (NCAI), established in 1944; the 1963 *Arizona v. California* Supreme Court decision; and the 1975 Indian Self-Determination and Education Assistance Act.

ahead," wrote Brenda Burman, commissioner for the Bureau of Reclamation, in the forward to the study (US Department of the Interior, Bureau of Reclamation, and Ten Tribes Partnership, 2018). Robinson and colleagues conclude, "All told, Colorado River Basin water management seems to be evolving (albeit very gradually) in terms of the visibility of tribes and their water rights" (Robinson et al., 2018, p. 871).

In 2017 the Ten Tribes Partnership collaborated with the other twenty Colorado River Basin tribes to form the Water and Tribes Initiative, with the goals of strengthening tribal capabilities in water resource management and active participation in water policy dialogues and fostering sustainable water use through cooperative, solution-oriented approaches (Water and Tribes Initiative, 2022).

The Water and Tribes Initiative launched several major projects, coalitions, and initiatives designed to leverage their collective power. In 2020, they published a policy brief entitled "A Common Vision for the Colorado River System: Toward a Framework for Sustainability," in which they outline the scope of tribal visions, initiatives, and leadership and identify common ground among the tribes. A framework to govern the Colorado River system emerged that incorporates several elements of an Indigenous water ethos, including ensuring "the spiritual, cultural, and ecological integrity of the River system" and integrating "traditional indigenous knowledge with western science to better understand the River system and the consequences of alternative management scenarios" (Water and Tribes Initiative, 2020).

The Colorado River Tribes appear to be developing more influence in water negotiations. In February 2022, the federal government allocated $1.7 billion for the tribes to settle their unresolved water claims. And in the fall of 2022, twenty tribes signed a letter imploring Interior Secretary Deb Haaland (Laguna Pueblo) to include the tribes in the negotiations for Colorado River management, set to expire in 2026.

Indigenous nations throughout the region have proven resilient in the face of ongoing cultural and environmental destruction. Take the Pueblo of Sandia people in central New Mexico, for example. The Rio Grande River played a critical role in agriculture and in the ceremonial life of the Pueblo of Sandia people. However, rapid industrial growth and lax federal and state environmental enforcement led to extreme deterioration of the health of the river. The tribe had no way of communicating their needs, nor mechanisms for having their voice and concerns heard. However, in 1987 with the passing of the Clean Water Act, the Pueblo of Sandia applied for and received "treatment of state" status, becoming the first Indigenous nation in the US to create and enforce their own water quality standards.

The Pueblo of Sandia's Water Quality Standards program enforces more stringent water-quality standards than the rest of New Mexico. Because of their efforts and the water-quality data they collect, they have a seat at the table of local water decision boards and have been acknowledged as serving as "a counterweight to pollution claims made by local dischargers" (Harvard Project American Indian Economic Dev, 1999). Following years of silence, the program has facilitated heightened dialogue and the exchange of information between the Pueblo and the state of New Mexico.

Indigenous organizations throughout the Southwest also promote Indigenous water justice. Organizations, like the Pueblo Action Alliance to protect Chaco Canyon and the Chaco Wash, have adopted business models that align with their values. These values include focusing on good stewardship, caring for ancestral lands, and prioritizing family and ceremony. For example, as the group's director Julia Fay Bernal (Sandia Pueblo and Yuchi) said, "You don't have to explain to me why you can't come to work today" (Devault, 2022). Trust and respect are honored over the dominant culture's focus on competition and efficiency.

Black Mesa Trust, founded in 1999 to address the devastating impact that Peabody Coal was having on Hopi and Navajo communities and people, was formed to

> educate and prepare our children for future leadership in regard to the stewardship of our land and sacred water. . . . We are dedicated to bringing back the traditional water ethics that have sustained our people for millenniums and creating new ways of caring for and healing the water . . . the lifeblood of all living things. (Masayesva, n.d.)

Through sustained campaigns to promote Indigenous water justice, Black Mesa Trust has been a leading voice for over two decades in the effort to impart Indigenous water knowledge and wisdom into conversations and decisions around water sustainability throughout the Southwest.[3]

---

3 For a comprehensive exploration of corporate and federal power that ultimately resulted in the forced relocation of numerous Navajo families to facilitate coal extraction from Black Mesa—an area inhabited and cherished by Navajo communities for generations—consult Judith Nies's thought-provoking book, *Unreal City*. This book delves into how the multifaceted interplay between global corporate interests and regional considerations led to a divisive situation where both Navajo and Hopi communities found themselves in conflict over access to the land of Black Mesa. Beyond the devastating social repercussions for

Nick Estes (Lakota), in his work on water justice for Indigenous people, argues that Indigenous communities face systemic water injustices resulting from colonialism, capitalism, and extractive industries. He contends that these injustices manifest through water contamination, resource exploitation, and the denial of Indigenous sovereignty over waterways. Estes emphasizes the need for Indigenous-led movements and decolonization efforts to challenge these injustices and regain control over their waters, advocating for environmental justice and the protection of Indigenous water rights. Estes's main argument centers on the urgent necessity of addressing water injustices as a crucial aspect of Indigenous liberation and self-determination (Estes, 2024).

We see such resistance and Indigenous water justice actions throughout the Southwest. The Pima Indians, also known as the Akimel O'odham or River People, are reclaiming their water rights in southern Arizona. They, historically, practiced irrigated agriculture but faced water scarcity and discrimination when homesteaders and profiteers diverted water from the Gila River, depriving the Pima of their water supply for irrigation. The federal government refused to recognize their water rights, discounting the Pima's claims of "time immemorial" water usage and allowed nontribal farmers to divert water away from the Pima's agricultural lands. Despite the region's severe drought and political injustices, the Pima now have the rights to more water than any other community in Arizona. The Pima-Maricopa Irrigation Project is central to this achievement. It aligns with Pima approaches to water by respecting water as a relation; reviving traditional farming practices such as cultivating maize, beans, and squash; constructing and maintaining canals in line with historical significance; fostering community involvement and cooperation; and promoting sustainable agriculture practices. These practices combine traditional wisdom with modern methods to honor the Pima's cultural bond with water, efficiently manage resources, and revitalize agriculture on the reservation, reflecting a commitment to both heritage and sustainability (J. Robbins, March 2023).

Dina Gilio-Whitaker (Colville Confederated Tribes) highlights how Indigenous activists have throughout history fought against environmental degradation, land dispossession, and resource exploitation. Standing Rock serves as a prominent contemporary example of this enduring commitment to protect water. This modern-day movement echoed the long-standing tradition of

---

many Navajo families, this corporate-driven venture had far-reaching environmental consequences, notably impacting local water resources (Nies, 2014).

"water protectors," who understand that water is not just a commodity but at the core of their cultures (Gilio-Whitaker, 2019).

Numerous Indigenous water justice movements have emerged in the American Southwest in recent times. Movements like Save the Confluence focus on protecting sacred sites and opposing commercial developments near the Colorado and Little Colorado Rivers. Protect the Peaks strives to preserve the San Francisco Peaks in Arizona from ski resort expansion and artificial snowmaking. The No More Delays campaign, led by the Gila River Indian Community, advocates for equitable distribution of Colorado River water resources. Haul No! protests uranium mining and transportation threatening Indigenous lands and water sources. The Havasupai Tribe has fought uranium mining near the Grand Canyon, which endangers their water supply. Lastly, Save Our Ceremonies challenges excessive groundwater extraction impacting sacred springs used in Indigenous rituals across Arizona.

Sarah, a Diné water activist involved in water advocacy on the Navajo reservation, emphasizes the critical role of Indigenous grassroots initiatives in addressing pressing water issues. She explains that these grassroots initiatives are born out of a deep connection to the land and the understanding that water is not just a resource but a sacred and life-sustaining entity. Sarah says, "Water is not a commodity to us. We're born from water; without water, we're not alive. It's sacred to us. When we fight for clean and accessible water, we're protecting the very essence of who we are." Please see textbox 4.1 to become further educated and involved in the work of decolonization and Indigenous water justice in the Southwest.

Indigenous leaders and Indigenous-led water justice movements continue to stand up in the face of threats not only for the waters that sustain their lives but also for their sovereignty as nations and as people under siege. Vernon Masaysva reflects on Hopi resilience and resistance:

> Hopefully there will be a Fifth World, but we have to do it. Create the Fifth World based on what you want your children to live in. . . . But resistance is not easy. What can we do? We have no money. We've written a U.N. proclamation for Hopis to sign so federal government does its job to protect Sípà. Us little people are doing a lot but we don't know how to get our message out to the world. We're going to stand. We're not going to let anyone cut off our umbilical cord. (Ellis, 2019)

CENTRALIZING INDIGENOUS KNOWLEDGE AND WISDOM

How might Indigenous wisdom and science rooted in thousands of years of ancestral knowledge move from marginalized and subjugated "out of sight" places to a central place, and serve as a guide for a water-sustainable future in the arid Southwest? Indigenous scholars are actively engaged in this transformative process. For example, Indigenous hydrologists like Karletta Chief (Diné) are at the forefront, emphasizing a distinctly Indigenous perspective on hydrology. Chief's research is grounded in values of respect for Indigenous cultures, active community involvement, tribal-driven research, mentorship of future generations, and coauthorship with tribal partners in hydrological research conducted on tribal lands (Chief, 2020). The multitude of Indigenous scholars whose research on water is referenced throughout this book serves as a testament to their leadership and guidance, offering valuable insights for shaping water sustainability throughout the region.

Indigenous communities often prioritize the health of rivers and ecosystems, serving as guiding examples for comprehensive water stewardship. As demonstrated by the Pueblo of Sandia's enforcement of their own water quality standards, which exceed state regulations to protect the Rio Grande River, and the White Mountain Apache Tribe's river restoration projects blending traditional ecological wisdom with modern science, Indigenous practices have effectively restored aquatic ecosystems. As Indigenous communities continue to demonstrate their expertise in comprehensive water stewardship, there is an opportunity for their leadership to become more centralized, serving as a prominent force in shaping the future of water quality and restoration work across the region.

Collaborative water policymaking and sustainable water collaboration represent another avenue through which Indigenous communities have showcased their leadership. They frequently engage in cooperative efforts with neighboring non-Indigenous entities, as exemplified by the Ten Tribes Partnership, the coalition of ten Colorado River Basin tribes described earlier. They actively participate in water policy dialogues, advocating for sustainable water practices, and their growing influence highlights their pivotal role in shaping regional water policy strategies.

In my environmental sociology graduate class in early 2023, students actively discussed the integration of Indigenous knowledge and wisdom into decision- and policy-making processes concerning water sustainability. Ailin,

BOX 4.1. SOUTHWEST INDIGENOUS WATER JUSTICE RESOURCES

BLACK MESA TRUST: blackmesatrust.org

"The mission of Black Mesa Trust is to safeguard, preserve, and honor the sacred land, culture, and water of the Hopi People, including the Grand Canyon, the Little Colorado Basin, and surrounding areas, for future generations."

BLACK MESA WATER COALITION: nativemovement.org/bmwc

"BMWC was formed in 2001 by a group of young intertribal, interethnic people dedicated to addressing issues of water depletion, natural resource exploitation, and public health within Navajo and Hopi communities."

INDIGENOUS ENVIRONMENTAL NETWORK: ienearth.org

The Indigenous Environmental Network (IEN) was founded in 1990 by grassroots Indigenous groups in the United States to confront environmental and economic injustices. Its mission involves strengthening the ability of Indigenous communities and tribal leaders to create protections for sacred places, natural resources, water, air, and public health. IEN also works toward the development of sustainable, economically resilient Indigenous communities that benefit both people and the environment.

PUEBLO ACTION ALLIANCE: puebloactionalliance.org

"Pueblo Action Alliance is a community-driven grassroots organization that protects Pueblo cultural sustainability and community defense by addressing environmental and social impacts in Indigenous communities." (puebloactionalliance.org/purpose)

See Karen Goodluck and Christine Trudeau's article "Indigenous Feminism Flows through the Fight for Water Rights on the Rio Grande" for an in-depth look at an intergenerational group of Pueblo women's water advocacy work (Goodluck and Trudeau, January 1, 2022).

WATER AND TRIBAL INITIATIVE—COLORADO RIVER BASIN: waterandtribes.org

"WTI facilitates connections among tribes and other leaders, builds trust and understanding, and creates opportunities to explore shared interests and take collaborative action."

Indigenous Water Relationships | 129

> **BOX 4.2. THE BLUFF PRINCIPLES**
>
> The Bluff Principles, which emerged from a series of conversations among the Hopi Tribe and other tribal leaders in 2016, are particularly noteworthy for the way in which they infuse an Indigenous water ethos into visions for sustainability.
>
> Central to these principles is the recognition of water as a fundamental right, with a commitment to ensuring clean water for all peoples (Principle 1). Emphasizing respect for sacred sites and diverse religious beliefs underscores the spiritual significance of water (Principle 2). A holistic approach to water management, centered on ecosystem health, is advocated (Principle 3), alongside public education on the intrinsic value of water as the essence of life (Principle 4). Collaboration and inclusivity are paramount in policymaking (Principle 6), guided by an ethic of concern for all, with a focus on equity, fairness, and stewardship (Principles 7, 8, and 9). Traditional wisdom, especially from elders, is valued (Principle 11), with a call for urgent action and foresight to safeguard future generations (Principles 12 and 13). Finally, water is revered as a sacred gift, deserving of reverence and shared with love and spirituality (Principles 15 and 16) (Water and Tribes Initiative, 2020).

a geography graduate student, raised the point that, out of calls for "inclusivity," a token Indigenous person is occasionally included on boards and other advisory and decision-making bodies. Yet as with other forms of tokenism, such practices disadvantage the minority representative, leading to higher visibility where they may feel scrutinized, stereotyped, isolated, and otherwise reminded of their differences. Such practices may alleviate guilt in the dominant group; meet calls for diversity, equity, and inclusion; and make members feel like they have given Indigenous people "a seat at the table," all without providing real space for Indigenous voices and perspectives to be heard and integrated.

Anna, an applied geospatial sciences graduate student, offered an intriguing possibility based on her research in environmental management: create parallel tribal positions with equal decision-making powers. For each water conservation position and water conservation board, develop a corresponding tribal position and tribal water board. Find the funding, double payroll budgets, and integrate tribal leadership into the very structure of decision-making processes.

Mariana, a sociology graduate student, wondered if such an approach would continue to reproduce the same system of domination at the root of many of the problems: "This assumes that Indigenous people want to lead and structure themselves in the same ways as the dominant society. Maybe what we need to do is ask Indigenous people how they want to participate." This reminds me of community-based organizing, where community members drive all aspects of their participation, from development of infrastructure and systems to organization of decision-making bodies. Mariana concluded, "We need to learn to listen to each other. This is the place from which we can start to envision alternatives."

We close this chapter with the words of Hopi elder Curious Coyote, whose childhood memories highlight some of the key dimensions of an Indigenous water ethos including respect, reverence, and gratitude, calling on ancestral and elder knowledge, and forging deep connections with water:

> I was taught by my grandpa, ahh, I was with him out in the farm and little raindrops start to come, and so he told me, he said, "Repeat after me." He said, "Water, thank you for visiting us, coming to visit us." And then he said, "Thank you for remembering us." See, we're talking to the Rain People, our ancestors—they came to visit, they remember us. They came to bless us with rain for our crops. So, he said, "That's what you say," and that's what I remember. I remember, of course, never waste water. He said, "When you see a rain storm up there, you go like this [sucks in air a couple times]. Inhale, you suck it, you want it to come to you." Then sometimes the wind will interfere, it'll stop it. So, you go like this: tisk tisk [signs with hands]. Go away, go away. Well, all Hopi kids are taught that, yeah. Those are very strong memories, childhood memories about water.

BOX 4.3. HOPI DECLARATION OF WATER

On October 23, 2003, the Hopi gathered for Hisot Navoti (Hopi Water Fair) as part of a global event to honor water. At the gathering, they adopted a Declaration of Water. In this declaration, we can see many of the Indigenous water values discussed in this chapter.

Declaration of Water

>As children of water,
>we raise our voices in solidarity to speak for all waters.
>
>Water, the breath of all life, water the sustainer of all life,
>water the voice of our ancestors, water pristine and powerful.
>
>Today we join hands, determined to honor,
>trust and follow the ancient wisdom of our ancestors
>whose teachings and messages continue to live through us.
>
>The message is clear: Honor and respect water
>as a sacred and life-giving gift from the Creator of Life.
>Water, the first living spirit on Earth.
>
>All living beings come from water,
>all is sustained by water,
>all will return to water to begin life anew.
>
>We are of water, and the water is of us.
>When water is threatened, all living things are threatened.
>
>What we do to water, We do to ourselves.
>
> (Hopi Hisot Navoti Gathering, November 19, 2016)

VOICES

How would you define a "water ethic"?

What does a "water ethic" look like to you?

What's an appropriate relationship between human beings and water?

Water benefits us and we can use the water to help us survive and do what we need to do. But the water also needs to be able to continue on its path and continue its water cycle as well.

—*Molly, environmental science project manager, Phoenix, Arizona*

I try to help the birds. I think that that's important. I change the water in the bird bath about every three or four days. Not overdo it, but I think about wildlife as part of our community too. And so, I think our relationship with water should be for personal use, for public use, and for the use by the animal community.

—*James, retired teacher, Albuquerque, New Mexico*

To me water ethics means helping people find ways to connect with their water source. This helps shift people's perspective, helping them see water is a living thing. This water allows for plants and trees to grow; animals rely on this water. I think connecting people with their water sources helps them have a little bit more respect for it.

—*Flash, field guide for an outdoor wilderness survival company, Utah*

In Buddhism there is an expansion of what it means to be a sentient being. So, a rock is a sentient being. Water is a sentient being. And if they're sentient beings, then in an ethical framework, water would be cared for more deeply and not be harmed. A water ethic is having a relationship with water where we don't see ourselves at the center of the conversation but rather as a kind of steward.

—*John, meditation teacher, Flagstaff, Arizona*

Water ethics should be a form of common sense. Water is part of our environment and a requirement for life, so I feel that it is appropriate to treat it well and not pollute or waste it, while being grateful for our ability to have clean, fresh water on demand. It is a human right, and it should be accessible to everyone.

—*Eric, construction project manager, Scottsdale, Arizona*

A water ethic looks like: don't build a damn golf course if you don't have the water. I don't care whether you reclaim it or not, there's got to be a better use of reclaimed water than a damn golf course. And don't do a reclaimed water project in Flagstaff. I mean, look how much trouble they got in taking reclaimed water up to the Snowbowl. You know, oh my God, you're peeing on the mountain; well you could probably drink that water, but you know. So how about we just don't use so much to start with? After all, it's a living being. It's got a lot of bacteria in it, and it's a living being.

—*Marie, ranch owner, Mormon Lake, Arizona*

There's a limited amount of water. A water ethic is about making choices. It doesn't have to be "one size fits all." But I think that every person needs to take a look at how they are using water and do it in a responsible manner that leaves some for the next generation.

—*Leah, hydrogeologist, Salt Lake City, Utah*

My vision is to have some kind of integrated rainwater harvesting system that brings water to every property. We could survive from rain that naturally falls on the ground; that would be a pretty well adapted landscape don't you think?

—*Billy, landscape architect and planner, Denver, Colorado*

5

Rethinking Water Relationships in the Arid Southwest

Over the last seven years, friends, family members, neighbors, and acquaintances have asked me about the topic of my most current research. I tell them that I'm researching how people throughout the arid Southwest think about their relationships with water. Most give me a sort of puzzled look. "What do you mean by 'relationship with water,'" they ask? This question surprises me. To me, it as though I've told them that I'm interested in understanding their relationships with their mother, and they're asking, "what do you mean by relationship with my mother?"

The way we see our relationships with the more-than-human world is critical. Do we have a healthy relationship with the land, water, trees, birds, and animals—one built on love and mutual respect? Or do we have a controlling relationship with the more-than-human world—one built on fear and opportunism? We know there is something terribly wrong if our relationship with our mother is built on fear, opportunism, and control. Some recognize that a society built on use and abuse of natural resources is not sustainable. But what would it mean for us to collectively recognize that we as a society have an "abusive relationship" with water? Furthermore, what happens when we don't even recognize that we are in relationship at all?

Conservation arose as an approach to settling the West where water was sparse. Rooted in a colonial mindset, steeped in utilitarian values, conservation was designed to make the West habitable for large-scale settlement and growth. However, the old systems are breaking down and, as explored in chapter 2, an overreliance on conservation is inadequate.

To forestall water crisis and see a way into a healthy water future, a dramatic shift is necessary in how we think about and relate to water. Ways of thinking about and relating to the world directly impact the world in which we live. If we continue to try to alter social institutions and social structures without attending to attitudes, values, and deeply embedded belief systems, we will continue to create more or less the same world that needs changing. True and lasting change comes from shifting perspectives. As Albert Einstein is attributed to saying, "no problem can be solved from the same level of consciousness that created it." A fundamental change in mindset is needed to address the underlying systemic and cultural issues driving water crises in the Southwest.

Water Ethics and Fostering Meaningful Connections with Water

Ethics are about developing caring relationships with others. Ethics guide us toward respectful behavior rooted in care and concern for others' well-being. Wildlife ecologist and conservationist Aldo Leopold called for the development of a "land ethic" in his 1949 classic *A Sand County Almanac*. Leopold's land ethic called for moral responsibility, namely, care and concern for the greater community. By "community" Leopold meant not only human groups but the community of all beings, including the water, soils, plants, and animals. The Aldo Leopold Foundation describes Leopold's vision of a land ethic in this way: "the relationships between people and land are intertwined: care for people cannot be separated from care for the land. A land ethic is a moral code of conduct that grows out of these interconnected caring relationships" (Aldo Leopold Foundation, 2022).

Extending Leopold's vision of a land ethic to water helps us consider how the relationships between people and water are intertwined. A water ethic recognizes that care for people cannot be separated from care for water. If we replace the word "land" with "water" in the Leopold Foundation's description, we may say something like the following: *A water ethic is a moral code of conduct that grows out of the interconnecting caring relations among water and the community of all beings.*

This book set out on a journey to understand our relationships with water via interviews and exploration of the various conservation ethos of people living throughout the Southwest. Two main water ethos shape our relationships with water. The prevailing one, the conservation ethos, continues to shape how we think about and relate with water. In the face of water crises, we continue to look for more and better ways to conserve water. Yet, the water issues of the Southwest continue to intensify.

Living throughout the Southwest are examples of communities with cultures that model resiliency in their ability to survive in these arid regions for thousands of years. Traditional Indigenous relationships with water point to other ways of living within this arid region of the world, ways that have worked. However, in the midst of the prevailing conservation ethos and its utilitarian ideals, Indigenous approaches to living in the arid Southwest often go unnoticed and undervalued.

Where does that leave us now? We find ourselves in a position where alternative approaches, perspectives, and connections with water are urgently needed. What we require is a relational water ethos, one that surpasses the perspective of viewing water solely as an object to be conserved for future use to perpetuate the growth and development ideals of the early twentieth-century reclamation project (See textbox 2.1. "History of Conservation and Utilitarianism in the Southwest"). Rather, we need a water ethos that supports all life, human and more-than-human, and that fosters a relationship of respect, even reverence, for water.

In this pivotal chapter, our focus undergoes a transformative shift, moving away from a conservation water ethos grounded in utilitarian values, economic development, and individualism. Instead, we embark on an exploration of a rich and interconnected relational water ethos. This perspective is rooted in the principles of deep ecology, drawing inspiration from Indigenous knowledge systems, promoting the empowerment of Indigenous leadership, and prompting a fundamental paradigm shift from a conquest mentality to a holistic and interconnected relational mindset.

Thinking about Relationships to Water: Deep Ecology

Coined in 1972 by Norwegian philosopher Arne Naess, *deep ecology* emphasizes the intrinsic worth of all life regardless of its instrumental and utilitarian value for human beings. Deep ecology focuses on organizing social structures to align with this essential understanding and promote policies and activities that support ecological integrity so that all life, including human life, may thrive. From a deep ecology perspective, humans are but one expression of the natural world, no better nor worse than other life-forms. Nature deserves respect, and all living beings and environments have a right to live and thrive. From a deep ecology perspective, humans are dependent upon and live in relationship with the more-than-human world. Deep ecology maintains a relational, interdependent worldview imbued with a sense of reciprocity. A deep ecology ethos honors the rights of nature and views nature as sacred, meaningful, and deserving veneration and respect.

Even though deep ecology emerged from Western traditions, it shares some values with Indigenous traditions. Indigenous water ethics offer deep ecology models that have stood the test of time. Deep ecology offers a potential bridge, facilitating a stronger connection with the more-than-human world and transcending the limitations of the conservation model.

INTERCONNECTION: A SYSTEMS APPROACH

Deep ecologists maintain that the survival of any part is dependent on the survival of the whole. We are intimately interconnected with one another. An understanding of interdependence offers guidance for understanding complex, interrelated systems and helps move us away from binary-type thinking that pits individuals against individuals, and "my rights" to water against "your rights" to water. Understanding interdependence offers insight into what scientists and social scientists call "systems thinking." Barry Richmond, who coined the term, defines systems thinking as "the art and science of making reliable inferences about behavior by developing an increasingly deep understanding of underlying structure" (Richmond, 1994, p. 139).

Systems thinking maintains that all systems are composed of interconnected parts. As F. Capra and G. A. Pauli wrote, "the more we study the major problems of our time, the more we come to realize that they cannot be understood in isolation. They are systemic problems—interconnected and interdependent" (Capra and Pauli, 1995). Systems thinking maintains that systems function based on their underlying structure, with a focus on the connections between parts. Systems are viewed as emergent, nonlinear, self-organizing, and counterintuitive.

Tentative steps have been taken toward a systems approach to water conservation in the West. The California Global Warming Solutions Act of 2006, or Assembly Bill 32 (AB 32), required California to reduce its greenhouse gas emissions below 1990 levels by 2020. The California Air Resources Board explained that AB 32 was necessary to mitigate climate change, as, among other effects, climate change impacts the quality and supply of water to California (California Air Resources Board, 2014). AB 32 recognizes that climate change impacts snowpack in the higher elevations, which supplies Northern California with its water. The recognition that climate change exacerbates drought, along with the passage of a bill to mitigate these affects, demonstrates a systems way of thinking whereby interconnections between systems are acknowledged and policy is put into place to drive change. Considered one of the most successful pieces of legislation to reduce greenhouse gas emissions, AB 32's goals were met four years ahead of schedule, in 2016. While AB32 is a conservation bill, it is one of the first water bills that demonstrates a shift in mindset, recognizing the connections between climate change, snowpack, and water, and integrating a systems way of thinking.

A systems way of thinking about conservation is a first step in recognizing and forming approaches to water that are based on interconnection. Yet conservation's utilitarian focus at best prioritizes the strategy of using renewable resources no faster than their rate of renewal. What has been missing is a deeper ecological ethic infused with an understanding of interconnection. As Michelle Nijhuis, coeditor of *High Country News*, writes,

> if conservationists are to protect ecosystems, the conservation movement must start acting more like an ecosystem, operating at many interconnected levels. Even as it advocates for laws and regulations . . . it must work to reorganize society—to support people and communities in living sustainably within ecosystems and alongside other species. (Nijhuis, November 2022, p. 3)

Understanding interconnection shifts one's perspective from seeing oneself as separate from the Earth and each other to seeing how our relationships with each other and the planet contribute toward the well-being of all. The recognition that we interconnect with others challenges the ethos of the rugged individual, which overvalues the individual, often at the expense of others. Vietnamese Zen monk and teacher Thich Nhat Hanh coined the term "interbeing" to refer to this relationship, writing, "'Interbeing' is a word that is not in the dictionary yet, but if we combine the prefix 'inter' with the verb 'to be,' we have a new verb, 'inter-be'" (Hanh, 2011, p. 413). Saying we "inter-are" with water means that we recognize the way water and other living beings interact with each other.

The documentary *DamNation* features the many ways that diverting water impacts fish (Knight and Rummel, 2014). As I watched these fish live and die based on how we direct waterways, I found myself mesmerized by images of fish swimming up and downstream, fish jumping, fish swimming in schools, fish thriving. I imagined the water without the fish and felt a sense of sadness overcome me. At first, I couldn't quite put my finger on why water without fish made me so sad. Then I realized it was because water without fish felt dead. I began to realize that the water itself is *alive*. The water and the fish inter-are. What are waterways without fish? And certainly, fish do not exist without water.

Drinking a glass of water can also reveal how we inter-are with water. We may mindfully drink a glass of water, realizing that that water came from deep within the Earth. We can feel the water become our bodies, directly experiencing the inter-dynamics of self and water. As we observe other beings, birds, insects, friends and family, we can recognize that we *all* inter-are with water. Textbox 5.1 offers a "water meditation" designed to help guide readers into a deep recognition of their interdependence with water and with the Earth as a whole.

Let's take rivers as another example of how interdependence functions. As Rina Swentzell (Santa Clara Pueblo) discussed in chapter 4, rivers are not independent, separate waterways but are rather part of dynamic, alive watersheds: members of a larger community of life. As a biologist at the Ridgeway Water Festival explained to me, the part of the Uncompahgre River that flowed behind us was, sadly, not alive. When we looked at a sample of the river through a microscope, we found no living organisms. Apparently metals from mining operations had gotten funneled through the watershed and polluted the river, causing a die-off. That part of the river was dead. In contrast, when we examined water from another stream, we found the water teeming with microorganisms. The stream is alive.

At what point does a system die and lose its ecological integrity? The river and the life depending on that river coexist. That includes human life. When

BOX 5.1. WATER MEDITATION

To experience this Water Meditation as a guided practice, readers can visit followingthealiveness.com/meditations

Let's begin by thinking like a system. To think like a system, recognize your connections with others. Bring to mind the network of homes all connected through a series of tunnels composed of pipes that deliver water to your home so that the instant you turn on the faucet, voilà, water comes pouring into your glass. Now bring to mind all of the services that enable this one public water system to function: the industry that manufactures the water pipes, the construction of water systems, and the shared responsibility of systems of regulation and enforcement that enables one water system to deliver fresh potable water to homes. Even further, reflect on all of the things that would have to shift if this system broke down. If you could no longer receive water in your home, how would you drink, shower, clean your floor, water plants, and so forth? What if your plumbing system, the system of pipes and infrastructure that removes excess water from your home, also broke down? Now the excess water and waste has nowhere to go. The land surrounding your home soon gets saturated with toxins. As we think like a system, we recognize, honor, and embrace the complex networks of beings and structures that support our lives.

Breathe in. Breathe out. As you exhale, become aware of releasing water vapor into the air. Notice the existence of water in the air, in the form of humidity. Even dry environments have some humidity, although when people find themselves in low-humidity environments like Death Valley, they find their mouths dry out very quickly. Notice how moist your mouth is right now. That is because you are surrounded by water in the form of humidity in the air. Without water in the air, you would not be able to take another breath.

Your body is also composed of water. Notice any moisture, particularly evident in your mouth but also interacting with your entire body. Feel any "dry skin" and you may further realize that your body is replete with water, from your skin, to the waterways coursing through your system as blood, to the molecules of water that you breath into and out of your lungs with every breath—you are made of water.

continued on next page

BOX 5.1.—*continued*

The Buddha liked to make this yet more vivid. When he spoke of the water element, he typically included that which is "water, watery; that is bile, phlegm, pus, blood, sweat, fat, tears, grease, spittle, snot, oil-of-the-joints, urine" (Bhikkhu Bodhi, n.d.) and so forth. Each and every cell in our bodies is composed of 60 percent water. We are not separated from water. We are water!

Let's now bring to mind a cloud. If your eyes were microscopes, you would not likely perceive a cloud but rather tiny ice crystals, their elegant forms moving among bits of dust. If your eyes were made of electron optical lenses, you would perceive the deeper structures of these crystals. Any one of these perceptual lenses—eyes, microscopes, electron optical lenses—helps us perceive particular forms, yet these "forms" depend upon our perceptual apparatus. It is merely convention to call the individual entity that I perceive through my human eyes a "cloud." From another perspective, this "cloud" is composed of infinite particles, including our perceptions of "it," and it changes form moment to moment, condenses, falls as rain, joins in rivers, oceans, temporarily becoming part of our bodies, and so forth. While we may perceive the cloud as an individual entity, it has no separate self.

Water directly reflects the transitory nature of form. Ever-flowing, changing form, moving through cycles, evaporating, condensing, water shape-shifts. We can envision a water molecule as the heat of the sun energizes it and it rises into the atmosphere, connects with other water molecules, becomes heavy, falls upon the ground as a raindrop, enters streams, brooks, waterfalls, and eventually gets integrated into our food and our bodies.

Spend a moment imagining the infinitely changing experiences that one molecule of water has on its trip into your glass of water or your next bite of food. Reflect on the ever-changing, dynamic, life-serving nature of water, allowing its transitory nature to infuse your understanding.

talking about human life, we also need to examine the larger systems that sustain human life. It's not just about 40 million people depending on the Colorado River. It's about the ways those people interact with the entire watershed, the more-than-human life that inhabits that watershed, the sense of place and community well-being that makes one care about that watershed, and the economic system that supports a secure future for those living among the watershed.

As we view our lives as connected with all other living and nonliving beings, it no longer makes sense to make choices based on what we think is best for ourselves alone. Recognizing our interconnections guides us to consider the impact of our actions on all other beings. When we view water as a resource to be distributed and used, we experience one set of outcomes. What would it look like if we recognized that we inter-are with water?

RECIPROCITY WITH WATER

As we recognize our interconnections with water, a sense of reciprocity may also develop. Reciprocity is the practice of building mutual well-being in relationships. In a healthy relationship, reciprocity is balanced. The idea that water is here for our use suggests that our relationship with water is one-way: that water gives to us, and we need not give anything to water, except in ways that we perceive as beneficial to us. In contrast, those who view themselves in a connected and reciprocal relationship with water express a sense that, just as water provides so much to us, we too must give to the water.

Carrie, a member of a local group of master gardeners working to clean up creeks around Tucson, Arizona, describes how the group is leading a campaign to return water to the aquifers. She says that the group does not return the water to the aquifers merely because humans depend on the aquifers for water, but also as an act of reciprocity, as an act of love for all beings who depend on water for their livelihood. Carrie explains,

> We are stewards of this world, and caregivers, and it is our job to take care of all the things: the land, birds, critters, and the water. We are to keep the water clean and keep it flowing. We are to use it sparingly, not waste it and not pollute it. And we are obligated to share it with all beings.

To Molly, an environmental science project manager, our human relationship with water is "mutualistic." This means "water benefits us, and we can use the water to help us survive and do what we need to do. But we also help the water to continue on its path and continue its water cycle as well." For Molly, we are not simply passive recipients of the gifts of water, rather we also play a crucial role in the water cycle and the life of water as it moves along its path.

Environmentalists like Carrie and Molly are not the only ones who maintain a sense of reciprocity with water. Paul, head coach of a college football team, views an appropriate relationship between human beings and water as one where "the relationship is beneficial to both parties. When water benefits us and we help the production and purification of water, I think it shows how much we care about water, and respect what it does for us." While a traditional conservation ethos underlies Molly's and Paul's words—we care for the water because we need the water—their notions of reciprocity also demonstrate a shift. They recognize water as more than a thing, as a living entity that deserves respect.

Other participants also view water as a living being with whom we are in relationship and owe respect. Sophie explains, "Water is kind of an entity, a live thing as opposed to just a resource. Just like a plant is breathing and growing, water also breathes and grows. I think of water as something beyond what I use every day to live. And respecting it for what it gives us." For Sophie, humans and water take care of each other.

Yaaxfin, a mother and ecology student, describes the relationship between humans and water as follows: "You take care of me, for me to serve you." Yaaxfin believes that water sustains us now and in the future. Likewise, we don't want to merely conserve it, "we want to protect it. Water is life, it's something sacred, and we want to respect and show our love for it."

Greg, a regional water specialist in Colorado, envisions a shift in conservation approaches, away from control and technological fixes:

> We will need to start to give the rivers with their natural hydrology way more credit than we have been giving them and think we can just engineer our way out of everything. We'll have to develop around how the rivers flow, just letting the river kind of do its thing and working around it rather than just conserving and distributing it.

Perhaps a paradigm shift is underway. Many respondents express a relational and reciprocal view of water. Aaron, a medical devices salesman from Apache Junction, maintains a fairly typical view of water conservation, viewing water as something we need to protect and save so that it will continue to meet our needs. However, Aaron also articulates a recognition of a reciprocal relationship with water, saying, "An appropriate relationship between water and humans is one where water is more respected. As humans, we shouldn't just take and take but also give back to this Earth. A form of reciprocity should exist!"

Robin Wall Kimmerer (Potawatomi) underscores the significance of cultivating a sense of reciprocity with water in her book *Braiding Sweetgrass: Indigenous Wisdom, Scientific Knowledge and the Teachings of Plants*. She writes that traditional Indigenous cultures have long understood the importance of reciprocity in their relationship with water, recognizing that it is not merely a one-way transaction but a mutual exchange of care and respect. Kimmerer encourages us all to adopt a similar mindset, where we give back to water as it gives to us. As Kimmerer writes,

> each person, human or no, is bound to every other in a reciprocal relationship. Just as all beings have a duty to me, I have a duty to them. . . . If I receive a stream's gift of pure water, then I am responsible for returning a gift in kind. An integral part of a human's education is to know those duties and how to perform them. (Kimmerer, 2015)

This reciprocity involves not only responsible water conservation practices but also a deep appreciation for the life-giving properties of water. By fostering this sense of reciprocity, we can begin to restore the balance in our interactions with the natural world and ensure that water, which sustains all life, is treated with the reverence and gratitude it deserves. By embracing an ethos of reciprocity, Kimmerer envisions a transformative path that goes beyond conventional resource utilization and conservation paradigms. This path leads us toward a sustainable coexistence with water and the entirety of the more-than-human world.

WATER'S RIGHTS

While nature's rights are integral to traditional Indigenous ways of knowing and seeing the world, as we have seen in previous chapters, non-Indigenous communities and governments view nature, including water, as property. Water laws have been and continue to be created and enforced around who owns the rights to nature. Nature is often perceived as a collection of separate components: a specific river, a particular forest, an individual mountain, and so on. Instead of recognizing nature as a vibrant, interconnected whole, this perspective leads to a mindset of commodification, ownership, and control, disregarding its inherent living and breathing essence.

As Deborah McGregor (Ojibwe) and colleagues note, in water justice literature influenced by Indigenous worldviews, water is perceived as a sentient being with responsibilities to safeguard life's welfare. This perspective sharply contrasts with viewing water merely as a resource, property, or commodity. McGregor and colleagues maintain that the concepts of water justice and security extend beyond merely ensuring equitable human access, a focal point emphasized by the United Nations in its discussions on the right to water. Instead, they advocate for a broader understanding that includes fairness and equity for water itself, recognizing it as a living entity with inherent rights and responsibilities (McGregor, Whitaker, and Sritharan, 2020).

William of the Laguna Pueblo highlights the intrinsic rights of water, emphasizing that it "was given to us by the Creator." This perspective highlights the significant value ascribed to water, extending gratitude not only to the water itself but also to its Creator for "allowing us to be able to ask for water" and emphasizes the fundamental rights that water possesses. A paradigm shift that recognizes the relational and interconnected dimensions of water will invariably be accompanied by a shift in how water rights are perceived.

Another value deep ecology shares with an Indigenous water ethos is the conviction that water has rights of its own, such as the right to be healthy and live, flow and thrive. For example, Darlene Sanderson speaks of the Water Protectors who have fought against the Dakota Access Pipeline and have taken action to protect other waterways that are being threatened with drilling, fracking, and development. Sanderson says, "It's a labor of love. Mother Earth has a right to be clean. The rivers have a right to be clean" (ITKI and UNESCO, 2016).

This points to a very different way of thinking. In her TED talk "Why Lakes and Rivers Should Have the Same Rights as Humans" (2019), Indigenous legal scholar and water protector, Kelsey Leonard (Shinnecock) calls for the legal rights of water. Acknowledging that those who are granted legal rights gain important protections under the law, Leonard challenges us to shift from thinking of water as a thing (rain or H2o, for example) to thinking of water as a being—asking not "what is water" but "*who* is water?" Recognizing the personhood of water transforms our relationship with water and our decisions around protecting water, similar, Leonard explains, to the way we would seek to protect our mothers, grandmothers, sisters, and aunts.

Leonard questions the moral compass of US society that recognizes the legal personhood of corporations, so that corporations receive all the protections that a citizen receives, but does not extend legal personhood to nature.

She explains that if we want to address the water crisis in our lifetime, we need to change: "We need to fundamentally transform the way in which we value water. . . . We need to do better, we need to . . . grant water the right to exist, flourish and naturally evolve." Leonard asserts that recognizing the legal rights of water "protects the water from us, from human beings that would do it harm." Furthermore,

> it reverses the accepted hierarchy of humanity's domination over nature. As human beings on this planet, we are not superior to other beings on this planet. We are not superior to the water itself. We have to learn how to be good stewards again.

Recognizing the legal rights of water protects water from human harm and "reverses the accepted hierarchy of humanity's domination over nature." Leonard offers steps we can take to transform our relationship with water.

1. Create laws in which we honor the rights of water.
2. Honor the original treaties between Indigenous peoples and non-Indigenous peoples for water protection.
3. Appoint guardians for the water that ensure that the water's rights are always protected.
4. Develop a holistic approach to measuring water quality standards to ensure the well-being of the water.
5. Work to dismantle exclusive property ownership over water.

Additionally, Leonard highlights successful examples of communities that have recognized the legal personhood of bodies of water within the United States and around the world. She calls on each of us to ask what we can do for the water and then act. Leonard recommends advocating for water by calling local politicians or attending town meetings. If these approaches are not successful, Leonard recommends crafting your own legislation as the residents in Toledo, Ohio, did in 2019 to recognize the legal personhood of Lake Erie. Furthermore, Leonard recommends learning

> about the Indigenous lands and waters that you now occupy and the Indigenous legal systems that still govern them. And most of all, you can connect to water. You can restore that connection. Go to the water closest to your home, and find out why it is threatened. But most of all, if you do anything, I ask that you make a promise to yourself, that each day you ask, what have I done for the water today? (Leonard, 2019)

BOX 5.2. RECOGNIZING THE "LEGAL PERSONHOOD" OF BODIES OF WATER

The Whanganui River made history in 2017 when it became the first water body in the world to be granted legal personhood. This was achieved after an extended legal battle in New Zealand, which resulted in the river being legally protected. Essentially, any individual who harms the river is held accountable to the same extent as they would be if they caused harm to a human being. To ensure compliance with the river's new status, two guardians were appointed by the local Maori tribe.

There are calls throughout the United States, from all political factions, to award legal personhood to waterways. The Little Wekiva River in Florida, situated close to Orlando, is one example of such a water body. This river has suffered from excessive nutrient pollution and has even dried up on occasion. In November 2020, the residents of the region voted in support of recognizing the legal rights of the Econlockhatchee and Wekiva Rivers.

The problem of nutrient pollution has had a detrimental impact on Lake Erie, resulting in toxic algal blooms that render the water unsafe for human and animal consumption. As a result, there have been instances where the authorities have had to issue "no drinking" water advisories. In an effort to combat this issue, the City of Toledo has introduced a law that permits its inhabitants to file lawsuits on behalf of the lake, thereby giving them the legal right to fight against any harm caused to it.

For a more detailed explanation on the increasing efforts to promote legal personhood for water bodies, please refer to the following citation in the *Chicago-Kent Journal of Environmental and Energy Law*. It contains further examples of this movement and its implications (Editor, 2021).

WATER IS SACRED

We see examples throughout the dominant culture of small shifts away from treating water as a commodity to treating water as sacred and worthy of our care, protection, and respect. While not as developed as Indigenous views of water as sacred, as discussed in chapter 4, the language of the sacred shows up in many of the non-Indigenous water narratives. While describing the need to conserve water because "we need it to survive," Yaaxfin also remarks, "water itself is something sacred. Because it contains that which is life."

Jacob, a retired teacher, describes water as sacred in relation to his Catholic upbringing:

> Water is sacred. I always think of water as an element, it washes things away. It washes dirt away and, in a religious sense, it washes our sins away. It's physical in that it washes our dirt away, but it's also used as a spiritual thing in baptism.

Darrah, community program coordinator for a small town in southern Colorado, reflects on water as life: "if water is life, I would want to treat water as the sacred life that life is."

Sonia, judge for a family court in Las Vegas says, "water really is sacred. We are over 60 percent water, aren't we? Everything is water, nothing can survive without water, nothing on this Earth. So, it is beautiful. It is precious."

Fifty years ago, deep ecology started as a marginal movement by a group of devoted environmentalists. Today some of the ideas and principles of deep ecology have trickled into the mainstream. While conservation continues to overwhelmingly guide the dominant culture, policies, and approaches to water issues, I see possibilities for further developing a deep ecology ethic. How may the collective mindset be shifted away from the instrumental utilitarian approach that is at the root of conservation, toward a deep ecology mindset that honors a shared ecology and promotes a truly sustainable water future?

Shifting Mindsets: From a Conquest Mentality to a Relational Mentality

"We have mastered the conquest mentality," notes Eric Nolan, who at the time of our conversation was running for a seat on the Flagstaff City Council. "We know how to conquer, fight, and take. Now it is time for us to learn something new, how to care, share, and connect." Water conservation may be thought of as the latest iteration of the conquest mentality, disguised as benign and filled with good intentions, but ultimately reinforcing the same mentality that has ravaged these lands and waterways since colonization. While recognizing limits on water resources, water conservation has asked: How may we optimize our water use with the least amount of damage? Or, put another way, and reflecting the conquest mentality, water conservation has asked: How may we take the most, and still continue to live the lifestyles we are accustomed to living?

A MODERN ALDO LEOPOLD

During the mid-twentieth century, Aldo Leopold offered a vision for a land ethic, viewing nature as a "community to which we belong" (Leopold, 1949/2020, p. 18). Leopold envisioned the land ethic during a time when people were increasingly cut off from their natural surroundings, when nature was viewed as a commodity belonging to us, and when land and water were viewed in strictly economic terms. He articulated an alternative relationship with nature, one that emphasized intimacy with and humility in nature, learning from nature, making place-based choices, and cultivating love and a sense of wonder with the more-than-human world.

I have come across a handful of contemporary Aldo Leopolds over the years, people with the rare ability to articulate a shift in approach and mindset, who seek to live in relationship *with* the more-than-human world, ushering in a fresh vision at the level of the dominant society, one that encompasses new ways of thinking, being, and relating with nature. Here I'd like to share the work and vision of one of them: Brad Lancaster.

Brad Lancaster, a teacher and advocate for rainwater harvesting, works to help people "to see, and act, in new conscious ways," (Lancaster, 2023). His organizations, the Neighborhood Foresters program and the Desert Harvesters program, work with people to shift their relationships with water in ways that help them cultivate native food within their neighborhoods. Lancaster's two-volume award-winning book *Rainwater Harvesting for Drylands and Beyond: Guiding Principles to Welcome Rain into Your Life and Landscape* offers an in-depth step-by-step guide for working with rain to sustainably landscape in arid environments (2019a, 2019b).

THE MAN WHO FARMS WATER

Reflecting on the perception of rainwater, Lancaster writes,

> Rather than treating it as our primary renewable source of fresh water
> we typically treat rainwater as a nuisance, diverting it to the storm drain,

drainage ditch, or pollutant-laden street. In its place we invest vast resources acquiring lower-quality, secondary sources of ground and surface water. Such contemporary water management contrasts sharply with rainwater-harvesting traditions. (Lancaster, 2019a, p. 7)

Lancaster advocates for a shift in perspective, moving away from the notion of rain as an inconvenience to be controlled (a conquest mentality) and toward perceiving rain as an essential partner in our lives. The conquest mentality treats water as an external force, sometimes a friend or ally when it suits our purposes and at other times as an adversary or irritation when it doesn't. This dualistic relationship with water, characterized by love during droughts and frustration during excess rainfall leading to floods, reflects our conflicted feelings. Lancaster emphasizes the importance of embracing a relational mindset. Rather than adhering to the conquest mentality, which revolves around maximizing water use to meet our needs and desires, Lancaster encourages us to shift our perspective and consider how we can establish a partnership with water.

The relational mentality is illustrated in his stories titled "The Man Who Farms Water," about Mr. Zephaniah Phiri Maseko, who Lancaster visited in 1995 in southern Zimbabwe. In 1964 Mr. Phiri was fired from his railway job and told he would never secure employment again, due to his political activism against the white minority–led government. Concerned about how to support his family of eight, Mr. Phiri turned to the only resources he had: the Bible and a 7.4-acre family landholding that had no water source. Using the Bible as a gardening manual, and recognizing that he didn't have the Tigris or Euphrates Rivers as did Adam and Eve, Mr. Phiri concluded, "I must also create my own rivers," on land that received less than twelve inches of rainfall per year. Mr. Phiri began educating himself on rainwater harvesting, or "water farming," and over a thirty-year period, landscaped in such a way as to meet all of his family's needs on rainwater alone.

Working with the slope of the land, Mr. Phiri devised a system by which to "plant the rain," partnering with the water to slow it down and distribute it so it could soak into and spread throughout the land and ultimately be used for growing fruits, vegetables, and other vegetation. Mr. Phiri explained his approach: "The land must harvest water to give to the trees, so before you plant trees you must plant water" (Lancaster, 2019a, p. 27).

Through careful observation of the water and the way the water moved throughout the land, Mr. Phiri developed an understanding of water and

> **BOX 5.3. HOPI DRY FARMING**
>
> Dry farming, a time-tested technique practiced by the Hopi people in the arid Southwest, exemplifies sustainable agriculture in a challenging environment. For centuries, the Hopis, residing in twelve villages on what is now the Hopi Reservation in northeastern Arizona, have thrived as skilled farmers despite the region's limited annual rainfall, averaging eight to twelve inches. Old Oraibi, dating back to before 1100 CE, on Hopi First Mesa, stands as the oldest continuously inhabited village in the United States, a testament to their resilience and enduring presence.
>
> Farming is central to the Hopi way of life and spirituality. As Rosanda Suetopka Thayer writes, "This dry farming method is based on faith, keen observation, Hopi science methods and what the ancestors say is a 'heart full of prayer'" (Thayer, 2010). Dry farming relies solely on natural precipitation, strategically sowing crops based on land contours. Fields are situated on mesas, in washes, and between mesas, allowing rainwater to naturally irrigate them. Intergenerational knowledge is passed down, with most farming tasks performed by hand.
>
> The Hopis cultivate various crops using dry farming techniques, including corn (which holds a position of utmost significance and sacredness to the Hopi people), squash, beans, sunflower seeds, peaches, watermelons, wild onions, tomatoes, and chilis.

partnered with water to co-create a thriving farm that supported him and his family.

The conquest mentality emphasizes controlling and bending resources to meet human needs. Water conservation reinforces this model through the efficient utilization of resources to meet human needs and desires. Alternatively, a relational mentality is one rooted in deep ecology, emphasizing connection and recognizing that what we want must be considered in relation to the needs and wants of others, including the water itself. For example, Mr. Phiri creates wells that are open and lined with unmortared stones. At first this seems counterintuitive. How can one create a well that doesn't contain and control the water? But, Mr. Phiri explains, "these wells are those of an unselfish man. The water comes and goes as it pleases, for you see, in my land it is everywhere" (Lancaster, 2019a, p. 29).

FIGURE 5.1. Dry farming: cornfield. (Ansel Adams)

Lancaster drew inspiration and lessons from Mr. Phiri's example, learning how to partner with the water. Like any healthy relationship, he developed an intimate understanding of his partner. Lancaster observed how raindrops are soaked up "by the living sponges of forests, prairies, and desert thornscrub. These, along with their associated leaf drop, topsoil, and the cavities created by burrowing animals, help hold onto that water and slowly release it" (Lancaster, 2019a, p. 41). Through these observations and many others, Lancaster turned the eighth-of-an-acre depleted plot that he and his brother bought in Tucson into a lush environment, complete with on-site power, fruit and vegetable trees, native vegetation, flood control, wildlife habitat, beauty, and, notably, a sustainable water source.

Lancaster's inspirational talks and example have resonated with diverse audiences across the country, including community groups, schools, engineers, architects, and city and regional planners, inspiring many to engage with his work. Even one of our respondents, Wukoki, a natural resource specialist for the National Park Service, reflects:

There's a guy based out of Tucson who has written one or two books about waterscaping. It's not just about arid-adaptive plants like I've been discussing. He's actually focused on reshaping the land so that the water, like these intense rainstorms, can be captured. The water will then sink into the ground instead of just running off and evaporating in a flash flood. So, I started applying a few of those principles on my land.

"I AM . . . [THE] BEAST CARRYING WATER TO ITS NEXT STOP."

Conservation is about efficiency, utilization, and maximizing resources. In contrast, a relational approach to water based in deep ecology is about interconnecting with water and how we interact and co-create the flow of life with water. In the *Secret Knowledge of Water*, Craig Childs writes,

> As I drink the last of my water, I believe that we are subjects of the planet's hydrologic process, too proud to write ourselves into textbooks along with clouds, rivers, and morning dew. When I walk cross-country, I am nothing but the beast carrying water to its next stop. (Childs, 2001)

This view decenters humans, from seeing ourselves as the ones that the water serves, to the ones in service to the water, beasts carrying water to its next stop. This resonates with Vernon Masayesva's perspective, as shared in chapter 4, where he emphasized the integral role we play in the hydrological cycle, likening our bodies to gourds which serve as vessels that transport water from one location to another and subsequently release it to the "Cloud People."

A relational approach to water recognizes the important role that all aspects of the water system play in the water cycle. Lancaster points out that even the plant roots have an important role to play: "The plants' roots create thousands of micro channels throughout the soil, speeding up infiltration of water into the soil and steadily increasing the soil's storage capacity as plant and soil life grows and diversifies" (Lancaster, 2019b, p. 17).

Building upon the understanding that we are integral parts of the planet's hydrologic processes, it becomes clear that our relationship with water extends beyond mere consumption and utilization. Sandra Postel, the founding director of the Global Water Policy Project, encourages us to shift our approach, from manipulating water to meet utilitarian demands, toward adopting sustainable solutions that align with the order of the natural world and the natural flow of rivers (Postel, 2017). Similarly, science journalist Melissa Sevigny locates water security in a recognition of the rights of a river's path. Sevigny argues that water security is possible when we accept the limits of living in the desert and develop a close relationship with the natural world (Sevigny, 2016).

WE ALL HAVE A ROLE IN THE WATER CYCLE

The water cycle involves more than water as it is released by clouds; collects in ponds, lakes, and aquifers; moves through waterways; and evaporates and then collects once again into clouds. Rather, a relational approach to water recognizes every entity on Earth for its role in the water cycle. In this approach, vegetation is "a spongy living welcome mat that induces rain to quickly infiltrate into soil. Vegetation turns storm water into a productive resource that irrigates plants for free, supports springs and creeks, and assists in groundwater recharge" (Lancaster, 2019b, p. 257). And plants are "*living*

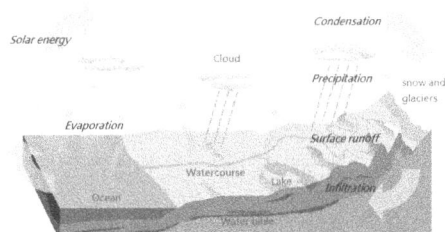

FIGURE 5.2. Consider this typical image of the water cycle taught in elementary schools and notice how plants and animals (including humans) are frequently omitted from our understanding of it. (Wikimedia)

pumps that access and draw soil water up into fruits and seeds. We in turn 'eat' this water in the form of a peach, pomegranate, olive, or mesquite pod" (Lancaster, 2019b, p. 257).

From plant roots, to vegetation, to topography, to animal and human bodies, a relational approach views the water cycle as much more than the "water cycle" taught in science curriculum. Google images for the term *water cycle*, and you will find hundreds of images, some more detailed than others, of the same basic model, arrows pointing to five main parts of the water cycle: precipitation, collection, travel, evaporation, and condensation. These are typically set within the image of a body of water, trees and a mountain, a blue

> **BOX 5.4. A WATER ABUNDANCE MODEL**
>
> In 1904 the Santa Cruz River still flowed year-round through Tucson, Arizona. The river was lined by forest, which acted as a sponge that would "absorb that rain and plant it into the soils," Lancaster explains. Yet a combination of overpumping and replacing vegetation with streets killed the Santa Cruz River. Similarly, pumping the Colorado River to support Phoenix's and Tucson's growing populations has killed the downstream stretch of the Colorado and the wetlands it once supported. Lancaster points out, "We squander the natural abundance that we already have, and we spend vast amounts of resources trying to replace that which we squandered by taking it from other people and other places, worsening scarcity for everyone" (Lancaster, 2017). However, rather than focusing on water sustainability, which implies maintaining what we already have, Lancaster proposes a water abundance model. When Lancaster realized that the city of Tucson receives more water in the form of rain (eleven inches per year) than the residents of Tucson consume, he developed approaches to working with the abundance of water that already naturally exists.

sky with clouds and the sun. Missing from most images of the hydro cycle are animals (including human beings), plant roots, stems, and other parts of the topography that help soak up and transport water. Missing from the typical model of the water cycle is a relational view of water that demonstrates how other forms of life interconnect with water. New questions arise when we view the water cycle relationally. For example, how do alpine forests or deserts or coastal communities interact differently with water?

Lancaster proposes that current models and understanding of water are based on a scarcity model: "We are a hydro-phobic society. We dehydrate ourselves" (ITKI and UNESCO, 2016). Lancaster explains:

> We drain our communities by diverting our rainwater away from rather than infiltrating it into our landscapes, waterways, and aquifers. We replace living nets of pervious vegetation and topsoil with impervious asphalt, concrete, and buildings, inducing rainwater to rush across the land and drain out of the system. (Lancaster, 2019a, p. 8)

Groundwater is excessively depleted, and water is swiftly drained from the land, preventing it from functioning as a vibrant sponge that absorbs water and fosters a beneficial cycle: vegetation absorbing water, nourishing itself, and promoting more vegetation growth. This rapid drainage contributes to escalated flooding. Additionally, substantial resources are expended on importing water that ultimately gets drained away, as exemplified by projects like the Central Arizona Project (CAP), which transports water over 300 miles from the Colorado River to Phoenix and Tucson, involving a 3,000-foot uphill journey. Rather than partnering with the rain, we drain the rain away, thereby exacerbating water scarcity. Lancaster encourages a shift from a water scarcity model to a water abundance model.

"COMMUNIFYING" VERSUS COMMODIFYING WATER

The pathway to water abundance involves what Lancaster calls "communifying," as opposed to commodifying, water. Rather than viewing water as a resource to be bought, sold, and hoarded, the abundance model views water as a member of the larger community, and our work together as essential to creating "community watersheds" that increase "the productivity and potential of our limited fresh water" (Lancaster, 2019a, p. 15).

Lancaster uses his own home and neighborhood in Tucson, Arizona, as a model of "communifying," demonstrating what is possible when water is viewed relationally and as part of the larger community. He refashioned the street in front of his home, from serving as a drain and moving water away from his home, to serving as an arroyo. Whereas most streets are designed to drain water away and prevent flooding (but consequently dehydrate the land), Lancaster saw the potential for the street to act as an arroyo (a waterway or channel to direct water onto arid or semiarid lands). He cut into the street in front of his home (at first illegally, but eventually worked with the city to legalize and incentivize the process) and redirected rainwater into his and his neighbors' yards. Inspired by the traditions of the Ak-Chin, who, similar to the Hopi practice of dry farming, position their farms at the ends of arroyos, Lancaster created a water-rich neighborhood with thriving vegetation, trees, and vegetables, all through working thoughtfully with rainwater. At the same time, he helped build community as neighbors visited in the streets while planting and landscaping together.

Besides creating water abundance, the process is also humanizing. Through planting the water and viewing water relationally, we recognize the importance of working with water on a human scale, in a way that generates life and supports our livelihoods and our well-being. This relational approach supports water abundance, challenging the consumer model of convenience and quick fixes. As Mr. Phiri explains, "it's a slow process, but that's life. Slowly implement these projects, and as you begin to rhyme with nature, soon other lives will start to rhyme with yours" (Lancaster, 2019a, p. 29).

This approach mirrors Indigenous scientists' approach to ecological restoration. As Josephine Woolington reports, many non-Indigenous scientists stress the urgency of addressing climate change and biodiversity loss, emphasizing quick action in restoring depleted landscapes. However, these approaches frequently lead to unsuccessful outcomes and neglect the significance of Indigenous methodologies, which prioritize patience and traditional practices. Woolington reports that Indigenous restoration approaches have been instrumental in revitalizing a web of connections, facilitating the resurgence of native plants and wildlife across numerous landscapes and waterways of the Pacific Northwest. However, public grants for restoration typically operate on short timelines, thereby favoring nontribal projects (Woolington, 2024).

Claudio Rodriguez, a community organizer with Tierra y Libertad, exemplifies the principles of communifying in his work on food and water justice in Tucson, Arizona. Similar to the communal approach demonstrated by Brad Lancaster in reshaping his neighborhood, Rodriguez's efforts focus on creating a sense of community ownership and responsibility for the land and water. Rodriguez explains,

> Like ants, our job is to bring back resources to the community. We need to ask the kids, what do you want to see? One had the idea of painting "Rain" on a cistern. Kids should never be absent from your work. Ask the moms, what resources are missing? Acknowledge the grandparents. (ITKI and UNESCO, 2016)

In this shared vision, children play a crucial role in shaping the future, with their ideas and perspectives valued alongside those of parents and grandparents. This holistic and inclusive approach echoes the ethos of working together with nature and with one another, recognizing that a gradual, symbiotic process leads to a more abundant and interconnected existence, both for human communities and the environments they inhabit.

ACEQUIAS: A COMMUNITY APPROACH TO WATER CONSERVATION

Many may not be aware, but there is a long history of communifying water in the Southwest. Influenced by Spanish, Arabic, and Pueblo irrigation systems, community-driven acequias developed throughout the Southwest as subsistence communities constructed with simple technologies similar to Hopi dry farming approaches (see textbox 5.3, "Hopi Dry Farming"). Physically, acequias are irrigation ditches primarily created by installing gravity chutes that work with the natural flow of water to irrigate land. As biological systems, acequias function to conserve water, soil, and energy, recharge aquifers, and preserve wildlife and plant habitats. As social systems, acequias "maintain the social fabric of the community" (Rivera, 1998, p. xviii). Through local knowledge and tradition, these irrigation systems use a community-based model to administer water usage based on equity and need.

Each acequia includes several commissioners and a mayordomo or ditch manager. While all other water systems in the Southwest follow a prior appropriation model—the first to use the water for "beneficial purpose" has first rights to the water—the acequia model overlays the prior appropriation system, ideally with fair and just models for community decision-making. Whereas prior appropriation views water as a commodity to be owned, acequias view water as a community resource to be shared. Furthermore, members of acequias view water not as a resource to be used but as an integral part of the community: "We don't control it. The land owns us. We're just a small part of it," says Joseph Padilla, a retired teacher who today irrigates his family's land through an acequia system in northwest New Mexico (Neuwirth, May 17, 2019).

Acequias are not merely water delivery systems but are also a way of life. Leanna Torres describes the acequia way of life in her own family, where her father gets up at two in the morning to check the water:

> Papa irrigates fields, brands cattle, repairs tractors, and never has enough daylight. The work he loves is also wearing him down, but he can't give it up, and so he laces on his boots every morning, devoting himself to a land that has never promised to sustain him. Water supply is shrinking, due to rising water demands and climate change, but still, he continues. (Torres, April 30, 2018)

Sylvia Rodriguez, professor emeritus of anthropology at the University of New Mexico, describes the power of the acequia model to bring people together to share scarce water supplies:

We have the wrong worldview here in the West, the idea of unlimited expansion, and it just doesn't work. I think land-based people who generally live on a small scale know that there's a limited good. The basic idea is that shortages are shared. (Rodriguez, May 29, 2016)

However, acequia communities also face challenges in these drought-ridden times. In the San Luis Valley, the local self-governed, communal water-management system based on acequias is not working. As journalist Nick Bowlin writes, "if the valley's farms and ranches, its towns and economies, are to survive . . . their relationship to water must change" (Bowlin, September 16, 2019). Kyler Brown, a potato and barley farmer, reflects on the local governance system, saying, "People thought the (acequia water management system) was the miracle, that was the amazing thing. . . . But implementing the system, forming committees and boards, that's the easy part. . . . Changing how people act, that's the real work" (Bowlin, 2019).

Unfortunately, the utilitarian mindset can still trump collective efforts. Those farmers with better water rights often use what they need and sell their extra water for credits. Meanwhile, corporations and wealthy farmers purchase the credits and pay groundwater pumping fees.

Additionally, values of individualism can also undermine the community approach. Beth, a water rights analyst in New Mexico, explains that while acequias are models of collaboration, individual competition also comes into play:

> There is definitely some competition that is involved with that system, because there is only so much water put in the ditch. You know, I am guilty of this too. If I do not wake up at 7:00 a.m. to get my share first, I might not get any at the end of the day. While there is a sharing component and you have to work with your neighbors, there is also a piece of who gets how much.

Sophie has firsthand experience living alongside an acequia in New Mexico. Sophie holds a nuanced perspective on these water channels. She acknowledges the significance of acequias for Pueblo communities, viewing them as integral to a communal tradition of shared water access. However, Sophie also observes a more individualistic approach to acequias among non-Indigenous residents in her area. She reflects on the utilization of acequias within her neighborhood:

> I used to reside in the North Valley, where homes were situated alongside an acequia, granting all the houses irrigation rights to access that water. Every Tuesday, residents could open their ditches and use as much water as they

needed until the acequia ran dry. In our case, we didn't actively cultivate anything, so we rarely used the water. However, our neighbor, who had a typical yard, would open his ditch every Tuesday, flooding his yard so extensively that it overflowed into ours. This led me to wonder whether acequias were really serving their intended purpose.

Community-driven acequias, with their consensus decision-making process, at times get undermined by economic structures, a culture of individualism, and a system of water rights designed for use, not for conservation. As Brown comments, "I have a decreed right to that water on paper, and I'm going to pump as much as I can, for as long as I can" (Bowlin, 2019).

Despite its challenges, to this day, acequia communities continue to govern water use, with seven hundred functioning acequias throughout New Mexico and several dozen in Southern Colorado. Although acequias may appear to be fragile and endangered systems, vulnerable to the destructive forces of modern market economies, they have persisted due to their foundation in tradition and community. Moreover, they present models for shifting relationships with water in arid regions facing increasingly dry futures as a result of climate change and overuse. Championing the resiliency and possibilities of acequias, journalist Simon Romero writes, "Making subsistence farming feasible in arid lands, New Mexico's communally managed acequias persisted through uprisings, epidemics and wars of territorial conquest, preserving a form of small-scale democratic governance that took root before the United States existed as a country" (Romero, July 13, 2021).

Developing a Relationship with Water

Recalling the introduction to this chapter, for those of us who were not raised to recognize water as a living being deserving of care, love, and respect as one would show a loved one, what can we do to develop our relationship with water? In my opinion, the most effective approach to developing a relationship with water is to consider qualities that are necessary for building any strong and healthy relationship: trust, respect, care, connection, and gratitude.

Placing our trust in water means believing that it will continue to sustain and provide for us, while acknowledging the need for our care and protection. It also means recognizing the power and potential of water to transform landscapes and shape ecosystems, while respecting its limits and vulnerabilities.

We can develop a respectful relationship with water by recognizing its intrinsic value and treating it with care and consideration. This means understanding that water is finite and precious and that it is essential to all forms of life on Earth. As discussed in chapter 4, respecting water is not only a matter of recognizing that water sustains our lives, but also includes revering water as a living, sentient being with its own will, drive for survival, and unique way of responding to threats. Respecting water also means acknowledging the cultural and spiritual significance of water to different communities throughout the world. It involves recognizing that water should not be treated as a commodity but rather as a living entity that plays a vital role in supporting ecosystems and biodiversity. Respecting water means treating it as a partner in our relationship with the rest of the living world and honoring its importance as a fundamental element of life. Ultimately, respecting water requires a shift in perspective toward water, from viewing it as a mere resource to be exploited, to a precious partner with whom we form a meaningful relationship.

When we care for and connect with water, we deepen our relationship with it even further. When we sit with water, listen to its sounds, and hear its songs (as in the epilogue to this book), we enter into a receptive learning state. Just as actively listening to a loved one can strengthen the bond between us, listening to water in any form can also develop our connection with it (see the water meditation in textbox 5.1 as a means to enhance connection with water). When we recognize water as a living entity and treat it with the same level of care and consideration as we would a loved one, we begin to develop a loving relationship with water.

As we cultivate a relationship with water, we may discover a sense of gratitude. As our gratitude for water increases, we become more attuned to the myriad ways that water enriches our lives and makes our existence possible. This heightened awareness allows us to recognize the powerful interconnectedness between ourselves and water, as the source of all life. As we dwell in this sense of connection with water and the immediacy of its gifts, our gratitude for it continues to deepen even further.

Social Change and Water in the Southwest

Although developing individual relationships with water is important, it is also important to consider how such relationships may be cultivated at the collective level. While it is impossible to predict the future, and I do not wish to engage in conjecture, I would like to conclude this chapter by posing some thought-provoking questions and considerations. In doing so, I hope to inspire readers to delve more fully into the topic of social change and water in the Southwest and to engage in further exploration and reflection.

Questions for Further Reflection

1. How may a new and healthy relationship with water bring about significant changes in laws, policies, economics, and infrastructure in the Southwest, changes that prioritize water stewardship, honor Indigenous traditional wisdom and leadership, and foster the well-being of communities and ecosystems?
2. In what ways might water infrastructure need to be reimagined in order to support healthy relationships with water?
3. What role can education and public awareness play in promoting healthy relationships with water?
4. How can marginalized communities, including low-income communities, communities of color, and Indigenous communities, be meaningfully included in decision-making processes concerning water stewardship and policy changes?
5. How can institutions, including educational, political, and environmental organizations, shift from a conservation-focused perspective to embrace a more relational approach to water?

What would water stewardship, which emphasizes developing and deepening relationships with water, look like? Such an approach would require a fundamental shift in the way we think about and interact with water, moving beyond a utilitarian perspective to one that values water for its intrinsic worth and recognizes its central role in our lives and communities. This shift would involve valuing traditional and Indigenous knowledge and practices; fostering meaningful and respectful relationships with water; acknowledging water's intrinsic value; honoring water's cultural, spiritual, and ecological significance; and prioritizing and promoting the long-term health and resilience of water systems.

Shifting models from utilitarianism to relationality, from management to stewardship, from conquest to respectful engagement with Indigenous ways of knowing and leadership, won't happen overnight. However, it is my hope that this book provides food for thought, inspires reflection, and raises questions that help each of us consider how we may contribute to new ways of seeing and relating with water. Little by little, we can contribute to shifts in society, moving from an abusive relationship with water to one that honors, respects, and reveres water—reflected both in the structures of our society and in our daily lives.

If you find the prospect of such social transformation daunting, consider how we have already witnessed significant changes in social systems and cultural attitudes toward water in just a few generations. Prior to the reclamation movement of the twentieth century, water was not viewed as a public resource in need of conservation. The idea of water conservation was not part of everyday life, and social structures were not designed to prioritize it. Over the course of the past century, there has been a remarkable and widespread transformation in the way society views and interacts with water. Previously, water was often regarded as an abundant resource, leading to wasteful practices. However, significant shifts in social structures, attitudes, and behaviors emerged, emphasizing the importance of water conservation. This collective shift demonstrates that we have the capacity to change. Even without prompting, every participant in our research spoke about the importance of water conservation. As discussed throughout the book, conservation has become deeply ingrained in society within a relatively brief period. The fact that ways of thinking, behaving, and organizing society can undergo such significant changes within just a few generations gives us hope that we can once again transform our relationship with water as a society.

And then there is the water itself.

What may the qualities of water itself—with its fluidity and permeability, its ability to traverse boundaries and connect regions, its continual movement from mountains toward oceans—teach us about how to live in healthy relationship with it on these arid lands?

BOX 5.5. WATER ETHICS: RESOURCES AND OPPORTUNITIES

In order for a new water ethic to take root, it must be put into practice. Ethics are principles by which we live and actions that we take. This will look different for different people and different communities. For those interested in taking further action to create a water ethic based in deep ecology and a relational mindset, here are some additional resources (see also textbox 4.1, "Southwest Indigenous Water Justice Resources" in chapter 4).

ALDO LEOPOLD FOUNDATION: aldoleopold.org

The Aldo Leopold Foundation works to inspire an ethical relationship between people and nature through Leopold's legacy.

WATER ETHICS NETWORK: waterethics.org

The Water Ethics Network provides a platform for individuals such as water professionals, business leaders, indigenous representatives, academics, civil servants, artists, philosophers, and anyone passionate about water to explore the values and principles— the ethics—that guide how we use, share, and care for water and its ecosystems.

THE RIVER NETWORK: rivernetwork.org

The River Network's mission is to empower and unite people and communities to protect and restore rivers and other waters that sustain the health of our country. Founded in 1988, they are a national watershed protection movement that includes nearly two thousand state, regional, and local grassroots organizations whose primary mission is to protect rivers and watersheds.

WATER-CULTURE INSTITUTE: waterculture.org

The Water-Culture Institute is committed to forging a new relationship between people and water that respects the rights and interests of both people and nature. Their premise is that cultural values and the health of water ecosystems are inextricably intertwined.

The rivers and the oceans sing their songs. Water is the melody of life.
—*Te Hurangi Wakerepunu, New Zealand Maori language activist and trade unionist*

We must begin thinking like a river if we are to leave a legacy of beauty and life for future generations.
—*David Brower, first executive director of the Sierra Club*

FIGURE 6.1. Song of the water. (Photograph by Janine Schipper)

EPILOGUE

The Song of the Water

I sit upon my favorite red rock, surrounded by flowing water. The water sings a sweet song as she travels toward the Verde River, flowing past towering sycamore trees. Sunlight shines through giant leaves and mingles with the water, creating a flickering lightshow upon the creek rocks above. Yellow warblers sing spring songs, while a water bug convention has gathered beneath my dangling feet. A zone-tailed hawk circles above.

I listen to the song of the water. As I listen closely, what at first sounded soft and soothing takes on a more urgent tone. She's flowing faster than I realized, rushing through a narrow band of rocks as she tumbles toward the Verde River. I sense that her song is much louder and fiercer than when I last spent time in the same spot. As I look around, I notice that the water flowing upstream seems higher along the rocky banks that line the creek, and a little pool has formed where the creek bed widens.

At first, I get excited. Maybe the snowmelt this past winter was enough to make a difference in the water levels. But the song tells a different story. I listen more carefully and realize that the rocks over which the water falls have been moved by human hands, creating a mini dam so that the water behind will collect and form into a swimming hole. The water tumbles over these rocks, singing a new song, one that is discernably louder. Had the rocks not been moved, the water in this part of the creek would sing a softer song. The water would not be in such a rush, crashing over rocks, but gently flow along, heading home to unite with the Verde, then with the Colorado, and eventually out to the ocean.

Yet, I know that these waters will never make it that far, never make it home to the ocean. Just as with the little swimming hole, we reorganize nature to suit our wants, needs, and desires. I wonder how things may be different if we were to begin listening more carefully to the song of the water?

Acknowledgments

Since embarking on this journey into our relationships with water in the Southwest, I've felt deep wells of gratitude for the countless individuals that have helped shape this exploration. I want to take some time here to honor as many as I can, acknowledging that any piece of writing is shaped by our myriad connections and influences over a lifetime—connections with both known and unknown individuals, all of whom contribute in tangible and intangible ways.

At the forefront of my acknowledgments, I wish to honor my beloved husband, Eliot, recognizing the invaluable role his support and insightful contributions played in shaping this book from beginning to end. It's impossible to enumerate all the countless ways Eliot supported me in this writing endeavor. From brainstorming initial research ideas, reading drafts, and exploring guiding frameworks, to the subtle nuances of our conversations shaping paragraphs and expressions, his impact has been immense. Yet perhaps his most influential contribution is simply who he is as a human being and how he relates to water and to the more-than-human world. With a heart full to overflowing, I thank you, Beloved.

I also wish to highlight the role a dear friend of thirty years, Deborah Cohan, has played in supporting me throughout the process of writing this book. Over the past few years, Deb and I walked astonishingly parallel writing paths. But what was perhaps most astounding was the way in which our hearts synced with each other every step of the way. I am grateful for the hours of conversations, processing, and indelible support. Thank you to my soul sister friend.

Many thanks to Roger Clark, who reached out to me many years ago after reading *Disappearing Desert* and encouraged me to write another book. This time, he suggested exploring water in the Southwest, emphasizing the need for a sociocultural examination of these issues, especially amidst the mounting water crisis.

I am grateful to Paula Stacey, who served as my developmental editor, helping me to revise the book with the intention of reaching a broad public audience. Paula's insightful vision contributed to establishing a cohesive flow and narrative thread throughout the book. Her creativity and perspective were instrumental in reorganizing and reframing the draft manuscript. I often liken this transformative process to that of a chrysalis: Paula took the manuscript, akin to a caterpillar, and with her expertise, shook up its contents to unveil something new and special. Although there were moments of apprehension during the book's metamorphosis, I am immensely grateful that we dove right into this work together. Thank you, Paula, for helping me create the type of book that I would want to read.

I extend my gratitude to Robert Ramaswamy, former acquisitions editor at the University Press of Colorado's University of Wyoming Press imprint. Robert's contagious enthusiasm immediately drew me in, endearing both him and his approach to building the environmental humanities collection. He grasped the essence of the book and understood my intentions behind it, supporting my aim to reach not only undergraduate students but also the wider public audience. Robert also embraced the interdisciplinary approach and the humanist and public sociology dimensions of the project. Robert embodied all I was looking for in an editor—warm, responsive, and supportive.

I thank Nate Bauer for stepping in to lead the project after Robert's departure from the press. I appreciate the support and additional effort put forth to bring this book to fruition, especially amidst an already demanding workload. Nate's dedication to this endeavor has not gone unnoticed, and I am thankful for his commitment to seeing it through to completion.

A heartfelt thank you goes out to the peer reviewers, whose insightful feedback contributed significantly to enhancing various aspects of the book and making it a more impactful read. My gratitude extends to all those involved at the University Press of Colorado for their contributions in bringing this book into its final form.

There's an abundance of gratitude to share and express. April Petillo and Michael Kotuwa Johnson offered invaluable insights regarding the chapters concentrating on Indigenous water relationships and the ramifications of the colonial mentality on Indigenous communities. Tasha Griffith reviewed initial drafts, bringing her editing skills to assist me in preparing sample chapters and a proposal for submission to publishers. I engaged in countless insightful and thought-provoking conversations with numerous individuals, which influenced my perspectives on various aspects of the book and how to meaningfully address the major water issues in the Southwest. I particularly want to emphasize the impactful discussions I had with Rachel Cox, Rachel Ellis, Tom Finger, Karla Hackstaff, Bob Hoffa, Chris Newell, Mike Robertson, Shelley Savage, Melissa Sevigny, and Angela Willeto. Special thanks go to my parents, Larry and Barbara Berkowitz, whose unwavering support, encouragement, and active involvement in the issues dear to my heart mean the world to me.

I wish to recognize the support provided by Northern Arizona University, my second home for the past twenty-seven years. NAU has played a pivotal role in nurturing my work and vision. I am especially grateful for the Department of Sociology, and the valuable support in pursuing my research endeavors extended to me by Jessie Finch and Yvonne Luna in their roles as department chairs. I am also deeply thankful for the Sustainable Communities program, where I have found not only support but also engaging discussions on critical environmental issues. These conversations have highlighted the significance of challenging fundamental assumptions and fostering meaningful dialogues with our students and communities. Special thanks go to Peter Friederici, Brian Peterson, Diana Stuart, and Nora Timmerman as well as previous directors Sandra Lubarsky and Luis Fernandez, all of whom epitomize the essence of questioning fundamental assumptions and advocating for just and sustainable communities, and whose approach is characterized by inclusivity and empathy.

And now for the grand finale of acknowledgments! Numerous graduate and undergraduate students contributed to the research underpinning this book. Graduate students, whom I trained, subsequently acted as mentors to undergraduates during the process of conducting in-depth interviews. I pause here to extend my heartfelt gratitude to each and every one of these students who dedicated their time and effort to collecting water narratives from individuals across the Southwest.

Thank you, graduate researchers! Blessings Chibambo, Kim Fessenden, Kaitlin Fitzgerald, Jorge Garza, Garold Johnson, Kelly Kusumoto, Madison Ledgerwood, Leann Leiter, Nicholas Martell, Nina Porter, Beth Vander Stoep, and Jennifer Williams.

Thank you, undergraduate researchers! Kolby Ah Sau, Ian Andersen, Kameryn Nichele Arnold, Katelyn Bergen, Sarah Birt, Emma Borkovich, Alethea Boulet, Grayson Bull, Sean Buechel, Audrey Bursek, Nicholas Bury, Bruno Calderon, Stella Carr, Kyle Chambers, Deziree Chamorro, Anastasia Cheifetz, Amber Chrisman, William Churchill, Taylor Clark, Aubrey Collins, Jonathan Colombo, Kristian N Cordell, Benjamin Corderman, Kira Darragh, Olivia Dawson, Charles DeWitt, Felix Delmar, Andrew Depaoli, Kate Dickerson, Matthew Doyle, Kelsey Dunst, Sarah Ellison, Jacob Encinas, Byron Evans II, Evan R Fazz, Maja O'Keeffe Fosmo, Tara M Fry, Shenhuimei Gao, Thalia Garcia, Natalie Gauvin, James Gleixner, Bianca L Gonzalez, Jeremy W Gooden, Emily Goodman, Samantha Gordon, Sarah Grams, Sydney Gregerson, Brendaya Grigsby, Meaghan Hager-Garman, Joshua Hallam-Burrows, Thomas Harris, Sydney Hausberter, Nicholas Havelock, Jacob Henderson, Lauren Herd, Jaime Hernandez-Cauthen, Todd Douglas Hoffman, Chloe Channing Hubbard, Connor Huenneke, Rachel Iliff, Rolonda Jumbo, Zoe Jordan, James Justham, Taelor Keyonnie-Begay, Kurtis Kerr, Gavin Kilcoyne, Riley Koldenhoven, Eleanor Krueger, Amanda Krigbaum, Emma Kukulski, Alexandra Kulig, Alex Klausen, Jackson Lange, Beatrice Lara, Thomas Laszlo, Jack Lenard, Dylan Lenzen, Sophia Licher, Rafael Lopez, Flavio Luna, Precious M Luster, Sarah Lydford, Leah Manak, Ana Manzano, Jake Max, Daityevon McFadden, Kate Meiner, Andrew Minard, Diego Mondragon, Connor Moore, Micah Mossman, Jasmine Meuller-Hsia, Kaylana Meuller-Hsia, Matthew Muilenburg, Travis Murakami, John Murphy, Jessica Nowak, Helen O'Keefe, Jacqueline Padilla, Daniel Pape, Zachary Paulsen, Erica Peeblex, Taylor Pennington, Kaylee Pershklakai, Dana Peters, Lauren Peters, Haley Phillips, Sheridan Pritchard, Meredith Prentice, Kevin Pugh, Caitlin A Reichel, Hannah Reyes, Walker Reznick, Ansley Roberts, Rebecca Rodriguez, Cameron Rood, Rachel Rose, Gabryl Sam, Deja R Sanders, Mallory Schaefer, Lindsay Schillo, Eric Schuller, Justin Sease, Clarece Sellers, Shawn Sharkey, Sydney Shaw, Sean Shoemaker, Armani Simmons, Michael Sloan, Lydia C Smart, Jake Smith, Tyler Soderman, Sarah Spainhower, Matthew C Spitzley, Matthew Stark, Hali Stauffer, Matthew C Stuebs, John L Stoops, Kurt Strauss, Elaina Thompson, Leighanne B Thompson, Sara Tilford, Jessica M Tramp, Hannah Urrutia, Isaiah

Vander, Austin Vanderveen, Kelly Verrinder, Gabriel Villarreal, Ryan Vogelsang, Chaz R Walters, Joshua Walker, Dalen Ward, Jennifer Weigley, Joyceline S Wero, Cade White, Kristi White, Summer White, Matthew Wilcox, Alexander Wille, Mariah Willadsen, Analise Williams, Carly Willson, Amanda Wolcott, Espen Yates, and Kevin Zamora.

Two cohorts of environmental sociology graduate students provided in-depth reviews of early drafts of *Conservation Is Not Enough*. Their insights and feedback played a pivotal role in shaping numerous ideas throughout the book. Many thanks to Justice Addai, Mariana Alvidrez, William Cannon, Cara Caruolo, Sarah Nizhoni Chacon, Towera Chirwa, Portia Griefenberg, Murshidha Jawaheer, Zoe Lawrence, David Lieder, Sirene Lipschutz, Hannah Maclean, Rebecca "Jade" McCullough, Brian Medina, Ailin McCullough, Kayla Shaffstall, Paola Silva, Sara Sprague, Emma Stanley, and Anna Vaughn.

Thank you to all of the participants in this research who offered your time, perspectives, and water narratives. The strength of this project lies in the power of your voices.

And finally, a deep bow of gratitude to the Song of the Water. As I listen to you, I cultivate ever-deepening connections with you and with this precious planet in which you flow.

APPENDIX A
Research Overview

My research interests revolve around the larger cultural stories and mythologies we tell ourselves about water—"water narratives." I began with the following research questions: What stories do we tell ourselves about water in the Southwest? How do our cultural stories impact the way we relate with water? How do we assign meaning to water, and what sort of a water awareness is necessary to achieve water sustainability in the Southwest?

Undergraduate students, graduate students, and I conducted in-depth interviews in order to explore these research questions and gather water narratives. The interviews created opportunities for individuals to share their stories, highlight their values, and explore how their ways of thinking about water have changed over time. We asked questions that offered us insight into peoples' stories, experiences, and relationships with water (see textbox 0.2 for the interview questions). The interviews took place over five semesters from the fall of 2015 through the fall of 2017. Northern Arizona University's institutional review board approved the research for this project.

I designed and facilitated a training process to prepare graduate and undergraduate students to conduct interviews. I began each semester by training

Master's in Sustainable Communities students on how to conduct in-depth interviews. After they had received the training and conducted their own interviews, they helped me to train undergraduate students in my upper-division Environment and Society classes. The training involved developing a research plan and a recruitment plan; engaging in institutional review board training and obtaining certification to work with human subjects; receiving instruction from me on approaches, methods, and strategies for conducting in-depth interviews; and role-playing and practicing conducting in-depth interviews.

Students were instructed to conduct their interviews in relatively quiet public venues. Prior to conducting the interview, students obtained informed consent, collected demographic information (see appendix B for demographic information), and asked respondents to share a pseudonym that they wanted used in any written and published materials. Each interview was audio-recorded for accuracy and lasted between one and one-and-a-half hours. Students were also required to transcribe their interviews and were trained on how to thoroughly document respondents' words. Undergraduate students were grouped in pairs, and each pair was responsible for recruiting one individual to interview for the study. In total, 165 undergraduate students and eleven graduate students conducted interviews for this research. I am grateful for each one of the students for their efforts and contributions to this research and have included all of their names in the acknowledgments.

Together, the students and I conducted ninety-five interviews. I took a sabbatical during the spring semester of 2018 in order to read, reflect upon, and analyze all of the interviews. I used a grounded theory process in order to code (identify key ideas and categories) and systematically analyze the interviews and explore emerging patterns. Grounded theory served as a means for reducing the influence of my own assumptions on the interviews and helped me to identify underlying values, assumptions, and perceptions of respondents.

I coded each interview twice using Dedoose, a qualitative software program. With Dedoose I was able to match people's own words with the codes. This proved critical when highlighting certain voices to illustrate themes throughout the book. The coding process involved identifying a set of initial codes and then engaging in open and focused coding. I underwent a detailed coding process of all of the interviews once and then recoded every interview a second time in order to apply the codes systematically throughout all interviews. I also took analytic memos to keep track of my initial assumptions, note changes in my understanding, and record insights that arose through the coding process.

Key themes emerged out of the process of coding and memo taking. Those themes became the central organizing principles of the book and are highlighted in the chapter titles and subtitles throughout the book.

APPENDIX B

Demographic Information

The following tables present demographic information about the participants in the research, offering insight into their backgrounds and characteristics.[1] This data provides context for understanding the diversity and perspectives represented in the study.

Age

18–30	31–45	46–60	61–75	76 or over	Unreported
24	18	25	12	5	11

Gender

Male	Female	LGBTAQ	Unreported
53	39	2	1

---

[1] There are inconsistencies in the demographic information obtained. Unfortunately, not all students collected demographic information on their respondents as instructed. Sometimes students reported some information (examples: age and ethnicity) while not reporting other information (examples: education and political orientation). Despite these drawbacks, these tables provide an overview of the diverse range of participants in this study.

Demographic Information

Race or Ethnicity

African American	European American	Indigenous American	Latino/Latina	Pacific Islander	Other	Unreported
3	59	8	11	1	3	10

Education (highest attainment)

Less than High School	High School	College Student	Associate Degree	BA	MA/Professional	PhD	MD	Unreported
1	14	12	1	27	23	3	1	13

Spirituality or Religion

Christian	Jewish	Buddhist	Traditional/Native	Spiritual/New Age	Atheist	Other	None	Unreported
31	2	3	2	8	3	1	18	27

Political Orientation

Republican/Conservative	Democrat/Progressive	Libertarian	Green	Independent	None/Undecided	Traditional (before colonialism)	Unreported
10	28	5	1	16	12	1	22

Current Home in the Southwest

CA	NV	UT	AZ	CO	NM	SW TX	Unreported
5	2	2	64	6	12	1	3

Respondents came from a variety of professional backgrounds, including the following:
    accountant for water sales and distribution company
    alfalfa farmer
    animal welfare professional
    assistant curator for a botanical garden
    beekeeper
    bicycle shop owner
    board member of aqueduct project
    businessman and property manager
    cataloger
    coach and owner of a fitness club
    college students (8)
    community initiatives facilitator
    community organizer for a nonprofit environmental group
    community organizer / digital marketing / hotel owner
    construction project manager
    county clerk of a superior court
    director of a state department of transportation
    director of sustainability for a resort
    emergency management
    English professor
    environmental science and policy graduate student
    environmental sciences lecturer
    family court judge
    farmer
    federal labor law enforcement
    fish restoration technician
    football manager / uber driver
    game and fish employee
    government
    head football coach
    housewife
    hydrogeologist
    hydrologist (2)
    improvement manager
    information and technology services technician (2)

landscape architect and planner
local ditch manager
manager of a water treatment facility
marine biologist
medical devices salesman
medical doctor
meditation teacher
mother
natural resource specialist for national park service
office personnel for a produce store
owner of seed corporation
pharmaceutical technician
potato farmer
president of a manufacturing company
program director for a nonprofit environmental organization
project manager
project manager for a ranching organization
project manager for construction / telecommunications
ranch co-owner and head rancher
rancher
restaurateur
retired (8)
river guide
sales manager
senior geologist
ski and snowboarding instructor
special education teacher
teacher
university instructor
university professor
vice president of operations for a manufacturing company
volunteer coordinator
waiter
water resource manager (2)
water rights analyst
wilderness guide

Works Cited

Abram, D. (2012). *The Spell of the Sensuous: Perception and Language in a More-than-Human World*. Vintage.
Aldo Leopold Foundation. (2022). *The Land Ethic*. Retrieved October 2022, from Aldo Leopold Foundation. https://www.aldoleopold.org/about/the-land-ethic/
American Rivers. (2013). *American Rivers*. Retrieved September 2020, from I Am Red—The Colorado River: https://americanrivers.org/rivers/films/i-am-red-the-colorado-river/
American Rivers. (2015). *America's Most Endangered Rivers of 2015*. Retrieved May 2021, from American Rivers. https://www.americanrivers.org/2015/04/most-endangered-the-colorado-river-in-the-grand-canyon/
Arax, M. (2019). *The Dreamt Land: Chasing Water and Dust across California*. Vintage.
Arellano, J. A. (2021). Decolonizing Mexican Americans. Retrieved from *Post45*. https://post45.org/2021/08/decolonizing-mexican-americans/
Arizona v. California, 373 U.S. 546 (U.S. Supreme Court January 8–11, 1962).
Basso, K. (1996). *Wisdom Sits in Places: Landscape and Language among the Western Apache*. University of New Mexico Press.
Belfi, E., and Sandiford, N. (2021). What Is Decolonization, Why Is It Important, and How Can We Practice It? Retrieved October 2022, from Decolonization Series Part 1: Exploring Decolonization. In S. Brandauer and E. Hartman (Eds.). https://globalsolidaritylocalaction.sites.haverford.edu/what-is-decolonization-why-is-it-important/

Bellagio MGM Resorts. (2018). Bellagio Las Vegas. Retrieved October 2018, from Fountains of Bellagio. https://bellagio.mgmresorts.com/en/entertainment/fountains-of-bellagio.html

Berry, W. (2006). *The Way of Ignorance and Other Essays*. Counterpoint Press.

Bhikkhu Bodhi. (n.d.). Majjhima Nikāya: The Greater Discourse on the Simile of the Elephant's Footprint. Retrieved October 2023, from *suttacentral.net*. https://suttacentral.net/mn28/en/bodhi?lang=en&reference=none&highlight=false

Boughton, S. (2024). *The Wild River and the Great Dam: The Construction of Hoover Dam and the Vanishing Colorado River*. Christy Ottaviano Books.

Bowlin, N. (2019, September 16). *High Country News*. Retrieved September 2019, from Colorado farmers fight to save their water and their community's future. https://www.hcn.org/issues/51.16/water-colorado-farmers-fight-to-save-their-water-and-their-communitys-future

Brown, D. (2001). *Insatiable Is Not Sustainable*. Praeger.

Bureau of Reclamation. (2022). Lake Mead Annual High and Low Elevations (1935–2022). Retrieved October 2023, from *Lake Mead Line*. https://www.usbr.gov/lc/region/g4000/lakemead_line.pdf

Bureau of Reclamation. (2023, April 20). Above-Average Snowpack and Projected Runoff Will Send More Water from Lake Powell to Lake Mead. Retrieved May 2023, from *News and Multimedia*. Press release: https://www.usbr.gov/newsroom/news-release/4492

Bureau of Reclamation. (2023, April 27). 5-Year Probabilistic Projections. Retrieved May 2023, from Bureau of Reclamation: https://www.usbr.gov/lc/region/g4000/riverops/crss-5year-projections.html

Bush, E. (2023, May 22). Three States Agree to Reduce Water Usage so the Colorado River Doesn't Go Dry. Retrieved October 2023, from *NBC News*. https://www.nbcnews.com/science/science-news/arizona-california-nevada-cut-water-usage-drought-hit-colorado-river-rcna85567

California Air Resources Board. (2014). *Proposed First Update to the Climate Change Scoping Plan: Building on the Framework*. California Air Resources Board for the State of California.

Capra, F., and Pauli, G. (1995). *Steering Business towards Sustainability*. Unipub.

Carlowitz, M. A. (2021, August 9). Lake Mead Drops to a Record Low. Retrieved from NASA Earth Observatory. https://earthobservatory.nasa.gov/images/148758/lake-mead-drops-to-a-record-low

Cheng, W., Lu, S., Jiao, W., Wang, M., and Chang, A. (2013). Reclaimed Water: A Safe Irrigation Water Source? *Environmental Development*, 8, 74–83.

Chief, K. (2020). Water in the Native World. *Journal of Contemporary Water Research and Education*, 169, 1–7.

Childs, C. (2001). *The Secret Knowledge of Water*. Back Bay Books.

Childs, C., and Derby, D. B. (2015, September 28). Water Maze. Retrieved March 2020, from *Orion Magazine*. https://orionmagazine.org/article/water-maze/

Colorado College State of the Rockies Project. (2023, February 15). The 2023 Survey of the Attitudes of Voters in Eight Western States. Retrieved March 2024, from Colorado College State of the Rockies. https://www.coloradocollege.edu/other/stateoftherockies/conservationinthewest/2023.html

Crifasi, R. R. (2016). *A Land Made from Water: Appropriation and the Evolution of Colorado's Landscape, Ditches, and Water Institutions.* University Press of Colorado.
Cronon, W. (1996). The Trouble with Wilderness; or, Getting Back to the Wrong Nature. In W. Cronon, *Uncommon Ground: Rethinking the Human Place in Nature* (pp. 69–90). W. W. Norton.
Cuaz, N. (2020). *Unearthing an Emancipatory Conservation: A Critical Ethnographic Study of Justice in Conservation.* Flagstaff, AZ: ProQuest 28257229.
Curley, A. (2019). Unsettling Indian Water Settlements: The Little Colorado River, the San Juan River, and Colonial Enclosures. *Antipode*, 53(4), 705–23.
Curley, A. (2021). Infrastructures as Colonial Beachheads: The Central Arizona Project and the Taking of Navajo Resources. *Environment and Planning D: Society and Space*, 39(3), 387–404.
Daigle, M. (2018). Resurging through Kishiichiwan: The Spatial Politics of Indigenous Water Relations. *Decolonization: Indigeneity, Education and Society*, 7(1), 159–72.
Dasgupta, S. (2016, March 30). 5 Reasons Why Many Conservation Efforts Fail. Retrieved May 2021, from *Mongabay*. https://news.mongabay.com/2016/03/5-reasons-why-many-conservation-efforts-fail/
Davis, W. (2023). *River Notes: Drought and the Twilight of the American West.* Greystone Books.
Dearen, P. (2016). *Bitter Waters: The Struggles of the Pecos River.* University of Oklahoma Press.
deBuys, W. (2013). *A Great Aridness: Climate Change and the Future of the American Southwest.* Oxford University Press.
d'Elgin, T. (2016). *The Man Who Thought He Owned Water: On the Brink with American Farms, Cities, and Food.* University Press of Colorado.
Deloria, V., Jr. (1988). *Custer Died for Your Sins: An Indian Manifesto.* University of Oklahoma Press.
Devault, K. (2022). A Growing Movement to Reclaim Water Rights for Indigenous People. Retrieved October 2022, from *Yes!* https://www.yesmagazine.org/environment/2022/05/31/water-justice-native-tribes
Dunbar-Ortiz, R. (2015). *An Indigenous Peoples' History of the United States.* Beacon Press.
Editor. (2021). Legal Personhood: The Growing Movement to Give Bodies of Water Their Day in Court. Retrieved May 2023, from *Chicago-Kent Journal of Environmental and Energy Law*. https://studentorgs.kentlaw.iit.edu/ckjeel/2021/04/05/legal-personhood-the-growing-movement-to-give-bodies-of-water-their-day-in-court/
Ellis, R. (2019, April 30). Community defense of thesis: Exploring Anticolonial Protective Pathways for the Confluence of the Colorado and Little Colorado Rivers (ProQuest 13884154). Flagstaff, AZ: Northern Arizona University.
Environmental Protection Agency (EPA). (2017). Water Sense. Retrieved October 2020, from State Water Facts. https://19january2017snapshot.epa.gov/www3/watersense/our_water/state_facts.html
Environmental Protection Agency (EPA). (2023). A Closer Look: Temperature and Drought in the Southwest. Retrieved March 2024, from EPA. https://www.epa.gov/climate-indicators/southwest
Environmental Protection Agency (EPA). (2024, February 13). ICLUS Data for the Southwest Region. Retrieved March 2024, from Global Change Explorer. https://www.epa.gov/gcx/iclus-data-southwest-region

Estes, N. (2024). *Our History Is the Future: Standing Rock versus the Dakota Access Pipeline, and the Long Tradition of Indigenous Resistance*. Haymarket Books.

Ferris, K., and Porter, S. (2021). *The Myth of Safe-Yield: Pursuing the Goal of Safe Yield Isn't Saving Our Groundwater*. Tucson: ASU Kyle Center for Water Policy at Morrison Institute.

Festinger, L. (1957). *A Theory of Cognitive Dissonance*. Stanford University Press.

Fixico, D. (2003). *The American Indian Mind in a Linear World: American Indian Studies and Traditional Knowledge*. Routledge.

Flavelle, C., and Healy, J. (2023, June 1). *New York Times*. Retrieved October 2023, from Arizona Limits Construction around Phoenix as Its Water Supply Dwindles. https://www.nytimes.com/2023/06/01/climate/arizona-phoenix-permits-housing-water.html

Fleck, J. (2019). *Water Is for Fighting Over, and Other Myths about Water in the West*. Island Press.

Fuller, A. A. (2010). Population Growth, Climate Change and Water Scarcity in the Southwestern United States. *American Journal of Environmental Sciences*, 6(3), 249–52.

Gilio-Whitaker, D. (2019). *As Long as Grass Grows: The Indigenous Fight for Environmental Justice, from Colonization to Standing Rock*. Beacon Press.

Glennon, R. (2009). *Unquenchable: America's Water Crisis and What to Do about It*. Island Press.

Good Food Finder. (2023, February 2). Criollo Cattle as a Solution for Ecosystem Regeneration. Retrieved March 2024, from Good Food Finder. https://www.goodfoodfinderaz.com/blog/2023/2/2/criollo-cattle-as-a-solution-for-ecosystem-regeneration#:~:text=Research%20conducted%20by%20the%20Sustainable,arid%20landscapes%20in%20the%20Southwest

Goodluck, K. (2022). Locked inside the U.S. Water Regime. *High Country News*, 14–15.

Goodluck, K., and Trudeau, C. (2022, January 1). Indigenous Feminism Flows through the Fight for Water Rights on the Rio Grande. Retrieved January 2023, from *High Country News*. https://www.hcn.org/issues/54.1/indigenous-affairs-water-indigenous-feminism-flows-through-the-fight-for-water-rights-on-the-rio-grande

Grafton, R. Q., et al. (2018). The Paradox of Irrigation Efficiency. *Science*, 361(6404), 748–50.

Hanh, T. N. (2011). *Awakening of the Heart: Essential Buddhist Sutras and Commentaries*. Parallax Press.

Hansman, H. (2022). *Downriver: Into the Future of Water in the West*. University of Chicago Press.

Harrison, C. S. (2021). *All the Water the Law Allows: Las Vegas and Colorado River Politics*. University of Oklahoma Press.

Harvard Project American Indian Economic Dev. (1999). The Harvard Project on American Indian Economic Development. Retrieved October 2022, from Water Quality Standards: Pueblo of Sandia. https://hwpi.harvard.edu/files/hpaied/files/water_quality_standards.pdf?m=1639579305

Hobbs, J. G. (2005). *History of Colorado River Law, Development and Use: A Primer on Development and Use; A Primer and Look Forward* [Conference paper]. Hard Times on the Colorado River: Drought, Growth and the Future of the Compact, Summer Conference, June 8–10, University of Colorado Law School, Boulder, CO.

Holland, A. (2014). Water Management in the American Southwest: Lessons for an Age of Climate Change. American Security Project.

Hopi Hisot Navoti Gathering. (2016, November 19). Crossing Worlds Hopi Projects. Retrieved March 2024, from Hopi Water Declaration. https://crossingworlds.org/hopi-water-declaration/

Hundley, N., Jr. (2009). *Water and the West: The Colorado River Compact and the Politics of Water in the American West*. University of California Press.

Inskeep, S. (2007, September 3). NPR. Retrieved January 2023, from Xeriscaping: A Hot Topic in Santa Fe. https://www.npr.org/templates/story/story.php?storyId=14136213

IPCC. (2021, August 9). Climate Change Widespread, Rapid, and Intensifying—IPCC. https://www.ipcc.ch/2021/08/09/ar6-wg1-20210809-pr/

IPCC. (2023). *AR6 Synthesis Report Climate Change 2023*. Geneva: Intergovernmental Panel on Climate Change. https://www.ipcc.ch/report/sixth-assessment-report-cycle/

Isakowitz, L. (2019, July 31). Restoring the Colorado River Delta. Retrieved August 2022, from The Nature Conservancy. https://www.nature.org/en-us/about-us/where-we-work/priority-landscapes/colorado-river/restoring-the-delta/

ITKI and UNESCO. (2016). ITKI UNESCO City of Gastronomy Conference—"Food and Water in Arid Lands." Tucson: University of Arizona College of Social and Behavioral Sciences.

James, I. (2020, December 23). Colorado River Tribes Seek Approval from Congress to Put Water on the Market in Arizona. Retrieved September 2022, from *azcentral*. https://www.azcentral.com/story/news/local/arizona-environment/2020/12/23/colorado-river-indian-tribes-lease-water-market-arizona/5794280002/

James, I. (2023, June 16). *Los Angeles Times*. Retrieved March 2024, from Tribes Seek Greater Involvement in Talks on Colorado River Water Crisis. https://www.latimes.com/environment/story/2023-06-16/tribes-push-for-greater-involvement-in-colorado-river-talks

Jenkins, M. (2007, February 5). *High Country News*. Retrieved August 2022, from The Efficiency Paradox: https://www.hcn.org/issues/339/16808/print_view

Kimmerer, R. W. (2015). *Braiding Sweetgrass: Indigenous Wisdom, Scientific Knowledge and the Teachings of Plants*. Milkweed Editions.

King, K. S. (2013, October 18). Enabling 101: How Love Becomes Fear and Help Becomes Control. Retrieved May 2021, from *GoodTherapy*. https://www.goodtherapy.org/blog/enabling-101-how-love-becomes-fear-and-help-becomes-control-1018134

Knight, B., and Rummel, T. (Directors). (2014). *DamNation* [Motion Picture].

Krol, D. U. (2023, January 6). Biden Signs Bills That Secure Long-Sought Water Rights and Land for 5 Arizona Tribes. Retrieved January 2023, from *azcentral*. https://www.azcentral.com/story/news/local/arizona-water/2023/01/06/5-arizona-tribes-gain-water-rights-land-from-biden-legislation/69784740007/

Kuhn, E., and Fleck, J. (2019). *Science Be Dammed: How Ignoring Inconvenient Science Drained the Colorado River*. University of Arizona Press.

Kuhne, C. (2017). *River Master: John Wesley Powell's Legendary Exploration of the Colorado River and Grand Canyon*. Countryman Press.

LaDuke, W. (1999). *All Our Relations: Native Struggles for Land and Life*. Southend Press.

Lancaster, B. [TEDxTalks]. (2017, March 6). *Planting the Rain to Grow Abundance* [Video]. YouTube. https://www.youtube.com/watch?v=I2xDZlpInik

Lancaster, B. (2019a). *Rainwater Harvesting for Drylands and Beyond* (Vol. 1, 3rd ed.). Tucson: Rainsource Press.

Lancaster, B. (2019b). *Rainwater Harvesting for Drylands and Beyond* (Vol. 2, 2nd ed.). Tucson: Rainsource Press.

Lancaster, B. (2023). Rainwater Harvesting for Drylands and Beyond. Retrieved January 2023, from *Harvesting Rainwater*. https://www.harvestingrainwater.com/

Lassiter, A. (2015). *Sustainable Water: Challenges and Solutions from California*. University of California Press.

Laurin, K., Shepherd, S., and Kay, A. A. (2010). Restricted Emigration, System Inescapability, and Defense of the Status Quo: System-Justifying Consequences of Restricted Exit Opportunities. *Psychological Science*, 21(8), 1075–82.

Leonard, K. (2019). Why Lakes and Rivers Should Have the Same Rights as Humans. Retrieved October 2022, from TED. https://www.ted.com/talks/kelsey_leonard_why_lakes_and_rivers_should_have_the_same_rights_as_humans?language=en

Leopold, A. (1949/2020). *A Sand County Almanac*. Oxford University Press.

Limerick, P. N., Travis, W., and Scoggin, T. (2010). *Boom and Bust in the American West*. Center of the American West.

Loeffler, J., and Loeffler, C. (2012). *Thinking Like a Watershed: Voices from the West*. University of New Mexico Press.

Marshall, R. M. (2010, July 21). Sustainable Water Management in the Southwestern United States: Reality or Rhetoric? PLOS One. https://journals.plos.org/plosone/article?id=10.1371/journal.pone.0011687

Martínez, R. (2012). *Desert America: Boom and Bust in the New Old West*. Metropolitan Books.

Masayesva, V. (n.d.). About Black Mesa Trust. Retrieved October 2022, from Black Mesa Trust. http://www.blackmesatrust.org/

Mather, M., and Jarosz, B. (2014, November 17). Where Poverty and Inequality Intersect. *Population Bulletin*, 69(2), 4–7.

Maupin, M. I. (2018). *Estimates of Water Use and Trends in the Colorado River Basin, Southwestern United States, 1985–2010*. US Geological Survey.

McGivney, A. (2009). *Resurrection: Glen Canyon and a New Vision for the American West*. Braided River.

McGregor, D., Whitaker, S., and Sritharan, M. (2020, April). Indigenous Environmental Justice and Sustainability. *Current Opinion in Environmental Sustainability*, 43, 35–40.

Meyer, R. (2018, December 18). The Southwest May Be Deep into a Climate-Changed Mega-Drought. Retrieved January 2020, from *The Atlantic*. https://www.theatlantic.com/science/archive/2018/12/us-southwest-already-mega-drought/578248/#Correction2

Milly, P. A. (2020, March 13). Colorado River Flow Dwindles as Warming-Driven Loss of Reflective Snow Energizes Evaporation. *Science*, 367(6483), 1252–55.

Moreno, A. (2017, November 6). The Adaptable Cattle Saving Ranchers from Drought. Retrieved October 2022, from *The Atlantic*. https://www.theatlantic.com/science/archive/2017/11/criollo-cattle-drought/544994/

National Association of Counties. (2022, October 11). NACo County Explorer. Retrieved January 2023, from NACO County Explorer: Demographic Shifts in American Counties. https://www.naco.org/blog/naco-county-explorer-demographic-shifts-americas-counties

National Geographic. (n.d.). Conservation. Retrieved September 2022, from National

Geographic Resource Library. https://education.nationalgeographic.org/resource/conservation

National Resource Council. (2007). *Colorado River Basin Water Management: Evaluating and Adjusting to Hydroclimactic Variability*. National Academies Press.

Nature Conservancy. (n.d.). Priority Landscapes: The Colorado River Basin. Retrieved January 2023, from The Nature Conservancy. https://www.nature.org/en-us/about-us/where-we-work/priority-landscapes/colorado-river/

Needham, A. (2016). *Power Lines: Phoenix and the Making of the Modern Southwest*. Princeton University Press.

Neuwirth, R. (2019, May 17). *National Geographic*. Retrieved October 2020, from Centuries-Old Irrigation System Shows How to Manage Scarce Water. https://www.nationalgeographic.com/environment/2019/05/acequias/

Nies, J. (2014). *Unreal City: Las Vegas, Black Mesa, and the Fate of the West*. Bold Type Books.

Nijhuis, M. (2022, November). Conservation Is an Ecosystem. *High Country News*, 3.

Nilsen, E. (2022, November 27). *CNN*. Retrieved January 2023, from Wells Are Running Dry in Drought-Weary Southwest as Foreign-Owned Farms Guzzle Water to Feed Cattle Overseas. https://www.cnn.com/2022/11/05/us/arizona-water-foreign-owned-farms-climate/index.html

O'Donnell, E. (2023, November 21). Water Sovereignty for Indigenous Peoples: Pathways to Pluralist, Legitimate and Sustainable Water Laws in Settler Colonial States. Retrieved April 2024, from https://journals.plos.org/water/article?id=10.1371/journal.pwat.0000144

Olmstead, E. P. (1997). *David Zeisberger: A Life among the Indians*. Kent State University Press.

Owen, D. (2018). *Where the Water Goes: Life and Death along the Colorado River*. Riverhead Books.

Parker, D., and Kearns, F. (2015, May 19). California's Water Paradox: Why Enough Will Never Be Enough. Retrieved September 2022, from *The Conversation*. https://theconversation.com/californias-water-paradox-why-enough-will-never-be-enough-40889#:~:text=This%20paradox%20%E2%80%93%20that%20enough%20water,to%20ensure%20a%20healthy%20environment

Partlow, J. (2024, February 11). *The Washington Post*. Retrieved March 2024, from Inside the Race to Grasp the Fate of the Colorado River. https://www.washingtonpost.com/climate-environment/2024/02/11/colorado-river-states-climate-change-future/

Patch, D. and Kowalski, T. (2020, May 4). azcentral. Retrieved May 2022, from Now, More than Ever, We Need Tribes at the Water Negotiating Table. https://www.azcentral.com/story/opinion/op-ed/2020/05/04/tribes-need-seat-colorado-river-negotiating-table/3061411001/

Pela, R. (2016, February 2). How Arizona Snowbowl Fakes Flakes for a Longer Ski Season. Retrieved October 2024, from *Phoenix New Times*. https://www.phoenixnewtimes.com/arts/how-arizona-snowbowl-fakes-flakes-for-a-longer-ski-season-8018927

Person, D. (2020, June 3). CAP: Know Your Waters News. Retrieved January 2022, from ICS—Three Little Letters That Signify Big Contributions and New Flexibility. https://knowyourwaternews.com/ics-three-little-letters-that-signify-big-contributions-and-new-flexibility/

Pinchot, G. (1947). *Breaking New Ground*. Harcourt, Brace.

Poor People's Campaign. (n.d.). Poor People's Campaign. Retrieved May 2022, from Wendsler Nosie Sr: The Holy Places Are Rumbling at What Is Happening in the World. https://www.poorpeoplescampaign.org/we-cry-power/wendsler-nosie/

Postel, S. (2017). *Replenish: The Virtuous Cycle of Water and Prosperity*. Island Press.

Postel, S., and Richter, B. (eds.). (2003). *Rivers for Life: Managing Water for People and Nature*. Island Press.

Regan, S. (2022, July 7). Running Dry in the American West. Retrieved September 2022, from PERC: https://www.perc.org/2022/07/07/running-dry-in-the-american-west/

Reisner, M. (1986/1993). *Cadillac Desert: The American West and Its Disappearing Water*. Penguin Books.

Richmond, B. (1994). Systems Thinking / System Dynamics: Let's Just Get On with It. *System Dynamics Review*, 10(2–3), 135–57.

Richmond, T., Mandell-Rice, J. R., and Lipinski, R. L. (2022, February 19). The Purposeful Tension within the Doctrine of Beneficial Use. Retrieved October 2024, from *National Law Review*. https://natlawreview.com/article/purposeful-tension-within-doctrine-beneficial-use

Richter, B. (2014). *Chasing Water: A Guide for Moving from Scarcity to Sustainability*. Island Press.

Riggs, S. (2021, November 2). Lifeways of the Little Colorado River. Retrieved October 2023, from Grand Canyon Trust. https://www.grandcanyontrust.org/blog/grand-canyon-little-colorado-river-native-voices

Rivera, J. A. (1998). *Acequia Culture: Water, Land, and Community in the Southwest*. University of New Mexico Press.

Robbins, J. (2023, March). This Native American Tribe Is Taking Back Its Water. Retrieved October 2023, from *Smithsonian Magazine*. https://www.smithsonianmag.com/innovation/native-american-tribe-pima-indians-taking-back-water-180981542/

Robbins, P. (2007). *Lawn People: How Grasses, Weeds, and Chemicals Make Us Who We Are*. Temple University Press.

Robinson, J., Cosens, B., Jackson, S., Leonard, K., and McCool, D. (2018, October 11). Indigenous Water Justice. *Lewis and Clark Law Review*, 22(3), 841–921.

Rodriguez, S. (2016, May 29). Greenhorns. Retrieved September 2020, from How Rural New Mexico Shares Water during Drought. https://greenhorns.org/blog/how-rural-new-mexico-shares-water-during-drought/

Romero, S. (2021, July 13). Drought Hits the Southwest, and New Mexico's Canals Run Dry. Retrieved January 2022, from *New York Times*. https://www.nytimes.com/2021/07/13/us/acequias-drought-new-mexico-southwest.html

Ross, A. (2011). *Bird on Fire: Lessons from the World's Least Sustainable City*. Oxford University Press.

Ross, J. F. (2018, May 24). Outside. Retrieved May 2021, from John Wesley Powell's Perilous Journey down the Colorado. https://www.outsideonline.com/2304721/john-wesley-powells-perilous-journey-down-colorado

Rothberg, D. (2022, August 4). The Coming Crisis along the Colorado River. Retrieved October 2022, from *New York Times*. https://www.nytimes.com/2022/08/04/opinion/drought-climate-colorado-river.html

Sadasivam, N. (2015, May 27). Killing the Colorado: What You Need to Know. Retrieved from *Pro Publica*. https://www.propublica.org/article/killing-the-colorado-what-you-need-to-know

Schipper, J. (2008). *Disappearing Desert: The Growth of Phoenix and the Culture of Sprawl*. University of Oklahoma Press.

Schneider, K. (2022, December 27). *New York Times*. Retrieved January 2023, from Thousands Will Live Here One Day (as Long as They Can Find Water). https://www.nytimes.com/2022/12/27/business/water-development-west.html#:~:text=In%201980%2C%20Arizona%20enacted%20a,of%20water%20that%20they%20withdraw

Scott, C., Vicuña, S., Blanco-Gutiérrez, I., Meza, F., and Varela-Ortega, C. (2014). Irrigation Efficiency and Water-Policy Implications for River Basin Resilience. *Hydrology and Earth System Sciences*, 18(4), 1339–48.

Sevigny, M. (2016). *Mythical River: Chasing the Mirage of New Water in the American Southwest*. University of Iowa Press.

Slow the Flow. (2023). Simple Ways You Can Conserve. Retrieved March 2024, from Slow the Flow. https://slowtheflow.org/

Smith, A. V., Blaeser, J., and Lee, J. (2022, December). Will Tribes Become Colorado River Powerbrokers? *High Country News*, 7–9.

Smith, A. V., Olalde, M., and Farooq, U. (2023, July). Waiting for Water. *High Country News*, 30–47.

Sneed, A. (2019, May 29). What Conservation Efforts Can Learn from Indigenous Communities. Retrieved May 2021, from *Scientific American*. https://www.scientificamerican.com/article/what-conservation-efforts-can-learn-from-indigenous-communities/

Southwest Climate Science Center Workshop. (2017, March 28–29). Ecological Drought in the Southwest United States: Confronting a Hotter Future. Fact Sheet. Retrieved September 2020, from Department of the Interior, Climate Science Centers. https://swcasc.arizona.edu/sites/default/files/2022-08/SWCSCworkshop%20FactSheet.pdf

Stromberg, J. C., and Tellman, B. (2012). *Ecology and Conservation of the San Pedro River*. University of Arizona Press.

Summitt, A. R. (2013). *Contested Waters: An Environmental History of the Colorado River*. University Press of Colorado.

Taylor, E. B. (2021). *Rivers Run through Us: A Natural and Human History of Great Rivers of North America*. Rocky Mountain Books.

Ten Tribes Partnership. (2022). The Ten Tribes Partnership. Retrieved October 2022, from Keepers of the River. https://tentribespartnership.org/#:~:text=The%20Ten%20Tribes%20Partnership%20is,River%20as%20water%20challenges%20persist

Thayer, R. (2010, June 29). *Navajo-Hopi Observer*. Retrieved July 2020, from Hopi Farmers Continue to Utilize Centuries-Old Dry Farming Methods. https://www.nhonews.com/news/2010/jun/29/hopi-farmers-continue-to-utilize-centuries-old-dr/

Thiel, A. (2013). Climate Change Impacts on Hydropower in the Colorado River Basin. Retrieved October 2020, from Center for Water Policy. https://uwm.edu/centerforwaterpolicy/wp-content/uploads/sites/170/2013/10/Colorado_Energy_Final.pdf

Tohono O'odham Community Action (TOCA). (2012, November 20). Attack of the Junk Food Zombies -Tohono O'odham Youth. Retrieved November 2020, from Pan Left Community Media Education Workshop. https://www.youtube.com/watch?v=Sly_VnCWfMw&t=4s

Torres, L. (2018, April 30). *High Country News*. Retrieved October 2020, from This Acequia Life. https://www.hcn.org/issues/50.7/water-this-acequia-life

Tory, S. (2017, August 30). *High Country News*. Retrieved March 2020, from Money-for-Water Programs Work—But for How Long? https://www.hcn.org/issues/49.17/water-theres-success-in-water-for-money-programs-but-for-how-long-colorado-river-fallow-fields

Tuck, E., and Yang, K. W. (2021). Decolonization Is Not a Metaphor. *Decolonization: Indigeneity, Education and Society*, 1(1), 1–40.

USDA Southwest Climate Hub. (2020). Focus on Croplands in the Southwest. Retrieved March 2020, from USDA Climate Hubs. https://www.climatehubs.usda.gov/hubs/southwest/topic/focus-croplands-southwest

USDA Southwest Climate Hub. (2021). Overview of Climate Change Impacts on Agricultural Crops of the Southwestern United States. Retrieved from USDA Climate Hubs. https://www.climatehubs.usda.gov/hubs/southwest/topic/focus-croplands-southwest#:~:text=The%20southwest%20produces%20more%20than,depend%20on%20good%20visual%20appearance

USDA Southwest Climate Hub. (2023a). Las Vegas Wash Water Recycling. Retrieved April 2024, from Water Adaptation Techniques Atlas. https://webapps.jornada.nmsu.edu/wata/#Las%20Vegas%20Wash%20Water%20Recycling

USDA Southwest Climate Hub. (2023b). Limited Irrigation Dryland (LID) Farming System. Retrieved April 2024, from Water Adaptation Techniques Atlas. https://webapps.jornada.nmsu.edu/wata/#Limited%20Irrigation%20Dryland%20(LID)%20Farming%20System

USDA Southwest Climate Hub. (2023c). Water Transactions to Support Riparian Ecosystems in the Isleta Reach of the Rio Grande. Retrieved April 2024, from Water Adaptation Techniques Atlas. https://webapps.jornada.nmsu.edu/wata/#Water%20Transactions%20to%20Support%20Riparian%20Ecosystems%20in%20the%20Isleta%20Reach%20of%20the%20Rio%20Grande

USDA Southwest Climate Hub. (n.d.). Water Adaptation Techniques Atlas (WATA). Retrieved March 2024, from USDA Climate Hubs. https://www.climatehubs.usda.gov/hubs/southwest/tools/water-adaptation-techniques-atlas-wata

US Department of the Interior, Bureau of Reclamation, and Ten Tribes Partnership. (2018). *Colorado River Basin Ten Tribes Partnership Tribal Water Study*. US Department of the Interior.

Utah Water Savers. (n.d.). Homepage. Retrieved March 2024, from Utah Water Savers. https://www.utahwatersavers.com/

Vaux, H., Jr. (2005). Water Management, Conservation, and Reuse in the United States. NRC Committee on US-Iranian Workshop on Water Conservation and Recycling. National Research Council.

Vegan Calculator. (n.d.). The Vegan Web Designer. Retrieved March 2024, from How Much Water Have You Saved? http://thevegancalculator.com/

Ward, F. A., and Pulido-Velazquez, M. (2008). Water Conservation in Irrigation Can Increase Water Use. *PNAS*, 105(47), 18215–20.

Warner, L. A. (2017). Using Audience Segmentation to Tailor Residential Irrigation Water Conservation Programs. *Journal of Agricultural Education*, 58(1), 313–333.

Water and Tribes Initiative. (2020, October). Policy Brief #3: A Common Vision for the Colorado River System: Toward a Framework for Sustainability. Retrieved October 2022, from *Natural Resources Policy*. https://naturalresourcespolicy.org/docs/policybrief3finalweb.pdf

Water and Tribes Initiative. (2022). Who We Are. Retrieved October 2022, from Water and Tribes Initiative: Colorado River Basin. https://www.waterandtribes.org/about-us

Whyte, K. (2018). Settler Colonialism, Ecology, and Environmental Injustice. *Environment and Society*, 9, 125–44.

Wildcat, D. R. (2009). *Red Alert! Saving the Planet with Indigenous Knowledge*. Fulcrum Publishing.

Williams, R. A., Jr. (2012). *Savage Anxieties: The Invention of Western Civilization*. St. Martin's Press.

Wilson, J. (2023). Feds May Cut Supply across Seven States to Keep Colorado River Afloat. Retrieved May 2023, from *Desert Sun*. https://www.desertsun.com/story/news/environment/2023/04/11/feds-may-cut-supply-across-seven-states-to-keep-colorado-river-afloat/70092965007/

Wilson, N. J., Montoya, T., Arseneault, R., and Curley, A. (2021). Governing Water Insecurity: Navigating Indigenous Water Rights and Regulatory Politics in Settler Colonial States. *Water International*, 46(6), 783–801.

Woolington, J. (2024, March). Regeneration Underground. *High Country News*, 32–42.

Yazzie, M. K. (2018). Decolonizing Development in Diné Bikeyah: Resource Extraction, Anticapitalism, and Relational Futures. *Environment and Society*, 9, 25–39.

Yazzie, M. K., and Risling Baldy, C. (2018). Introduction: Indigenous Peoples and the Politics of Water. *Decolonization: Indigeneity, Education and Society*, 7(1), 1–18.

Zulauf, C., and Brown, B. (2019, July 24). Cover Crops, 2017 US Census of Agriculture. Retrieved January 2023, from *Farmdoc Daily*. https://farmdocdaily.illinois.edu/2019/07/cover-crops-2017-us-census-of-agriculture.html

Index

Page numbers followed by f indicate figures, page numbers followed by n indicate notes, and page numbers followed by t indicate tables.

A'aninin, 85
Abram, David, 22
acequias, 20; community-driven, 158–59; water conservation and, 157–59
agriculture, 6, 16, 24, 46; arid lands and, 80; culturally based, 104; development of, 56; Hopi, 104, 112; irrigated, 31, 66, 125; population growth and, 74; supporting, 56; sustainable, 125; water for, 19, 30–31, 42, 52, 65, 87
Ak-Chin Indian Community, 155
Akimel O'odham (River People), 125
Albuquerque, 35; Rio Grande and, 10; water conservation in, 64
Aldo Leopold Foundation, 134, 135, 163
alfalfa, 21, 87
All-American Canal, 80n1; adverse consequences of, 68, 76; leakage from, 69, 70
All-American Canal Lining Project, 69
allocation, 31, 39n3, 60, 61, 65; problems with, 82

American Rivers, on Colorado River, 9
American Security Project, 43
Andrade Mesa Wetlands, 69, 70
Apache Country, place names in, 114
Apache Junction, 142
Apache, 108, 117; *Dzil Ligai Si'an* (Mount Baldy), 117; Goshtl'ish Tu' Bil Sikane, 113; Water Serpent, 120
aquifers, 59, 67, 70, 78, 141; groundwater, 94; recharging, 67, 157
Arellano, José Antonio, 101
aridity, 28, 48, 78; efficiency and, 68
Arizona Department of Water Resources, 73–74
Arizona Republic, 98
Arizona Snow Bowl, 29, 87
Arizona-Sonora Desert Museum, 114
Arizona v. California (1963), 85, 122n2
Arizona v. Navajo Nation (2023), 90, 91
Attack of the Junk Food Zombies, 121
Audubon New Mexico, 42

Balenquah, Lyle, 18, 120; on ancestors/resource bases, 114; on Hopi farming techniques, 109
barley, 21
Basso, Keith, 108, 109, 113
behavior: attitudes and, 38; conservation, 35; values and, 34
Belfi, E.: on decolonization, 101
Bernal, Julia Fay, 124
Berry, Wendell: on rugged individualism, 71
Biden, Joseph, 39, 98
biodiversity loss, 16, 156
Black Mesa, 95; coal mining on, 96, 124n3
Black Mesa Trust, 96, 124, 128
Black Mesa Water Coalition, 128
block caving, 94
block pricing, 59–60
Bluff Principles, described, 129
Boone and Crockett Club, 92
Boulder Canyon Project Act (1928), 80n1
Bowlin, Nick: on water management, 158
Braiding Sweetgrass: Indigenous Wisdom, Scientific Knowledge and the Teachings of Plants (Kimmerer), 143
Brower, David, 165
Brown, Ben, 48
Brown, Douglas, 74
Brown, Kyler, 158, 159
Buddhism, water ethic and, 132
Burman, Brenda, 123

Calexico, Colorado River and, 68
California Air Resources Board, 137
California Global Warming Solutions act of 2006 (Assembly Bill 32), 137
California Gold Rush, 84
California Highway 98, 68
California Institute for Water Resources, 67
Canyonlands, 6
CAP. *See* Central Arizona Project
capitalism, 125; free-market, 74; resisting, 102
Capra, F.: on systemic problems, 136
Cave Creek, 70
Central Arizona Groundwater Replenishment District, 72
Central Arizona Project (CAP), 44, 45f, 155; authorization for, 80n1; Indigenous people and, 98; pumping station, 55f; water management and, 45
ceremony, 20; connections and, 117–18; relationships with water and, 118
Chaco Canyon, 124
Cheng, W.: recycled water and, 65
Chief, Karletta, 98, 114, 127
Chihuahua, Mexico, 24
Childs, Craig, 55, 152
Christianity, Pueblo people and, 93
cistern system, 61
City of Toledo, Lake Erie and, 146
civilization, 82, 84
clan names, 117
Clean Water Act (1987), 123
climate change, 5, 6, 22, 52, 63, 156; water and, 137
Cochise County, 48
coding process, 176–77
cognitive dissonance, 32–37
colonial mentality, 19, 80–82, 94, 96, 102; conservation management and, 97; internalizing, 99–100; resisting, 101; subtle forms of, 100
colonial-capitalist expansion, 90
colonialism, 86, 87, 92, 96, 125, 134; dismantling, 101; settler, 93; tribal-state water conflicts and, 88–91
colonization, 51, 85, 147; European, 86, 94; missionary, 39; of Navajo people, 95
Colorado Plateau, 26
Colorado River, 4, 16, 64, 68, 69, 73, 78, 80–81, 98, 126, 154, 168; allocations from, 10, 39n3, 60, 61, 67, 70; analysis of, 122–23; CAP and, 44; climate change and, 5; conflicts over, 88; decolonization efforts for, 101; depending on, 141; depletion of, 5, 6, 8–11; hydraulic infrastructure for, 55; hydropower from, 9; integrity of, 123; Leopold on, 8–9; litigation over, 10; management of, 82, 91; population served by, 9; rights to, 64, 122; snowmelt for, 23f; Southern Nevada and, 42; sustainability of, 48; water flow of, 15, 122; water from, 6, 82

Colorado River Basin, 63, 64, 98, 127; agricultural withdrawals in, 66; attention for, 31; map of, 2f; tribes within, 90–91; water management on, 123
Colorado River Basin Project (1968), 80n1
Colorado River Basin States, 39n2
Colorado River Compact (1922), 45, 63, 67, 80–81, 88; allocation and, 61, 83
Colorado River Delta, 5, 69, 76; described, 9; restoring, 70
Colorado River Drought Contingency Plan (2019), 83
Colorado River Indian Tribes (CRIT), 64–65, 98, 110
Colorado River Initiative, 98
Colorado River Storage Project Act (1956), 80n1
Colorado River Water Conservation District, 82
Colorado River Water Use Plan, 69
commodification, 102, 106, 143
communifying, 157; commodifying versus, 155–56
Community-Based Global Learning Collaborative, 101
connections, 139; ceremony and, 117–18
conquest mentality, 20; shift from, 147–59; water conservation and, 148, 150
conservation: addiction and, 74; approaches to, 18, 54; attempts at, 37; call for, 41–43; construction and, 24; domestic, 71; economic development and, 58, 63; emphasis on, 30, 40; Extraordinary Conservation (term), 44; lessons of, 53; modeling, 42; monetizing, 57–60, 74, 76; as moral philosophy, 33; overreliance on, 134; practices/perspectives on, 30; rationalizing, 32–37; roots of, 93, 147; social construction of, 17; theoretical dimensions of, 16–18; tools for, 45; understanding, 16–18; utilitarianism and, 55, 56; values of, 49, 53–54; water rights and, 60–62, 63; water use and, 91–93; water waste and, 34
Conservation District of Southern Nevada, 42
conservation districts, 97, 98
conservation efforts, 11, 17, 19, 20, 36–37, 65, 72, 74; developers and, 73; utilitarian, 55–56
conservation ethos, 13, 15, 19, 33, 49, 56, 102, 105, 135; developing, 59; internalization of, 54; roots of, 77, 80–82; wasting water and, 68
conservation movement, 110; early, 91–92; modern, 92–93
conservation paradigms, 15, 53, 143
conservation projects, 46, 57, 59
construction, conservation and, 24
cornfield, dry farming, 151f
corporations, personhood of, 144
COVID-19 pandemic, 88
Criollo cattle, arid conditions and, 48
CRIT. *See* Colorado River Indian Tribes
critical engagement, promoting, 11
Cromwell Morely, Basso and, 108
Cronon, William: on wilderness, 82
cultural issues, 31n1, 134
cultural revitalization projects, 121
culture, 11, 22, 30, 32, 72, 74, 93, 120, 175; conservation, 18–19, 34, 37–51; dominant, 53, 53n1, 70, 105, 106, 107, 146; generational knowledge and, 115; Indigenous, 20, 95, 100, 102, 107, 112, 119, 127, 128; mestizo, 115; technological, 95–96; traditional, 86
Curecanti Unit, 80n1
Curley, Andrew: water agreements and, 90
Custer Died for Your Sins (Deloria, Jr.), 100

Daigle, Michelle, 119
Dakota Access Pipeline, 144
DamNation, 138
Dartmouth, Lord, 94
Dawes Act (1887), 86
Dead River, Rio Grande and, 78
Death Valley, 139
deBuys, William: economic interests and, 31
decision-making, 40, 54, 97, 122, 129, 130, 161; community, 157; environmental, 32, 52
decolonization, 101–2, 126; water justice and, 102

"Decolonization Is Not a Metaphor" (Tuck and Yang), 102
deep ecology, 15, 16, 20, 135, 147, 150; challenges of, 17; relationships to water and, 136, 138–41; social structures and, 136; water ethos and, 144, 152
Deloria, Vine, Jr., 95, 100
demographics, 13, 179–82
desalination plants, 47
Desert Harvesters, 148
desertification, 6
development: blaming, 52; resisting, 101; water, 43, 81. *See also* growth
Dickey, Sonia, 95
Diné Nation. *See* Navajo (Diné) Nation
Disappearing Desert (Schipper), 71
dominance, 51, 100, 107, 116–19, 130
drinking water, 59, 67; access to, 89; fighting over, 43; safeguarding, 41
drought, 6–11, 26, 52, 54, 63, 78; acknowledging, 30; drylands and, 45; extended, 6, 38, 40; facing, 37–39, 67; prolonged, 16, 59; rainfall and, 36; severe, 8, 125; water shortages and, 52
dry farming, 151f, 155, 157
Dunbar-Ortiz, Roxanne, 79

Earth protectors, 96
ecological integrity, 136, 138, 141
Econlockhatchee River, legal rights of, 146
economic development, 31, 32, 74, 75, 135; Colorado River and, 9; conservation and, 63; supporting, 88; values of, 95–96; water and, 43, 87, 88
economic strategies, 58–59
economic systems, 74, 141
ecosystems, 6, 137, 161; interconnectedness/interdependence within, 15; regeneration of, 48; water and, 159–60
education, 24, 161, 180; conservation, 28
efficiency, 13, 24, 31, 33, 35, 47, 61, 64, 74, 110, 142, 147–48, 162; acequias and, 157; agricultural, 66; approaches to, 19, 21, 42–43, 46, 68, 157–59; aridity and, 68; assumptions about, 11; colonial mentality about, 19; communifying approach to, 157–59; community-driven, 20; conquest mentality and, 150; conservation, 65, 70, 76, 152, 279; culture of, 15–16, 38, 50–51; economic, 15, 56; efforts at, 38–39, 41–42; growth and, 67–68; household, 72; importance of, 27–28, 63; improving, 67–68; individualism and, 71; initiatives for, 42; irrigation, 76; municipal, 76; paradox, 64, 66–67; practicing, 13, 28, 36, 143; rationalizing, 37; river, 56; scientific solutions for, 46, 47; social dynamics in, 12; understanding of, 17; valuing, 65–70, 107, 109; water conservation and, 70, 152; water management and, 45
Einstein, Albert, 134
electricity, generating, 63
environment, 56; term, 22; water security and, 52
environmental degradation, 56, 95, 114, 125; impact of, 18
environmental impact studies, 47
environmental issues, 11, 17, 18, 32, 47
environmental justice, 17, 18, 125
Estes, Nick, 125
ethics, 120, 134, 135
ethnicity, 13, 80, 180
Euphrates River, 149
evaporation, 6, 153
Evelyn, John, 91
extractive industries, 125

farming techniques, Hopi, 109, 115. *See also* dry farming
Farooq, Umar, 88
Ferris, Kathleen, 73–74
Festinger, Leon, 32, 36
Fixico, Donald, 108, 119, 120, 121
Flagstaff, 26, 29, 36, 116, 132; described, 3; Red Gap Ranch and, 47
Flagstaff City Council, 147
Flaming Gorge Dam, 80n1
Fleck, John, 64, 82
flooding, 8, 155, 159
Flores, Amilia, 110
Food and Water in Arid Lands Conference, 107n1, 120
Fort Belknap Indian Reservation, 85

Fort Yuma Indian Reservation, 98
47 Ranch, 48
Fountain Hills, 25, 26; fountain at, 27f
Fountain Park, 25
Freeport-McMoRan, negotiations by, 90

gabions, 104
Garcia, Jesus, 114, 115
gardens, watering, 46
gasoline, water for production of, 46
Gila River Indian Community, 98, 126
Gilio-Whitaker, Dina, 125
Glen Canyon Dam, 80n1, 81f
global warming, 29
Global Water Policy Project, 152
golf courses, 95
Gonzales, Patrisia, 112
Goodluck, Kalen, 64, 128
Grafton, R. Quentin, 66, 67
Grand Canyon, 6, 126
Grand Falls, 106f
grassroots initiatives, 126
gravity chutes, 157
Great Aridness, A (deBuys), 31
Great Basin Water Network, 47
greenhouse gas emissions, 137
Grinnell, George Bird, 91–92
grounded theory process, 176
groundwater, 55, 67, 72, 73, 78, 94, 149; decline in, 6, 155; over-extraction of, 30; pumping, 59, 158; recharging, 153
Groundwater Management Act (1980), 72
growth: conservation and, 74, 75, 76–77; economic disparity and, 75; slowing of, 73; unlimited, 73; valuing, 72–74, 76–77; water and, 72, 87. *See also* development
guilt, 50; feeling, 26–28, 30
Gulf of California, 8
Gulf of Mexico, 10

Haaland, Deb: Colorado River and, 123
habitats: preservation of, 57; restoration of, 70
Hanh, Thich Nhat: interbeing and, 138
Haul No!, protests by, 126
Havasupai Tribe, uranium mining and, 126

Henry, Charles, 108, 120; Basso and, 109, 113; on place names, 114; water names and, 119
High Country News, 88, 137
Hobbs, Greg, Jr.: on Law of the River, 61
Hobbs, Katie: on water management, 73
Hohokam people, irrigation system by, 80
Hoover Dam, 16, 80n1
Hopi Declaration of Water, 131
Hopi Nation, 16, 97, 104, 107, 124, 126, 128, 130; Bluff Principles and, 129; Cloud People, 118, 152; Old World and, 96; Rain People, 130; Sípàapu and, 96; water rights and, 90
Hopi Water Fair, 131
housing projects, 46, 72, 73
Hualapai Tribe, 89–90
humans-over-nature mentality, 52
hydro cycle, images of, 154
hydrology, 11, 110, 142, 152
hydro-phobic society, 154
hydropower, 9, 63

identity: cultural, 101, 119; Indigenous, 121; political, 119
Imperial County, agriculture in, 24
Imperial Dam, 68
Imperial Irrigation District, 69
Imperial Valley, Colorado River and, 69
Indian Citizenship Act (1924), 122n2
Indian Reorganization Act (1934), 122n2
Indian Self-Determination and Education Assistance Act (1975), 122n2
Indigenous communities, 15, 92, 102, 117, 122, 127, 134, 135, 141, 161; colonial mentality and, 99–100; shaping, 86
Indigenous Environmental Network (IEN), 128
"Indigenous Feminism Flows through the Fight for Water Rights on the Rio Grande" (Goodluck and Trudeau), 128
Indigenous people, 13, 90, 96, 97, 112, 116, 117, 129, 130; compacts and, 82; interviews with, 107; marginalization of, 86, 92; partnering with, 100; rights of, 87, 99; subjugation of, 94; term, 22; values of, 108; water conservation and, 102

Indigenous Peoples' History of the United States, An (Dunbar-Ortiz), 79
Indigenous voices, 101, 107, 129; marginalization of, 18
Indigenous World Forum on Water and Peace, 106
individualism, 80, 135; rugged, 71, 76, 137; valuing, 70–72, 158
Industrial Revolution, 109
industry, 67; development of, 56, 123; water for, 31
infrastructure, 80, 88, 130; hydraulic, 55; water, 63, 91, 161
injustices, 86, 92, 125, 128
Insatiable Is Not Sustainable (Brown), 74
Integrated Climate and Land Use Scenarios (ICLUS), 73
Intentionally Created Surplus (ICS), 44
inter-are/inter-be, 138, 141
interconnections, 20, 117; recognition of, 118, 141; as systems approach, 136–38, 141; water and, 144, 160
interdependence, web of, 119
Intergovernmental Panel on Climate Change (IPCC), 8
interviews, 54, 58; conducting, 175–76
irrigation, 16, 65, 67, 80, 157; districts, 39; efficiency in, 76; rights, 158
Irrigation Efficiency (IE), 66–67
Isleta Reach, 42
ITKI and UNESCO City of Gastronomy Conference (2016), 104

James, Ian, 9, 98
Jenkins, Matt: on aridity/efficiency, 68
Jicarilla Apache Nation, 91
Joaquin, Jordan, 98
Johnson, Michael Kotutwa, 106, 115, 118; on knowledge/sustainability, 112

Kachina Wetlands Preserve, 103f
Kady, Roy, 110–11, 116; on corn, 117; on technological culture, 95–96
Kearns, Faith, 67
Kimmerer, Robin Wall, 143
King, Kyle, 74
knowledge: ancestral, 112–15, 127; centralizing, 127, 129–30; deep cultural, 107; ecological, 114; generational, 112, 114, 115; high-context, 113–14, 115; Indigenous, 15, 16, 18, 107, 108–9, 115, 127, 129–30, 143, 161; integration of, 127, 129; naming and, 114–15; traditional, 104, 113, 115, 161; valuing, 112–15. *See also* water knowledge
Kowalski, Dennis, 98
Kuhn, Eric, 82

labor law, enforcing, 58
LaDuke, Winona, 116, 117
Lake Erie, legal personhood of, 145, 146
Lake Mead, 9–10, 42, 45, 83; drought conditions for, 10, 63; water level at, 38, 39
Lake Powell, 9, 83; drought conditions for, 10, 63; water level at, 39
Lancaster, Brad, 151; communifying and, 155; conquest mentality and, 149; hydro-phobic society and, 154; rainwater harvesting and, 148–49, 154
land: arid, 80, 102; colonization and, 147; dispossession of, 90, 125; domination of, 51, 93; Indigenous, 87, 145; preservation of, 57; rights of, 28–29; sustainability, 95; water and, 21, 64–65
land exchange, 94–95
landscapes, 15; changing, 24; connections to, 120; dry, 40; human-built, 65; sustainability, 148; water and, 159–60; water-saving, 41, 71
Las Vegas, 26, 42, 47, 59, 147; Colorado River and, 5; water conservation and, 64
Las Vegas Valley, 42
Las Vegas Valley Water District, 71
Las Vegas Wash, 42
Laurin, Kristin, 33
law, science and, 96–97
Law of the River, 61, 82
Lawn People (Robbins), 30
leadership, Indigenous, 15, 16, 18, 102, 121–27, 129–30, 161
legal personhood, 20, 144–45, 146
Leonard, Kelsey, 144, 145
Leopold, Aldo, 21, 134, 163; on Colorado River, 8–9, 70; land ethic and, 20, 134, 148

Levine, Ketzel: xeriscaping and, 40
Lewis, Stephen Roe, 98
lifestyle: adjustments to, 37, 50, 72; choices, 19; valuing, 70–72; water and, 28
"Limited Irrigation Dryland" (LID) system, 42
Little Colorado Basin, 128
Little Colorado River, 106f, 126
Little Colorado River Settlements, 90
Little Wekiva River, legal personhood and, 146
Loeffler, Celestia, 107n1
Loeffler, Jack, 107n1
Lopez, Camillus, 117
Los Angeles, Colorado River and, 5
Los Angeles Times, 98
low-flow fixtures, 16
Lower Colorado Basin, 39, 39–40n3, 61

Manifest Destiny, 79, 80
"Man Who Farms Water, The" (Phiri), 149
Maori, 146
marginalization, 18, 86, 92, 127, 161
Martínez, Rubén, 75
Masayesva, Vernon, 121, 126, 152; on CAP, 98; colonial mentality and, 97; on Ocean Mother, 119; on water/commodity, 96; on water gourds, 118
McCain, John, 94
McDowell, Nora, 99
McGregor, Deborah, 144
meat, water footprint and, 46
memory, water and, 118–19
Mexicali: All-American Canal and, 69; water sources for, 70
Mexicali Valley, 69, 70
Middle Rio Grande Pueblos, 42
Milk River, diversion of, 85
monsoon rains, 3, 5f, 36, 37, 61
more-than-human world, 22, 133, 148; wisdom/guidance from, 115
Morelos Dam, 70
Moroney, Dennis and Deb, 48
Mother Earth, 95, 112, 117, 144; Sípàapu and, 96; water and, 104
Mother Nature, 52
Mushkegowuk Cree, 119

Naess, Arne, 136
Nakoda Tribe, 85
naming, place-based knowledge and, 114–15
National Congress of American Indians (NCAI), 122n2
National Defense Authorization Act (2015), 94
National Law Review, 63
National Park Service, 151
National Public Radio, 40
National Weather Service, 36
natural resources: abuse of, 133; conserving, 92; tribal governments and, 95. *See also* resources
nature, 114; domination of, 80, 93; personhood for, 144; relationship with, 17, 148, 153; reorganizing, 168; rights of, 143; term, 22; untamed, 84, 93; working with, 156
Navajo (Diné) Nation, 16, 22, 90, 91, 107, 124, 128; Bike'yah, 95; Bitter Water Clan, 117; COVID-19 and, 88; resistance by, 101, 102; resource extraction and, 101
Navajo Dam, 80n1
Navajo-Gallup Water Supply Project, 91
Navajo Reservation, 95, 106
Neighborhood Foresters, 148
Nevada Independent, 39
Nevada Water Authority, 40
New Mexico Xeriscape Council, 40
Newberry, Teresa, 113–14
Nies, Judith, 124n3
Nijhuis, Michelle, 137
No More Delays campaign, 126
NOAA National Marine Sanctuaries, 37
Nolan, Eric, 147
Northeastern Arizona Indian Water Rights Settlement Agreement, 91
Northern Arizona University, 175
Nosie, Wendsler, Sr., 94
Nuvangyaoma, Timothy, 90

Oak Flat, 94
Ogalla Aquifer, 48
Olalde, Mark, 88
Old Faithful Geyser, 25

Old World, Hopis and, 96
Owen, David, 56, 68, 83
ownership, 143; ethos, 84; land, 94; property, 145; valuing, 60–65; water, 84–85, 87–91, 94

Pacific Islanders, 13
Padilla, Joseph, 157
Parker, Doug, 67
Pascua Yaqui Tribe, 91
Patch, Dennis, 64–65, 98
Pauli, G. A., 136
Peabody Western Coal Company, 89, 124
PERC Reports, 63
Phelps Dodge, 89
Phiri Maseko, Zephaniah, 156; water partnering and, 149–50, 151
Phoenix, 25, 26, 72, 80; Colorado River and, 5, 52, 154, 155; growth of, 73, 75
Phoenix Active Management Area, 73
Pima Indians, 125
Pima-Maricopa Irrigation Project, 125
Pinchot, Gifford, 92
politics, 30, 32, 54, 74, 180
pollution, water, 105, 125, 146
population growth, 56, 57; agricultural production and, 74; impact of, 47; water rights and, 63; water supply and, 30
Postel, Sandra, 152
Powell, John Wesley, 56, 82
power grid, Colorado River and, 9
precipitation, 6, 9, 36, 45, 49, 83, 153. *See also* rainfall
prior appropriation system, 84–85, 87–91, 157
ProPublica, 66, 88
public health, 41, 89
public shaming, 34–35
Pueblo, 87, 116; Christianity and, 93; cultural history of, 93; dances, 118; land/water and, 94
Pueblo Action Alliance, 124, 128
Pueblo of Laguna, 111, 118, 123, 144; Creator, 118, 144
Pueblo of Sandia, 123; enforcement by, 127; Water Quality Standards of, 124
Pulido-Velazquez, M., 67

Quenchan Tribe, 88, 98

rainfall, 8, 152; droughts and, 36. *See also* precipitation
rainwater, 4–5; collecting, 61–62; diverting, 154; drought and, 36; farming, 148–52; harvesting, 61, 62, 76, 132, 148–49
Rainwater Harvesting for Drylands and Beyond: Guiding Principles to Welcome Rain into Your Life and Landscape (Lancaster), 148
Reagan, Shawn, 63–64
reciprocity, 20, 24, 141–43; ethos of, 143
reclaimed water, 65, 95
recycled water, 41, 56, 65
Red Gap Ranch, Flagstaff and, 47
Reisner, Marc: on water development, 43
relationality, 135, 147–59; radical, 102; utilitarianism and, 161
relationships: community of, 24; ethics and, 134; government-Indigenous, 86; health, 119; Indigenous, 135
religion, 129, 180
reservoirs, 32, 44; groundwater, 73; levels/decline in, 6, 10
resiliency, 65, 112, 126, 135; long-term, 31
Resolution Copper, 94
resource exploitation, 51, 57, 95, 101, 106, 125, 143
resources: economic, 60, 88; managing, 57. *See also* natural resources; water resources
respect, 105, 109, 120, 143
restoration, 127; ecological, 42; Indigenous, 156; projects, 46
Richmond, Barry, 63, 136
Ridgeway Water Festival, 138
rights: individual, 116–19; property, 62. *See also* water rights
Riley, Mary Velasquez, 117
Rio Grande, 42, 78, 123; danger for, 10; future of, 97; water from, 6
Rio Grande Water District, 59
Risling Baldy, Cutcha, 102, 106
River Network, The, 163
Robbins, Paul, 30
Robinson, Jason, 81, 122, 123

Rocky Farms, 48
Rodriguez, Claudio, 156
Rodriguez, Sylvia: on water scarcity, 157–58
Romero, Simon, 159
Roosevelt, Theodore: conservation movement and, 91–92; US Reclamation Service and, 56
Ross, Andrew, 31
Rothberg, Daniel, 39

Sadasivam, Naveena, 66
salinity, impact of, 65
Salt River Pima-Maricopa Indian Community, 75
Salt River Project, 75, 89
Salton Sea, 7f
San Carlos Apache, 94
San Felipe Pueblo, 116
San Francisco Peaks, 3, 4, 5f, 126; ski resort on, 29
San Juan River, 90, 97
San Juan River Settlement, 90
San Luis Valley, 48, 59, 158
San Xavier Apache Tribe, 89
Sand County Almanac, A (Leopold), 134
Sanderson, Darlene, 106, 112, 144
Sandiford, N.: on decolonization, 101
Santa Clara Pueblo, 93
Santa Clara River, 78
Santa Cruz River, 154
Santa Fe, 35, 87
Santa Fe National Forest, 34
Santa Fe Reporter, 34
Santa-Maria, Bernadette Adley, 117
Savage Anxieties (Williams), 84
Save the Confluence, 126
Save Our Ceremonies, 126
Schneider, Keith: on developers/conservation initiatives, 73
science, 50, 127; ancestral knowledge and, 112–15; benefits of, 48–49; geospatial, 129; law and, 96–97
Sea of Cortez, 5
Secret Knowledge of Water, 152
self-determination, Indigenous, 86, 95, 125
Sevigny, Melissa, 153
sewage effluent, reusing, 29

showers: low-flow, 46; short, 38–39, 46
Sierra Club, 165
Sierra Nevada, snowpack in, 47
Sípà, 126
Sípàapu, 96, 97, 126
Smith, Anna V., 88, 89, 99
Snake's Water, 120
snow: artificial, 29–30; diminishing levels of, 22
snowmaking, water for, 30
snowmelt, 4, 6, 9, 22, 64
snowpack, 47, 137
social change, water and, 160–62
social dynamics, 11, 12, 38
social existence, water for, 71
social issues, 11, 31n1, 34
social structures, 16, 50, 74, 97, 134; changes in, 162; deep ecology and, 136
soil conservation, acequias and, 157
song of the water, 166f
Sonora, 8
Sonoran Desert, 115
Southeast Arizona Land Exchange, 94
Southern High Plains, 42
Southern Nevada, water utilities of, 42
Southern Nevada Water Authority (SNWA), 47
specialty crops, high value, 66
Spell of the Sensuous: Perceptions and Language in a More-than-Human World (Abram), 22
spirituality, 18, 117, 180
sponge bathing, 39
sprinklers, installing smart, 71
Standing Rock, 125
stewardship, 129, 161
storm drains, 28
storm water, vegetation and, 153
storytelling, 20, 119–21
structural factors, 6, 11, 72
Suina, Phoebe, 97
surface water, 78, 149; evaporation of, 6
sustainability, 11, 12, 17, 20, 32, 46, 99, 168, 175; decisions about, 124; future, 76, 127; Indigenous approaches to, 109; knowledge and, 112; policy-making processes on, 127, 129; water and, 36, 95, 105–6, 147

Swentzell, Rina, 116, 117, 118, 138; on Pueblo, 93, 94
"Sylva: Or a Discourse of Forest-Trees and the Propagation of Timber" (Evelyn), 91

technology, 24, 50; ancestral knowledge and, 112–15; benefits of, 48–49; hope with, 47–48; strategies with, 47–49
Ten Tribes Partnership, 122, 123
Teravalis, 73
Tesuque Pueblo, 87, 118
Thinking Like a Watershed: Voices from the West (Loeffler and Loeffler), 107n1
Tigris River, 149
timber, overexploitation of, 91
Tohono O'odham, 80, 104, 117
Tonoho O'odham Community Action (TOCA), 104, 121
Tohono O'odham Community College, 113
toilets, 58, 71; low-flo, 46
Tonto Apache Tribe, 88
Tonto Forest Service, 94
Torres, Leanna, 157
Touton, Camille, 64
trade-offs, 40; challenges and, 30–32
training process, 175–76
Treaty of Guadalupe Hidalgo (1848), 86
Treaty with Mexico (1944), 80n1
tribal sovereignty, 86, 95, 99, 125, 126
Trudeau, Christine, 128
Tuck, Eve, 102
Tucson, 151, 152; Colorado River and, 5, 154, 155; communifying in, 155, 156; Yaquis and, 91

Uncompahgre River, 138
Uncompahgre Valley, 62
United Nations, 126, 144
University of Arizona, 112
University of California, Berkeley, 54
University of New Mexico Water Resources Program, 82
Unreal City (Nies), 124n3
Upper Basin Compact (1948), 81–82
Upper Colorado Basin, 39–40n3, 61, 82
uranium mining, protesting, 126
US Bureau of Reclamation, 39, 64, 82, 123; forecast by, 10; overreach by, 122

US Department of Agriculture, 42, 48
US Department of the Interior, 39, 122
US Environmental Protection Agency, 72, 73
US Forest Service, 92
US Geological Survey, 65, 82
US National Academy of Sciences, 66
US Reclamation Service, 56
US Supreme Court, 90, 122n2; Indigenous water rights and, 85; *Navajo Nation* and, 91
"use it or lose it" laws, climate change and, 63
Utah Division of Water Resources, 71
utilitarianism, 55, 56, 102, 161
utilities, 42

values: behavior and, 34; conservation, 19, 33, 35, 49, 53–54, 74, 76–77, 80, 107; core, 109; Indigenous, 20, 102, 108; intrinsic, 160; monetary, 111; utilitarian, 134, 135; Western, 20
Varner, Scott, 40
Vaux, Henry, Jr., 54
vegetation, 153, 155
Verde River, 78, 167, 168

Wakerepunu, Te Hurangi, 165
Walton Family Foundation, 98
wastewater, 24, 73, 103
water: access to, 38, 90–91, 158; as being, 111; beneficial use of, 63, 84–85, 132, 157; carrying, 152–53; changing forms of, 140; collecting, 24, 153; commodification of, 106; as commodity, 57, 110–11; connections with, 116–19, 134–35; contemporary approaches to, 102; cultural perceptions of, 21; domination of, 93; engagement with, 37; fighting over, 85, 87–88; gratitude for, 119; interdependence with, 116–19; Indigenous, 87, 145; interacting with, 161; as life, 11, 60, 110–11, 142; memory of, 14, 118–19; monetization of, 58–59, 60, 68, 76; partnering with, 51, 149–50; preservation of, 57; reciprocity with, 141–43; relationships with, 19, 20, 72, 80, 116, 119, 132, 133, 134,

Index | 205

135, 136, 138–41, 144, 145, 148, 152, 156, 159–60, 161, 162; respecting, 109, 160; rights of, 145; rights to, 60–65, 71, 132, 136; sacredness of, 122, 146–47; saving, 57–60, 73; stealing, 61–62; thinking about, 14, 26–32, 112, 161; toilet, 58; understanding, 76–77; valuing, 17, 20, 57–60, 110–11, 145; wasting, 28, 33, 34, 35, 37, 38–39, 42, 68; wealth generation and, 19
water abundance model, 154, 155–56
Water Adaptation Techniques Atlas (WATA), 41
Water and Tribes Initiative, 123, 128
water management boards, 70, 130
water challenges, 15, 47; tribal-state, 88–91
"Water Conservation in Irrigation Can Increase Water Use" (Ward and Pulido-Velazquez), 66
water consumption, 53, 66, 76, 95; agricultural, 66; decreasing, 41, 46; focusing on, 46; increasing, 68; savings and, 68
water crisis, 6, 12, 16, 32, 64, 135; addressing, 41, 145; averting, 13; in Southwest, 76–77; systemic/colonial issues driving, 134
Water-Culture Institute, 163
water cycle, 8, 153, 154; image of, 153f; role in, 142
water ethic, 14, 118, 124; connections with water and, 134–35; defining, 132; Indigenous, 109, 111; as moral code, 135; resources/opportunities in, 163
Water Ethics Network, 163
water ethos, 76–77, 135; deep ecology and, 144; Indigenous, 20, 106, 107, 121, 129, 130; sharing, 119–21
"water for money" strategies, 59
Water Guzzler's Report, 34
water issues, 73, 93, 119–21; addressing, 19, 50, 72, 126; social dimensions of, 11, 12
water justice, 143, 156; decolonization and, 102; Indigenous, 124, 125, 126, 128; movements, 102, 121–27, 129–30; resources for, 128

water knowledge, 20; ancestral/multi-generational, 112–15; Indigenous, 19, 93–100, 124
water management, 6, 11, 16, 54–57, 97, 123, 149, 158; conservation via, 43, 45; practices for, 42–43, 50; water utilization and, 45
"Water Management in the American Southwest: Lessons for an Age of Climate Change" (Holland), 43
water masters, 55
water meditation, 138, 139–40, 160
water narratives, 146; gathering, 12–13, 175
water policy, 59, 70, 97; dialogues on, 123, 127
water projects, 80–81, 122, 132
water protectors, 96, 126, 144
water quality, 105, 127
Water Quality Standards, 124
water resources, 125n3, 141, 162; access to, 74; bringing back, 156; dominance over, 51; essential, 88; maximizing, 152; as objects, 54; protecting, 16, 145; responsibility for, 52; saving, 68; scarcity of, 88–89; term, 19
water rights, 20, 66, 84, 89, 100, 122, 123, 143–45, 158; conservation and, 60–62, 63; first, 85; holders, 42, 63; Indigenous, 65, 85, 87, 88, 88n2, 90, 125; ironic aspects of, 62; issues over, 90–91; law of the river and, 61; Mexican, 69; paradoxes of, 62–65; population growth and, 63; reviewing, 99; securing, 60; transfer of, 90; tribal, 88, 91
water saving, 17, 65, 71
water scarcity, 8, 30, 54, 71, 76, 88–89, 125, 157–58; addressing, 47; escalation of, 73; model, 155
water security, 52, 153
water settlements, 91, 122, 134; Indigenous, 65, 89; Navajo-Hopi, 89, 90
water shortages, 32, 65, 158; addressing, 14; drought and, 52; severe, 41
water supply, 76, 157; diminishing, 59, 97; population growth and, 30; renewable, 29
water systems, 64, 139

water treatment, 56, 103
water use, 19, 24, 41, 60, 67, 87; approaches to, 73; behaviors related to, 38; community issues related to, 14; conservation and, 91–93; reducing, 28, 45; regulating, 16, 40, 158; sustainable, 39, 123; water management and, 45
Weber, Max, 109
Weiner, Jay, 88
Wekiva River, legal rights of, 146
Western Apache, 113
westward expansion, 9, 63
wetlands, human-created, 103
Whanganui River, legal personhood of, 146
Where the Water Goes: Life and Death along the Colorado River (Owen), 83
White Mountain Apache Tribe, river restoration project by, 127
White Pine County, 47
"Why Lakes and Rivers Should Have the Same Rights as Humans" (Leonard), 144

Whyte, Kyle, 82
Wildcat, Daniel R., 120
wilderness, 19; taming, 82, 84
wildfires, 38
wildlife preservation, acequias and, 157
Williams, Park, 8
Williams, Robert A., Jr., 84, 92
Winters v. United States (1908), 85, 90, 122n2
Wisdom Sits in Places (Basso), 108
Woolington, Josephine, 156
worldview, 53, 93, 158; eco-centric, 17; Eurocentric, 60n2, 80; Indigenous, 85, 144

xeriscaping, 16, 35, 40, 58, 59, 72

Yang, K. Wayne, 102
Yazzie, Melanie K., 101, 102, 106
Yellowstone National Park, 25

Zulauf, Carl, 48
Zuni Edgewater, 116–17

About the Author

Janine Schipper is professor of sociology at Northern Arizona University. She is the coauthor of *Teaching with Compassion: An Educator's Oath for Teaching from the Heart* and author of *Disappearing Desert: The Growth of Phoenix and the Culture of Sprawl.*

www.ingramcontent.com/pod-product-compliance
Lightning Source LLC
Chambersburg PA
CBHW051543020426
42333CB00016B/2074